GUIDE to

WOMEN PHYSICIANS

in the Washington DC area

by Judy Grande

First edition

Rocky Run Publishing, Inc.
PO Box 456
McLean, Va 22101
July 1993

Guide to

WOMEN PHYSICIANS

in the Washington DC area

by Judy Grande

Published by:

Rocky Run Publishing

PO Box 456
McLean, Va. 22101

"Library of Congress Catalog Card Number:" 93-83832
Grande, Judy
Guide to Women Physicians in the Washington D.C. area
ISBN 0-9636565-0-3

TO LANI

ACKNOWLEDGMENTS

When you put together a book of this type, there are so many people to acknowledge because it is truly a collaborative effort. First, I would like to thank the hundreds of doctors who took the time to fill out the lengthy questionnaire sent to them, and the dozens of them who enthusiastically supported the effort and offered their assistance.

For their help and invaluable support, I thank my family, particularly my husband, Brian Gallagher and our daughter, Lani; my brother-in-law/graphics designer, Ed Butera and my father-in-law/advisor, Wes Gallagher.

As always, thanks to Marj and Frank Grande and Joan Grande-Butera.

There would probably be no physicians' guide were it not for the help of Eric Wolferman, a computer whiz who taught (though he would debate this) a computer-illiterate how to work with a data base program. Many thanks also for all types of help to Pat Wolferman, Kathryn Kahler, Cheryl Hussey, Veronica Martinez, Kathy Bonk, Josh Kaufman, Rep. Patricia Schroeder, Edie Adam, Betty Gallagher, Chris Gallagher, Bruce Huber, Jane Gallagher, Jack Gillis, Dr. Frank D. Grande, Dan Taylor, Northern Virginia Press, Joel Mackower, Dr. Denise Fraser, Dr. Mary L. Keszler, Dr. Mona Ellis, Debbie Zildjian, Norita Rehrig, Helene Whitaker, Arlene Koumjian, Bob and Mary Rand, Washington Book Distributors, Dr. Sidney Wolfe, Andrea Camp, Thomas Brazaitis, Keith Epstein; and to some special physicians, Drs. Linda MacDonald, Devra Marcus, Janet Schaffel, Richard Rosenthal, Roger Snyder and Marilee Cole.

ATTENTION

All the information contained in this directory has come from the doctors listed herein and their staffs. The names, addresses and phone numbers were updated in early 1993. The professional information has not been independently confirmed. No medical boards were contacted regarding the certifications or licenses issued or any claims asserted against any particular physician. The writer and publisher have no financial relationship or affiliation with any physician listed in this book. Nothing in this book should be considered an endorsement or rating of any physician. The author and publisher accept no responsibility or liability for the actions of any physician listed in this book. The reader accepts full responsibility for investigating and choosing his or her own physician.

TABLE OF CONTENTS

PREFACE

Women physicians vs. men physicians. Is one better than the other? Does a doctor's sex really make a difference in the type of care he or she gives?

Except in the case of my obstetrician/gynecologist, I'd never really given it much thought. In my mind, it just made sense to have a woman gynecologist, who would be more sensitive to the problems associated with female organs and psyche. This became only too clear after a highly recommended male gynecologist in New York City tried to explain away my minor problem this way: "Just try to think of your body as a television set. Right now, you are experiencing technical difficulties."

No doubt, he thought this would put me at ease. Instead, it unnerved me, though far less than a comment minutes earlier. While examining me for breast tumors, he feigned surprise and "joked" that he had always heard women from my college were flat chested.

I was 20 years younger then and too horrified to say or do anything about his behavior. I quickly left his office and began my search for a woman doctor. Had this happened today, I would tell him exactly what I thought of his locker room humor and report him to the county medical society or state medical board.

When I moved to Washington D.C. in 1981, I found a wonderful group of women obstetrician/gynecologists and didn't really think much about the differences between male and female physicians again until about four years ago. That is when my then three-year-old daughter balked when she had to see the male doctors in her pediatricians' office.

It is not that they were bad doctors. How could she possibly know if they were? It is just that despite her age, she was already much more comfortable with the women physicians in the group.

About the same time, I noticed more of my female colleagues around town asking not only for names of women obstetrician/gynecologists but also internists, psychiatrists, dermatologists or other specialists. I found I had little information to offer.

Recommendations of friends or family had worrisome limitations. Few knew the credentials of their doctors. Where did they go to medical school? Where did they intern and do their residency? Did they receive the required additional training to make them eligible for board certification as specialists?

Even some women physicians said they lacked enough information for referrals to women in other specialties.

Area hospitals will help with referrals, but they are limited in that you will receive only the names of doctors affiliated with their particular hospital. You are also relying on a stranger - whoever may answer the phone - to find the right doctor for you.

Neither the hospital nor other telephone referral services can replace a handy reference guide that allows you to examine the backgrounds of hundreds of women doctors in the Washington metropolitan area personally.

When a search through local bookstores failed to turn up a consumer-oriented reference book on hospital-based or private practice physicians, the task of putting together such a guide fell into my lap serendipitously.

I had just quit working as a newspaper reporter, my occupation for nearly 20 years, to do some freelancing. But the notion of putting together a regional guide to women physicians captured my imagination. It fit not only my interests but skills developed as a journalist specializing in consumer health issues.

It was not a simple task. With the exception of the local American Medical Women's Association, I got little cooperation from the medical establishment in obtaining the names of the local women doctors in private practice. The women's division of the Medical Society of the District of Columbia denied my request for a list of its members, basing its rejection on the premise it was an invasion of its members' privacy.

The American Medical Association, which has computerized lists of its members by gender, region or specialty, among other categories, refused to provide its list, citing copyright protection. Any pharmaceutical company in the world can get a list of AMA doctors to hawk their wares, but I could not get a list that would help consumers make informed choices about their medical care.

Through a database service, I finally was able to obtain a fairly up-to-date list of women doctors who bought the Physicians' Desk Reference, a drug guide. I supplemented that list by writing to doctors with apparent women's names, finding them in the Yellow Pages, the Washington Physicians' Directory (sold primarily to doctors) and any other source imaginable, including names of friends' doctors who were not on any of my lists.

I then sent questionnaires to each of them (three mailings in all), beginning with about 1500 names. The number was reduced to approximately 1200 after letters were returned with no forwarding addresses or doctors responded they were retired or not seeing private patients. Many doctors in Group Health Associations or Health Maintenance Organizations, as well as in government service, such as local military bases, the National Institutes of Health and the Food and Drug Administration, were deliberately excluded from the guide either because they are not practicing physicians or consumers often have no choice in their selection.

A few doctors simply said they did not want to be part of the guide. Some thought it was sexist and a few said they did not want any more women patients. But most were enthusiastic about the project because they thought it would benefit patients and themselves. Many of the doctors said they don't even know many of their colleagues and would use the guide to make referrals for patients requesting women doctors.

Inevitably, this directory misses some doctors, but I believe it is by far the most comprehensive list available to consumers in the Washington area. I received some 540 responses from office and hospital-based physicians and the information is now being shared with you, as they provided it. I am making no recommendations or judgments on competence and abilities. I am simply offering you the mechanism by which you can choose yourself.

You will find most of the doctors represented are obstetricians and gynecologists, pediatricians, family practitioners, internists, and psychiatrists, a reflection of the proportion of women to men in medical specialties generally.

Women now make up roughly 20% of all doctors. But for a variety of reasons, they still shy away from some specialties, leaving general surgery, neurology, anesthesiology and gastroenterology largely to the men.

This brings me to a point about male physicians. Many do listen and care, and I have been fortunate to be treated by a few of them here in the Washington area. Patients should not automatically rule out men as caregivers, just as they should not automatically accept all women.

This guide is an attempt to help you find the best women physicians in the Washington area if that is what you are seeking.

I have purposely left out any information on medical insurance plans in which the doctors participate. I did this because I found during my research that the various plans are added or dropped by the doctors at seemingly a moment's notice, and I feared too much of the information would be outdated and inaccurate. Health insurance questions are best handled by calling the individual doctor's office.

I also apologize to those physicians not included. A few women doctors who filled out questionnaires, such as hospital-based neonatologists, anesthesiologists and radiologists, were excluded because patients usually have no choice in their selection. I also limited the list to nearby suburbs of Washington. For those unaware of this project who would have liked to participate, apologies. I probably could not find their names from any publicly available source and do not know of their existence.

Judy Grande
McLean, VA
July, 1993

CHAPTER ONE

GENDER BIAS IN THE MEDICAL COMMUNITY

If you believe there is a problem in the way some male physicians treat women, you just might place some of the blame on Sigmund Freud.

Despite his 30 years of research into the "feminine soul," the noted psychiatrist once acknowledged he had no idea what a woman really "wants." Nevertheless, he presented himself as an expert on female sexuality.

There are many who dispute this claim and some who would go so far as to say his writings left a very distorted view of women that permeates medicine to this day. The result: Some male physicians see women as highly emotional and let that impression color their diagnosis and treatment.

"There is the notion that women have this hysterical part of themselves and that accounts for their symptoms," says Arlington psychotherapist Dr. Cheryl Hussey.

Indeed, the American Medical Association reported in 1990: "There is evidence that physicians are more likely to perceive women's maladies than men's as the result of emotionality."

In its report on "Gender Disparities in Clinical Decision-making," the AMA also said many researchers attribute the greater utilization of health care services by women to "overanxiousness." As an example, it cites a study of heart catheterization rates, in which a disproportionate share of women's abnormal test results were attributed to psychiatric or non-cardiac causes, potentially compromising their care.

The AMA went on to a cite a number of areas in which women are receiving inadequate care, as compared to men:

• Though women and men with similar smoking practices are at equivalent risk for lung cancer, doctors order sputum studies twice as often for men as women.

• Though heart disease is the number one killer of women, 40% of male patients with abnormal heart scans in one study were referred for cardiac catheterization, while only 4% of the women were referred for further testing.

- Women in every age category receiving renal dialysis were 30% less likely to receive kidney transplants than men, according to one study. Another study found that men in the 46-60 age group were twice as likely to receive a kidney transplant as women the same age.
- Despite a government finding that female dialysis patients have a slightly better survival pattern than males, a 1987 study found that among patients with end-stage renal disease, women are less likely to receive kidney dialysis than men.

Perceiving men's utilization practices as normal and women's as overanxiousness may be doing a disservice to both sexes, the AMA concluded.

One study found that women's greater concern with health matters may actually contribute to women's lower mortality rates. Rather than women being overanxious, men may tend to be underanxious about their health and ignore illnesses, it said.

Gender bias may not be overt, the AMA reported. "Rather, societal attitudes, including stereotypes, prejudices and other evaluations based on gender roles may play themselves out in a variety of subtle ways."

The differences in the treatment of men and women stem from medical lore, not sexism, says Dr. Devra Marcus, a long-time Washington internist. For instance, in the past more men smoked than women, and doctors came to view lung cancer as a male disease.

"It is ignorant, not sexist, " says Marcus.

Ignorant or not, the gender bias has had a dramatic effect on women's health that will extend far into the future because of a lack of medical research on women's problems.

Much has been written in recent years about a study of 22,000 physicians that found aspirin could help prevent heart attacks. But while doctors were hailing the breakthrough and busily encouraging their male patients to take an aspirin a day, little could be said to women because not one was included in the study.

Similarly, women were excluded from a federally funded heart disease study of 15,000 people, appropriately known by the acronym Mr. Fit.

Medical sexism is not confined to heart researchers, however. When the National Institutes of Health (NIH) embarked on its largest study ever on health of the nation's elderly, no women were included for the first 20 years of the study.

The exclusion of women from medical research is not uncommon, though federal health officials and the medical establishment now acknowledge it and are trying to rectify it.

For years, Reps. Olympia J. Snowe, R-Maine and Patricia Schroeder, D-Colorado, co-chairs of the Congressional Women's Caucus, have been pushing NIH to concentrate more of its funding on women's health issues. They have rejected the excuse that women are often left out because their reproductive cycles make studies more costly and complex. It is precisely for this reason that they say women must be included in studies. Women do have reproductive cycles that make their health problems unique.

In 1987, NIH found only 13.5% of its $6 billion research budget was spent on diseases unique to women, such as cancers of the reproductive system. The study findings prompted Snowe to compare the medical community to Henry Higgins in "My Fair Lady," bemoaning in song, "Why can't a woman be more like a man?"

The analogy apparently has not been missed by the federal government or the AMA.

NIH initially defended itself by noting the 13.5% spent on problems unique to women was misleading, because so much of the remaining research involves diseases affecting women as well as men. (No study has been done on research spending unique to men.) But NIH also acknowledged it was slow to react to the congressional push for greater attention to women's health needs.

NIH has now responded by creating an Office of Research in Women's Health and the Women's Health Initiative, the largest study of women's health ever in the United States. More than 150,000 women will be followed and more than $600 million spent to research three chronic diseases in women over the age of 50 - coronary artery disease, cancer and osteoporosis.

Change comes slowly, but it is coming. And women are now in a position to be sure it does not stop. Former President Bush began the process by appointing Dr. Bernadine Healy as the first-ever woman director of NIH and Dr. Antonia Novello, the first woman surgeon general.

President Bill Clinton replaced both of them, but has put even more women in important policy-making postitions that could affect women's health, notably Donna Shalala, former chancellor of the University of Wisconsin at Madison as secretary of the Department of Health and Human Services, of which NIH is a part.

Testifying before Congress in February, Shalala said she supported the goals of the women's caucus and planned to make women's health one of her "personal priorities." She also cited the lack of research on minority health issues and said she would work to reverse it.

Schroeder, testifying at the same congressional hearing, said she was thrilled to see the support for the women's caucus agenda and declared, "Finally, NIH will be working for everyone."

In addition to Shalala, President Clinton has appointed women to other posts that impact the U.S health agenda. They include the administrator of the Environmental Protection Agency, which has jurisdiction over not only the quality of the air and the seas, but also the use of pesticides and other chemicals that find their way into the food supply. He also named another woman to replace Antonia Novello as surgeon general.

Perhaps most importantly, Clinton appointed his wife, First Lady Hillary Rodham Clinton, to oversee and coordinate the president's overhaul of the health care system.

At the grass roots level, there is hope as well. Family physicians and specialists can't help but notice the outcry by women for more caring, competent and equal medical treatment, as evidenced by the growing numbers of patients seeking women doctors.

In concluding its report, the AMA's Council on Ethical and Judicial Affairs made several recommendations:

- Physicians should examine their practices and attitudes for social or cultural biases.
- More research on women's health problems should be pursued and results of medical tests on males should not be generalized to females without evidence that results apply to both genders.
- The numbers of female physicians in leadership positions in teaching, research and the general practice of medicine should be increased.

The AMA's final recommendation was to study further the causes of gender disparities. "It is important to ascertain to what extent gender disparities in medical care are the result of biological differences between the genders and to what extent utilization practices and physician/patient interactions are influenced by cultural and social conceptions of genders."

For those who care to wait no longer for the answers, many believe a first step toward equal medical treatment is to fire the male physician and hire the woman.

CHAPTER TWO

WHY A WOMAN DOCTOR?

You may ask why a woman doctor? Given equal or comparable educational backgrounds and technical skills, should a woman be preferred over a man?

Opinions certainly vary, but those who answer an unequivocal yes readily offer a multitude of reasons for their conviction.

Women doctors for the most part are better listeners and more attentive to patients' problems, say many doctors and patients in the Washington metropolitan area. They say women doctors are often more forthright, direct and willing to take time with patients than their male colleagues. And they believe women physicians tend to establish a personal connection with the patient, often treating them more as a friend than a medical statistic.

Some also view the choice between a man and a woman in more feminist terms, citing the desire to support a woman doctor from an economical standpoint.

But the communication skills of women doctors usually top the list.

"Certainly some of my male colleagues are just as good, but generally women are better listeners," says Dr. Mona Ellis, a family physician in suburban Maryland. "It's more of a female trait."

Women also are likely to hold a hand to comfort someone, says Ellis. "Men have more of a problem with this. If they reach out to hold a shoulder, some women might not like it....The message would not be clear."

A report published in the Jerusalem Post in 1991 said the researchers at the Sackler School of Medicine at Tel Aviv University predict medicine will become "more humane and caring" as more women become doctors. They found women doctors in Israel are compassionate and better able to communicate with patients and their families while male doctors are motivated by power, competitiveness and higher status.

Approximately 20% of doctors in the United States are women, and the number is expected to exceed 30% early in the next century as more women enroll in medical schools. In some schools today, more than 40% of the medical students are women.

There is also the growing perception, supported by some studies, that women doctors spend more time with their patients. In this book's survey of local women doctors, many boasted they do not overbook appointments and emphasized they treat the "whole patient" not just the ailment of the moment.

Take the case of Dr. Denise Fraser, a northern Virginia general surgeon. She has always taken plenty of time with her patients when making hospital rounds. But one day she noticed, "My male colleagues were getting done in 1/3 the time it was taking me. So I started to speed up a little."

It didn't last long. The patients began to complain, and Fraser returned to her slower bedside manner.

"They expect me to take more time with them," Fraser says of her patients.

Edie Adam, a journalist from Burke, Va., is one patient who expects not only more time, but also understanding from a woman doctor. As a woman in a high-pressure, male-dominated industry, Adam says it is her hope that "another woman will understand instinctively the stresses we encounter daily."

"...And finally, I was fed up with being patronized by male doctors. There's no guarantee a woman will be a more understanding doctor, but I'm determined to give her the opportunity."

Several doctors interviewed say women who prefer women physicians tend to be middle-aged or younger, well educated and professional. But they also say they are starting to see more men who are seeking empathetic listeners and are finding it in a woman physician.

The doctors add that much of the large gay population — male and female — in the Washington area demands to see women doctors.

Many gay males say they are not comfortable seeing a straight male doctor, Ellis says. And her lesbian patients say some of the male doctors just don't get the message that they are gay. "Their first question is 'What kind of birth control are you using' ?" When the gay woman answers she doesn't have intercourse, the male doctors still don't understand.

For gay women, "I think it's a safety issue. They feel less at risk emotionally and professionally," says Dr. Cheryl Hussey, an Arlington psychotherapist.

Hussey, whose practice is 95% women, said her patients and colleagues tell her women doctors tend to be more empathetic and more interested in everything about the person, not just the symptoms. "My experience has been and certainly the experience of my patients is that women doctors tend to answer questions more honestly and directly."

"I work with a lot of male physicians, but some won't even talk to me because I'm not a medical doctor," says Hussey. "They may be top notch technicians but empathically...they have no idea how to take care of the total patient."

Is choosing a woman sexist?

"I don't think so, " says Hussey. "The attributes of empathy and sensitivity are part of the skills package patients are looking for in a physician. They're usually contained in a woman."

A 1988 study by the federal Office of Technology Assessment (OTA), entitled, "Quality of Medical Care: Information for Consumers," concurred that when rating physicians, "Americans place a high value on a physician's knowledge and technical competence, but they also place a high value on the interpersonal aspects of the quality of care, including the communication of information."

OTA reported that 96% of respondents in another national survey said it was very important for physicians to be able to answer questions honestly and completely. At least 92% of respondents felt it was very important to have access to clear explanations of medical problems and to have a physician willing to spend sufficient time to diagnose and prescribe. They also said the absence of these qualities was cited by a majority of people who changed physicians.

Despite women's communication skills, some male doctors have complained that women physicians may not be as qualified or competent as men because women still bear the burden of child bearing and rearing, and for the most part, responsibility for the home. They feel women doctors cannot spend as much time as necessary in honing their skills and keeping up with the medical literature.

This impression is hotly debated by women physicians, who say it is a sexist and ignorant point of view. It also flies in the face of the strides by women in the Washington medical community in recent years.

Women cardiologists direct the Coronary Care Unit at Washington Hospital Center, the Cardiac Arrythmia Service at Georgetown University Hospital, and the Echocardiography lab at Howard University Hospital, all highly respected medical facilities.

Women sit on the powerful executive committees of area hospitals, including Holy Cross Hospital and Columbia Hospital for Women.

Dr. Constance Bohon, who serves on the board of the Women's Health Resource Center, is also co-chair of maternal-fetal medicine at Columbia. Dr. Elliece S. Smith chairs the department of obstetrics and gynecology at Prince George's General Hospital and Dr. Nicolette Horbach directs the division of gynecology and urogynecology at George Washington University Medical Center.

Dorothy Moga, though not a physician, is the executive vice-president of the sprawling Inova Health Systems, which comprises Fairfax, Mt. Vernon and Fair Oaks Hospitals, as well as 6 urgent care centers, two nursing homes and three Access medical centers.

Dr. Carol W. Garvey is the president of the Montgomery County Medical Society and Dr. Kathy S. Brenneman chairs the section of geriatric medicine at Washington Hospital Center.

Women also chair the plastic surgery departments of several area hospitals, and Dr. Mary McGrath of George Washington University is the first woman chair of plastic surgery in a U.S. medical school.

It comes as no surprise, therefore, that several women doctors interviewed say they are able to compete head to head with their male colleagues anytime.

Dr. Devra Marcus, among the first handful of female internists in downtown D.C., flatly rejects the notion that women who are mothers must sacrifice skills as a physician. Even those who do cut back on their work hours can still be top notch physicians, she says.

A reduction in hours does not translate to a reduction in competence or skills, Marcus says. "You're competent if your conscientious."

Marcus, the mother of three children, works four days a week now. She cut her hours by 1/3 when her children were little.

"Working part-time can help with stress," adds Dr. Mary Lenore Keszler, a part-time neonatologist at Holy Cross Hospital in Maryland. Keszler says she not only keeps up her continuing education credits, but lectures at Georgetown and devotes a large amount of time each week to medical literature.

"I've seen a lot of burnout with men in their 40s and 50s," says Keszler. She asks if patients would not be better off with a doctor in a position similar to hers than someone who is "harried or hurried and doesn't even have time to answer a question."

The atmosphere surrounding a highly stressed physician affects family, staff, patients, says Keszler. "I would caution them: 'Wouldn't you like to have a have a half afternoon off to be able to read an article and remember what you read'?"

Nevertheless, discrimination still exists and there is much more to be accomplished by women. Most current female doctors are still clustered in the lower paying specialties, such as family practice, pediatrics and internal medicine. Only about 1% of surgeons are women.

"There are a lot of older surgeons who have told me we don't want women in this specialty," says Fraser, one of the few women surgeons in the DC area. "In surgery, sometimes you have to prove you're better than the guys just to hold your own."

Complaints of discrimination are hardly confined to the Washington area. There was the much publicized 1991 case of a renowned neurosurgeon at Stanford University Hospital who resigned, citing frustration from years of sexist remarks and discriminatory treatment by her colleagues. She later returned to Stanford.

And a February 1992 article in The Washington Post said sexism in the nation's medical schools still exists, despite the fact that women comprised nearly 40% of first year medical students. It said women are promoted less, are less accepted by their male colleagues in the more prestigious specialties, and are still the object of sexist remarks and slurs.

But times and attitudes will change as more women come into the medical system and make their opinions known and their abilities are accepted.

In the meantime, here is a suggestion from doctors and other health care experts on how best to select a physician.

Generally, those interviewed suggested asking friends or physicians for 2 or 3 names. Then check out the backgrounds of those doctors and if satisfied with their level of ability, make an appointment and go to see them. You don't have to tell them you're interviewing them.

One preliminary consultation should be enough to tell you if you can establish a meaningful relationship with this physician.

In the words of one doctor:

"I encourage people to interview doctors. Be consumers. Doctors are not god-like creatures as they were once thought of. If you don't like them, fire them. It's as important as childcare. You're putting your trust in this person. It's like you're interviewing an applicant for a job."

CHAPTER THREE

FINDING A QUALIFIED DOCTOR

One of the best measures of a doctor's competence is whether she is "board certified" in the specialty she is practicing. This means the doctor has completed a required amount of training (usually two or three years beyond residency) to enable her to pass an examination by one of 23 boards recognized by the American Board of Medical Specialties and the American Medical Association. Some specialties require oral as well as written exams and recertification after a certain number of years.

As defined by the American Board of Medical Specialties (ABMS), a specialist is a doctor who concentrates on certain body systems (such as heart or lungs), age groups or medical techniques to treat various types of disorders. Specialties range from allergy/immunology and family practice to pediatrics and urology.

A subspecialist completes training in a general specialty then goes on to additional training in a more specific subgroup. For example, a board certified pediatric gastroenterologist first must complete training and certification in pediatrics, then further training in disorders of the digestive systems of infants, children and adolescents.

Although there can never be guarantees of a physicians' competence or technical abilities, board certification is at least an indication of not only a physician's desire to practice a particular specialty, but also successful completion of years of training in that specialty. Any doctor can call himself or herself a cardiologist or a dermatologist simply by hanging out a shingle. But only those who are certified can produce a piece of paper that tells the patient he or she has passed the tests and learned the skills necessary to treat the problems associated with that specialty.

"Board certification is reasonable to expect," said Dr. Devra Marcus. "It is hard to get. It makes the club reasonably small."

Of course, there are a lot of boards with fancy sounding names that are not among the 23 recognized by ABMS and the AMA, and patients need to be aware of which board is doing the certifying. (A list follows.)

To find out if a doctor is certified prior to making an appointment, patients can check the ABMS Compendium of Certified Medical Specialties, which is found in most public, hospital, university and medical libraries. ABMS also publishes lists of its specialists in Yellow Pages directories and operates an 800 number to verify the status of an individual's certification.

I recommend using this number to confirm certification information in this guide or checking with the doctors' offices. Many doctors, particularly the younger ones, were in the process of certification at the time of publication and their status may be changed by the time you read this. For instance, several doctors had completed the educational training and were board eligible for certification but had not yet taken and passed all the required exams. The toll-free number to call for verification is 1-800-776-2378.

The following is a list, with descriptions, of the recognized specialties and subspecialties, including addresses and phone numbers. The information comes primarily from brochures provided by the American Board of Medical Specialties, Evanston, IL.

ALLERGY AND IMMUNOLOGY

The allergist/immunologist treats disorders affecting the immune system, including asthma, eczema and reactions to food, drugs or insect bites.

American Board of Allergy and Immunology
University City Science Center
3624 Market St.
Philadelphia, PA 19104
(215)349-9466

ANESTHESIOLOGY

An anesthesiologist, following at least four years of post-graduate training, is responsible for pain relief and maintenance of a stable condition during and following a surgical or diagnostic procedure. An anesthesiologist may receive additional training in CRITICAL CARE MEDICINE.

American Board of Anesthesiology
100 Constitution Plaza
Hartford, CT 06103
(203)522-9857

COLON AND RECTAL SURGERY

A board certified colon and rectal surgeon completes at least five years of training in general surgery and an additional year of colon and rectal surgery. Written and oral boards are required for certification.

American Board of Colon and Rectal Surgery
20600 Eureka Rd #713
Taylor, MI 48180
(313)282-9400

DERMATOLOGY

A dermatologist specializes in the treatment of disorders of the skin, mouth, external genitalia, hair and nails, with extensive training in skin cancers and other tumors. Subspecialties include DERMATOPATHOLOGY, involving the evaluation of tissue samples, and IMMUNODERMATOLOGY, expertise in the study of skin diseases involving the immune system.

American Board of Dermatology
Henry Ford Hospital
2799 West Grand Blvd
Detroit, MI 48202
(313)871-8739

EMERGENCY MEDICINE

This specialty involves decision-making to prevent death or disability in emergency situations. These specialists are usually hospital-based.

American Board of Emergency Medicine
200 Woodland Pass, #D
East Lansing, MI 48823
(517)332-4800

FAMILY PRACTICE

A family physician treats a wide variety of ailments in patients of all ages and may subspecialize in GERIATRIC MEDICINE, treating disorders common to the elderly.

American Board of Family Practice
2228 Young Drive
Lexington, KY 40505
(606)269-5626

INTERNAL MEDICINE

The internist manages all types of illnesses in adolescents, adults and the elderly, and has training in emergency internal medicine and critical care. Subspecialties include CARDIOVASCULAR MEDICINE, CLINICAL CARDIAC ELECTROPHYSIOLOGY, CRITICAL CARE MEDICINE, DIAGNOSTIC LABORATORY IMMUNOLOGY, ENDOCRINOLOGY, GASTROENTEROLOGY, GERIATRIC MEDICINE, HEMATOLOGY, INFECTIOUS DISEASES, MEDICAL ONCOLOGY, NEPHROLOGY, PULMONARY DISEASES, RHEUMATOLOGY, ALLERGY AND IMMUNOLOGY.

American Board of Internal Medicine
University City Science Center
3624 Market St.
Philadelphia, PA 19104
(215)243-1500 or (800)441-ABIM

NEUROLOGICAL SURGERY

This specialty involves the surgical treatment of disorders of the nervous systems, including their supporting structures and vascular supply.

American Board of Neurological Surgery
Smith Tower, #2139
6550 Fannin St.
Houston, TX 77030
(713)790-6015

NEUROLOGY

The neurologist treats all disorders of the brain, spinal cord, nervous systems and related blood vessels and structures. The neurologist is certified in neurology by the American Board of Psychiatry and Neurology, Inc. and can subspecialize in CHILD NEUROLOGY AND CLINICAL NEUROPHYSIOLOGY.

American Board of Psychiatry & Neurology
500 Lake Cook Rd. #335
Deerfield, IL 60015
(708)945-7900

NUCLEAR MEDICINE

The specialist in nuclear medicine uses radioactivity diagnostically, therapeutically and in research.

American Board of Nuclear Medicine
900 Veteran Ave. #12-200
Los Angeles, CA 90024
(213)825-6787

OBSTETRICS AND GYNECOLOGY

The obstetrician/gynecologist treats disorders of the reproductive system and manages its care. Certified subspecialties are GYNECOLOGIC ONCOLOGY, MATERNAL-FETAL MEDICINE, which involves complications of pregnancy, AND REPRODUCTIVE ENDOCRINOLOGY, which manages problems of endocrinology and infertility.

American Board of Obstetrics & Gynecology
936 N. 34th St. #200
Seattle, WA 98103
(206)547-4884

OPHTHALMOLOGY

An ophthalmologist, after three or more years of training in an accredited ophthalmology residency program, manages all aspects of eye and vision care.

American Board of Ophthalmology
111 Presidential Blvd. #241
Bala Cynwyd, PA 19004
(215)664-1175

ORTHOPAEDIC SURGERY

This specialist medically and surgically treats disorders of the extremities, the spine and associated structures.

American Board of Orthopaedic Surgery
400 Silver Cedar Court
Chapel Hill, NC 27514
(919)929-7103

OTOLARYNGOLOGY

The otolaryngologist, a head and neck surgeon, treats disorders of the ears, the respiratory system and head and neck generally.

American Board of Otolaryngology
5615 Kirby Drive #936
Houston, TX 77005
(713)528-6200

PATHOLOGY

A pathologist specializes in the causes and nature of disease, using laboratory methods to diagnose and recommend treatment. There are numerous subspecialties, including CYTOPATHOLOGY, the study of cells, and DERMATOPATHOLOGY, an expert in monitoring diseases of the skin by examination of tissue sections and skin scrapings.

American Board of Pathology
5401 W. Kennedy Blvd.
PO Box 25915
Tampa, FL 33622
(813)286-2444

PEDIATRICS

A pediatrician treats a variety of childhood ailments, from birth through adolescence. There are certified pediatric subspecialties in CARDIOLOGY, CRITICAL CARE MEDICINE, ENDOCRINOLOGY, GASTROENTEROLOGY, HEMATOLOGY-ONCOLOGY, NEONATAL-PERINATAL MEDICINE, NEPHROLOGY AND PULMONOLOGY.

American Board of Pediatrics
111 Silver Cedar Court
Chapel Hill, NC 27514
(919)929-0461

PHYSICAL MEDICINE AND REHABILITATION

This specialist treats patients with disabilities involving the musculo-skeletal, neurologic, cardiovascular and other body systems. A physiatrist may use a variety of treatments, including mechanical and electrical devices.

American Board of Physical Medicine and Rehabilitation
Norwest Center #674
21 First St. SW
Rochester, MN 55902
(507)282-1776

PLASTIC SURGERY

This specialty deals with the repair and reconstruction of body defects, including limbs, breasts, face and external genitalia. Minimum training is five to seven years. SURGERY OF THE HAND is a certifiable subspecialty.

American Board of Plastic Surgery
Seven Penn Center #400
1635 Market St.
Philadelphia, PA 19103
(215)587-9322

PREVENTIVE MEDICINE

This specialist works to promote and maintain good health and well-being and to prevent disease and death.

American Board of Preventive Medicine
9950 W. Lawrence Ave. #106
Schiller Park, IL 60176
(708)671-1750

PSYCHIATRY

A psychiatrist treats mental, addictive and emotional disorders, including depression, anxiety, sexual dysfunction and substance abuse. After obtaining a medical degree, a psychiatrist needs four years of additional training to be certified.

American Board of Psychiatry & Neurology
500 Lake Cook Rd. #335
Deerfield, IL 60015
(708)945-7900

RADIOLOGY

Therapeutic radiology, or radiation oncology, uses radiant energy to treat diseases, particularly malignant tumors. Several subspecialties include DIAGNOSTIC RADIOLOGY AND MEDICAL NUCLEAR PHYSICS.

American Board of Radiology
2301 W. Big Beaver Rd #625
Troy, MI 48084
(313)643-0300

SURGERY

A general surgeon treats a broad variety of conditions affecting all body parts through surgical means. Subspecialties include GENERAL VASCULAR SURGERY, PEDIATRIC SURGERY, SURGICAL CRITICAL CARE AND SURGERY OF THE HAND.

American Board of Surgery
1617 John F. Kennedy Blvd #860
Philadelphia, PA 19103
(215)568-4000

THORACIC SURGERY

This specialty involves the care of patients' chest disorders, including the surgical care of coronary artery disease, and cancers of the lung and esophagus.

American Board of Thoracic Surgery
One Rotary Center #803
Evanston, IL 60201
(708)475-1520

UROLOGY

A urologist treats disorders of the adrenal gland and reproductive and urinary systems.

American Board of Urology
31700 Telegraph Rd #150
Birmingham, MI 48010
(313)646-9720

CHAPTER FOUR

HOW TO REPORT A BAD DOCTOR

"Despite the medical miracles that we hear about almost daily, medicine is not an exact science — there are no guarantees." So warns a brochure of the Medical Society of the District of Columbia.

Hundreds of thousands of patients each year are testament to that statement, according to health experts fighting for states to improve policing of the medical profession.

A leader in the charge is Dr. Sidney Wolfe, executive director of Public Citizen's Health Research Group in Washington. Wolfe is a long-time critic of often underfunded and understaffed state boards that he says identify and punish only a minute portion of the bad doctors practicing in the United States.

Wolfe estimates there are as many as 300,000 medical negligence cases each year in hospitals alone, yet a 1991 report by the Health Research Group said fewer than one-half of 1% of the nation's half million doctors face disciplinary actions by state boards each year.

"There are only a handful of states that do a really good job," says Wolfe. Unfortunately they are not in this area, he adds.

The Health Research Group in 1991 ranked Maryland 49th among 50 states and the District of Columbia in total disciplinary actions by state boards per 1,000 medical doctors. The District of Columbia was ranked 40th and Virginia just ahead at 39th.

The Maryland Board of Physician Quality Assurance took 24 actions against doctors, including license revocations and probations, in 1988, the most recent data available at the time of the survey. But since that time, Maryland has increased its staff and upgraded the requirements for investigators, according to the state board's compliance chief, Barbara Vona.

In 1992, she said Maryland revoked the licenses of 12 physicians, accepted the voluntary license surrender of 22 doctors, placed 30 physicians on suspension and reprimanded 19 others.

In the district, the Board of Medicine disciplined 23 doctors in 1992, a slight improvement over past years. From January through October 3, 1989, the Health Research Group reported the District of Columbia had taken 9 actions against doctors, compared to 16 in all of 1988. Four of these actions in 1989 involved revocation of medical licenses.

The state of Virginia took 56 actions against doctors in 1989, according to Wolfe's group. In 1992, there were 67 sanctions against doctors, chiropractors, osteopaths and other medical professionals licensed by the board.

Wolfe's group criticized all three jurisdictions for case backlogs, limited funding for the medical boards and their generally poor national rankings. But he also praised Virginia for hiring investigators who scout out misprescribing doctors by looking through pharmacy records and for conducting audits of disciplined physicians' practices to identify those who are not adequately correcting their deficiencies.

Wolfe says Virginia also has an excellent public information branch, which sends out news releases announcing disciplinary actions and publishes them in a newsletter. The release of information, however, occurs only after action has been taken, sometimes years after a complaint is filed. In the meantime, the doctors may continue to treat unsuspecting patients.

This is the case across the nation. Patients have great difficulty getting access to information about their doctors because boards are secretive and most consumers would find it quite difficult to search for their physicians' malpractice cases in local records offices.

In 1974, the Health Research Group published the nation's first consumer directory of local physicians in Prince George's County. In it, Wolfe wrote, "Most people can find out more about a car they plan to buy than they can about a doctor who may hold their life in his hands."

The federal government has taken a step toward rectifying this problem with the creation of a National Practitioner Data Bank, which contains records of state actions and malpractice awards. But it, too, is off limits to consumers. Its purpose is to help hospitals check physicians' backgrounds before hiring.

The Health Research Group says this data bank should be opened to the public, but this would require action by Congress.

So what can you do in the meantime to become better informed or to deal with a problem?

To check out a prospective doctor's record, consumers can go to the court records office in the county in which the doctor practices to look up malpractice cases filed against him or her. But expect it to be a time consuming effort. Also, one or two cases filed against a particular doctor may be more misleading than helpful. Malpractice litigation is common and only a pattern of many cases against an individual physician may reveal a true competency problem.

In the case of serious medical negligence involving your current physician, go directly to your state board or local medical society.

In its brochure entitled "Complaints about Medical Care," the D.C. medical society encourages patients to discuss their concerns, questions or problems with their physicians first. If their differences cannot be ironed out, the D.C. society will refer complaints to one or more of the following medical society committees:

- Grievance Committee, which considers complaints from physicians or patients related to their relationship with each other.
- Medical Ethics and Judicial Committee, which handles complaints related to the ethical conduct of physicians, as set out in the opinions of the Judicial Council of the American Medical Assn.
- Peer Review of Utilization Committee, which deals with all aspects of the provision of quality medical care.
- The Voluntary Arbitration Committee, which provides for a voluntary and non-binding resolution of disputes involving fees.
- Committee on Impaired Physicians, which receives complaints from any source involving suspected physician impairment, such as alcohol or substance abuse, psychosexual disorders or other mental disabilities. If you have questions in this area, the society operates a confidential hotline at 202-466-1809.

Janet Heatwole, director of professional standards for the D.C. society, said the most complaints, 70 or 80 per year, involve minor matters, such as the doctor's repeated failure to return phone calls or poor bedside manner. These usually do not result in disciplinary actions and are resolved informally through an intermediary.

Since 1981, more than 115 cases involving physicians impaired by drugs or alcohol have been reported to the society. Ordinarily, the society will ask to evaluate the physician and if he or she needs treatment, will enter into an agreeement under which the doctor is monitored for five years, must attend monthly meetings and submit to urine tests. If a physician does not cooperate, his or her case is referred to the D.C. Board of Medicine, Heatwole said.

Patients can file an informal complaint by calling the Professional Standards Department at the Medical Society at 202-466-1800. A formal complaint must be sent in writing to the Medical Society of the District of Columbia, Professional Standards Department. The society will not consider complaints if formal litigation is being contemplated or has begun.

Generally speaking, a medical society is a voluntary organization and has no control over physician licensing. It tries to resolve disputes informally and can only reprimand, supsend or expel a physician from membership in the society. In DC, the most serious cases are referred to the Board of Medicine for the District of Columbia, which is the official state licensing authority.

The smaller Virginia and Maryland county medical societies mostly handle complaints by referring cases directly to their respective state medical boards.

The following are the names, addresses and phone numbers of the state medical boards, which have jurisdiction over physician licensing, and the local medical societies. In addition to receiving complaints, the state boards will tell consumers if a particular physician has been reprimanded or disciplined in some way. It will not confirm, discuss or divulge any cases under investigation.

The District of Columbia Board of Medicine
605 G St. NW, Rm. 202LL
Washington DC 20001
(202)727-5365

Maryland Board of Physician Quality Assurance
PO Box 2571
Baltimore Md. 21215
(410)764-4777

Virginia State Board of Medicine
1601 Rolling Hills Dr.
Richmond Va. 23229
(804)662-9908

MEDICAL SOCIETIES

Alexandria Medical Society
101 S. Whiting St. #210
Alexandria VA 22304
(703)751-4611

American Medical Association
Washington office
1101 Vermont Ave. NW
Washington DC 20005
(202)789-7400

Arlington Medical Society
4615 Lee Highway
Arlington VA 22207
(703)528-0888

Fairfax County Medical Society
8100 Oak St.
Dun Loring VA 22027
(703)560-4855

Medical Society of the District of Columbia
1707 L St. NW, #400
Washington DC 20036
(202)466-1800

Montgomery County Medical Society
15855 Crabbs Branch Way
Rockville MD 20855
(301)921-4300

Prince George's County Medical Society
6307 Landover Rd
Cheverly Md 20785
(301)341-7758

CHAPTER FIVE

DOCTORS' DIRECTORY

The typical woman doctor in the Washington metropolitan area is in her early 40s, according to this book's survey of 540 women physicians. She works in a group practice with one or more associates and specializes in either internal medicine, pediatrics, obstetrics/gynecology or psychiatry.

Of the four predominant specialty groups, obstetrician/gynecologists are the youngest at nearly 40 years of age and are twice as likely to work in a group practice than solo.

The average internist and pediatrician is about 44 years old and also works with one or more partners. Psychiatrists tend to be slightly older, averaging about 47 years, and are four times more likely to work alone than in a group.

The following is a directory of 540 doctors, who responded to a two-page questionnaire about their practice and educational background. The names, addresses and phone numbers were updated by telephone early in 1993 and many new doctors were added to the directory. The professional information is reprinted as provided by the physicians or their staffs, and in many cases, includes personal comments on their philosophy of medicine, type of practice or special aspects of their care. The doctors have not been rated or reviewed in any way by the author.

The doctors are listed by specialty areas, which are then broken down into geographic locations by zip code, beginning with the District of Columbia, followed by suburban Maryland and Virginia. Within each zip code, the doctors names are alphabetized. The category of hospitals includes any type of affiliation, including full-time or attending physician, courtesy privileges and faculty positions.

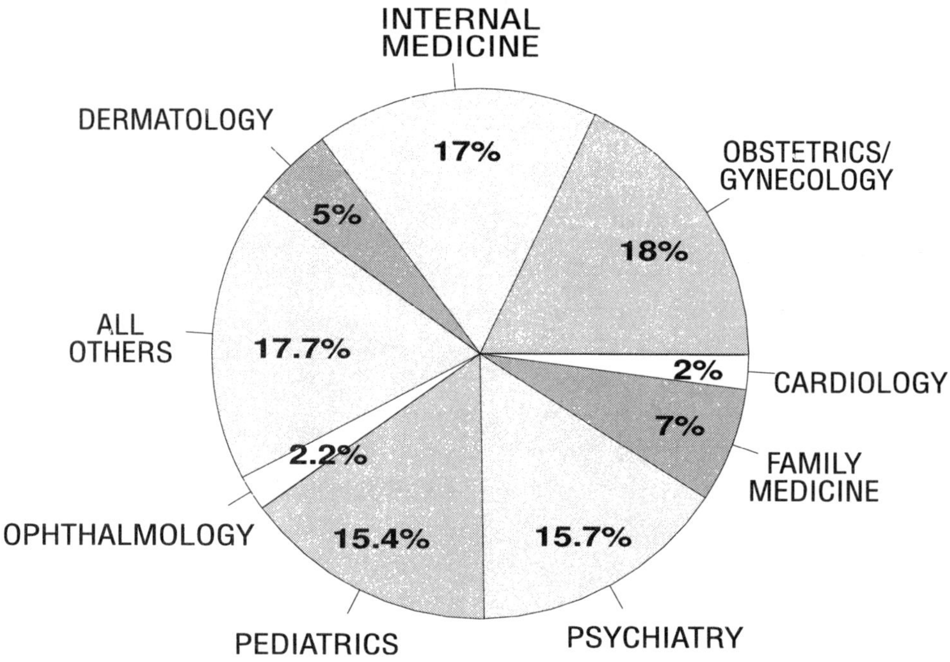
INTERNAL MEDICINE
17%
DERMATOLOGY
5%
OBSTETRICS/ GYNECOLOGY
18%
ALL OTHERS
17.7%
2%
CARDIOLOGY
7%
FAMILY MEDICINE
2.2%
OPHTHALMOLOGY
15.4%
15.7%
PEDIATRICS
PSYCHIATRY

DIRECTORY

DISTRICT OF COLUMBIA

Denise Chevalier, MD
650 Pa. Ave. SE #370, Washington DC 20003
(202)546-0062
MED. DEGREE: Howard University 1981
TRAINING: Howard University, pediatrics '81-'84, allergy and immunology fellow Howard Univ. '86-'88
BOARD CERT.:Pediatrics '86
HOSPITALS:Providence and Greater Southeast
COMMENTS: Pediatric and adult patients with allergies and asthma
SEE NE DC and Mitchellville, Md offices also

Cheryl C. Rosenblatt, MD
526 6th St SE, Washington DC 20003
(202)544-7785
MED. DEGREE: State Univ. of New York at Buffalo, '69
TRAINING: State Univ. NY - Ped. '70-'72; Fellow - Allergy/Immun. '82-'84 Walter Reed Army Med. Center; Cardiac Life Support 3/90; Allergy/Immun - New Visions for the 90s 11/90, New York Academy
BOARD CERT.:Allergy/Immun. '85; Pediatrics '75
HOSPITALS:Fair Oaks and Fairfax
SEE offices in Maryland and Virginia also

Denise Chevalier, MD
1140 Varnum St. NE #208A, Washington DC 20017
(202)529-4233 SEE SE DC office for background

Doina Zuba, MD
916 19Th St NW #214, Washington DC 20006
(202)223-2905
ASSOCIATES: L.B. Bolle, M.D., Otolaryngology /Plastic Surgery
MED. DEGREE: '66 Romania
TRAINING: Mercy Catholic Med. Center, Darby, Pa.; Georgetown Univ. Hosp., 2 yr. fellow allergy/immunology
LANGUAGES: Romanian COMMENTS: I like the patient to be informed of his medical problem and understand the process of healing, this way the treatment is followed properly.

Nirupma Rohatgi, MD
908 New Hampshire Ave NW, Washington DC 20037
(202)223-8999
MED. DEGREE: All India Institute of Medical Sciences
TRAINING: DC Gen. Hosp. - Ped.; Allergy/Immunology fellow Children's National Med. Center, Walter Reed Army Med. Center
BOARD CERT.: Pediarics '80; Allergy/Immun. '81
HOSPITALS: Asst. Prof. at George Washington; Shady Grove and Children's National Med. Center
LANGUAGES:Hindi and Urdu
COMMENTS: Low key, good patient-physician relationship, easily accessible.
SEE office in Gaithersburg also

Gloria R. Werth, MD
3 Washington Circle #208, Washington DC 20037
(202)785-0668
MED. DEGREE:Johns Hopkins Univ. '53
TRAINING: Washington Hosp. Ctr.; Walter Reed Army Med. Ctr.
BOARD CERT.:Allergy/Immunology '79
HOSPITALS: George Washington, lecturer; Providence, Sibley
COMMENTS: I spend as much time as needed to obtain the history and teach patients with asthma, hay fever, anaphylaxis etc. how to manage conditions.

MARYLAND

Denise Chevalier, MD
10274 Lake Arbor Way, Mitchellville Md 20721
(301)336-0005 SEE SE DC office for background

Joanne F. Domson, Md
9135 Piscataway Rd #240, Clinton Md 20735
(301)868-9313
SPECIALTY: pediatric & adult allergy, asthma
MED. DEGREE: Women's Medical Coll., Philadelphia '69
TRAINING: Fitzgerald Mercy Hosp., Medical Coll. of Pennsylvania
BOARD CERT.: Allergy/immun. '81; Pediatrics '75
HOSPITALS: Greater Southeast Comm., Southern Maryland, Mt. Vernon, Children's
LANGUAGES: French (little) SEE office in Alexandria, Va. also

Jyothi Gadde, MD, PA
7525 Greenway Center Dr. #214, Greenbelt Md 20770
(301)474-8118
MED. DEGREE: Gandhi Medical College '79
TRAINING: Prince George's Gen. Hosp.; Fellow Allergy/Immun. Johns Hopkins Univ. '83-'85
BOARD CERT.: Internal Med. '83; Allergy/immun. '85
HOSPITALS: Chief of Allergy, Prince George's Gen. Hosp.
LANGUAGES: Hindi SEE office in Silver Spring also

Jeanne M. Barbera, MD
50 W. Edmonston Rd #301, Rockville Md 20852
(301)251-3704
ASSOCIATES: Vincent J. Vaghi, MD (husband)
MED. DEGREE: Georgetown Univ. '79
TRAINING: Children's National Med. Center Pediatrics '79-'82 and Allergy fellow '82-'84
BOARD CERT.: Pediatrics '84 and Allergy/immun. '85
HOSPITALS: Children's LANGUAGES: Spanish-speaking nurse
COMMENTS: Adult & pediatric allergy - practiced by two caring/competent physicians, very cordial staff
SEE office in Germantown also

Jeanne M. Barbera, MD
N. Lake Med. Park, 19519 Doctors' Drive, Germantown Md 20874
(301)972-9433 SEE Rockville office for background

Nirupma Rohatgi, MD
9015 Shady Grove Ct., Gaithersburg Md 20877
(301)963-0196 SEE NW DC office for background

Cheryl C. Rosenblatt, MD
849-C Quince Orchard Boulevard, Gaithersburg, Md 20878
(301)948-7002
SEE SE DC office for background; Offices also in Virginia

Jyothi Gadde, Md
2415 Musgrove Rd #306, Silver Spring Md 20904
(301)989-9232 SEE Greenbelt office for background

VIRGINIA

Cheryl C. Rosenblatt, MD
3650 Joseph Siewick Dr., Fairfax Va 22033
also 8316 Traford Lane, Springfield Va 22152
(703)648-0030
SEE SE DC office for background; Office also in Maryland

Joanne F. Domson, MD
7906 Andrus Rd # 7, Alexandria Va 22307
(703)360-8881
SEE Clinton, Md. office for background

DISTRICT OF COLUMBIA

Nancy Lonsdorf, MD
Maharishi AyurVeda Med. Center
4910 Mass Ave NW #315, Washington DC 20016
(202)244-2700
ASSOCIATES: Nicholas Placenta, DO
MED. DEGREE: Johns Hopkins Univ. '83
TRAINING: Stanford Univ. '84-'86 (psychiatry)
COMMENTS: Specializing in nonpharmacologic, natural approaches to treatment of chronic illnesses, prevention and promotion of health. Special interest in women's health.

DISTRICT OF COLUMBIA

Elizabeth Ross, MD
2021 K St. NW #315, Washington DC 20006
(202)775-0955
ASSOCIATES: Kenneth Lee, MD
MED. DEGREE: Univ. Of Maryland '78
TRAINING: Univ. of Maryland '78-'81; cardiac path. fellow, National Inst. of Health '83-'85; cardiology fellow '85-'88 Wash. Hosp. Center
BOARD CERT.: Internal med.'81; Cardiovascular med. '89
HOSPITALS: Washington Hosp. Ctr., Wash. Adventist, Sibley, George Washington LANGUAGES: Spanish

Cynthia M. Tracy, MD
Georgetown Univ. Hosp., Director, Cardiac Arrhythmia Service
3800 Reservoir Rd Main Bldg, 4N, Washington DC 20007
(202)687-8903
SPECIALTY: electrophysiology/cardiology
ASSOCIATES: Drs. Jean T. Barbey, Allen Solomon
MED. DEGREE: Medical College of Ohio at Toledo '79
TRAINING: Georgetown Univ. Hospital
BOARD CERT.: Int. med '84; Cardiovascular med. '85
HOSPITALS: Georgetown Univ. Hosp., dir. Cardiac Arrythmia Serv.
COMMENTS: We strongly believe that a confident, well informed patient will fare better under any circumstance. Our team approach reflects this belief. Cardiologists, surgeons, nurses and technicians all communicate carefully with patients and their families to insure a fuller level of understanding and comfort.

Susan O'Donoghue, MD
Cardiac Arrhythmia Center, Washington Hospital Center
110 Irving St. NW, Washington DC 20010
(202)877-7685
SPECIALTY: Cardiac electrophysiology only
ASSOCIATES: Edward Platia, MD
MED. DEGREE: Georgetown Univ. '81
TRAINING: Emory Univ. Atlanta; cardiology fellow - Emory and Washington Hosp. Center; also electrophysiology fellow
BOARD CERT.: Cardiovascular med. '87; Int. med. '84
HOSPITALS: Washington Hosp. Ctr., George Washington
COMMENTS: Cardiac electrophysiology deals with patients with heart rhythm problems, fainting spells, pacemakers and other devices.

Esther Ocuin, MD
106 Irving St NW #119, Washington DC 20010
(202)882-1203
SPECIALTY: Consultative and invasive cardiology
MED. DEGREE: Univ. of Bologna, Italy '76
TRAINING: Washington Hosp. Center; Fellow card. - George Wash. Univ.; invasive card. - Washington Veterans Administration Hosp.
BOARD CERT.: Int. med '81; Cardiovascular med. '83
HOSPITALS: Asst. clin. prof. George Washington; Wash. Hosp. Ctr.
LANGUAGES: Hebrew, Spanish, Italian
COMMENTS: Strong rapport with patients and families. Orientation toward screening, prevention and reducing risk factors. Aggressive treatment of existing heart disease. Special interest in interventional and invasive cardiology and acute care.

Lucy Van Voorhees, MD
Washington Hosp. Center, 110 Irving St. NW, Wash. DC 20010
(202)877-6264
ASSOCIATES: Dept. of Cardiology, Washington Hosp. Center
MED. DEGREE: Univ. of Tenn. '76
TRAINING: City of Memphis Hosp, Georgetown Univ Hosp.; Card. fellow Vanderbuilt Univ Hosp. '79-'80; Georgetown/ Washington Veterans Admin. Hosp. '80-'81
BOARD CERT.: Int. med '79; Cardiovascular med.'85
HOSPITALS: Director coronary care unit, Washington Hosp. Center
LANGUAGES: French (a little)

Judith Hsia, MD
George Washington Univ. Medical Center
2150 Penn Ave NW, #4-414, Washington DC 20037
(202)994-5461
ASSOCIATES: Faculty of George Washington Univ.
MED. DEGREE: Univ. of Illinois '78
TRAINING: Tufts - New England Medical Center
BOARD CERT.: Int. med '81; Cardiovascular med. '87
HOSPITALS: Asst. prof of med., George Washington Univ.

Elizabeth M. Kingsley, MD
Cardiology Assoc., P.C., 2141 K St. NW #206, Wash. DC 20037
(202)822-9356
ASSOCIATES: Drs. Stuart Seides, Joel Rosenberg, James Ross, Benjamin Lee, Jonathan Altschuler
MED. DEGREE: Univ. of Maryland '78
TRAINING: Boston Vet. Admin. Hosp., Beth Israel Hosp., Boston
BOARD CERT.: Int. med.'84; Cardiovascular med. '89
HOSPITALS: Washington Hosp. Center, Anne Arundel General
LANGUAGES: Portuguese

Jannet F. Lewis, MD
Howard Univ. Hosp., 2041 Georgia NW, 6C-11, Wash. DC 20060
(202)865-1326
SUBSPECIALTY: echocardiography (sonograms of the heart)
MED. DEGREE: Louisiana State Univ. '77
TRAINING: Louisiana State Univ./Charity Hosp. of New Orleans
BOARD CERT.: Int. med '80; Cardiovascular med. '83
HOSPITALS: Howard Univ Hosp., assoc. prof., dir. of echocardiography

VIRGINIA

Anne E. Summers, MD
3289 Woodburn Rd #320, Annandale Va 22003
(703)820-2800
SEE Falls Church office for background: Office in Reston also

Anne E. Summers, MD
5201 Leesburg Pke #204, Falls Church Va 22041
(703)820-2800
SUBSPECIALTY: echocardiography
ASSOCIATES: Drs. Allan Simpson, Kenneth Brooks, Andrew Keller
MED. DEGREE: Medical College of Pa., Philadelphia '80
TRAINING: Northwestern Mem. Hosp., Chicago: also Cardiology fellow '83-'85
BOARD CERT.: Int. med. '83; Cardiovascular med. '85
HOSPITALS: Fairfax, Reston, Alexandria
COMMENTS: I believe that every patient should be treated as an individual with their special needs assessed and treated. Listening carefully and answering all questions are the mainstay of the doctor-patient relationship. I enjoy the wonderful people that are my patients. I love being a doctor.
SEE offices in Annandale and Reston also

Anne E. Summers, MD
1830 Town Center Dr. #405, Reston Va 22090
(703)481-9191
SEE Falls Church office for background; Office in Annandale also

Anne M. Safko, MD
The Cardiology Group, Inc.
611 S. Carlin Springs Rd #203, Arlington Va 22204
(703)671-8200
ASSOCIATES: Drs. Fritz Andersen, Jay Kalan
MED. DEGREE: Georgetown Univ. '81
TRAINING: Veterans Admin. Hosp., DC; Card. fellow Georgetown
BOARD CERT.: Int. med '87; Cardiovascular med.'88
HOSPITALS: Fairfax, Arlington, Northern Va. Doctors
COMMENTS: My practice involves general cardiology and includes echocardiography, stress testing and diagnostic catheterization (angiography). My approach to medicine involves active patient participation in all aspects of diagnostic testing and treatment. I believe patients should be thoroughly informed about treatment options and choices in diagnostic testing.

DISTRICT OF COLUMBIA

Valerie Callender, MD
650 Penn. Ave SE #360, Wash. DC 20003
(202)547-9405
SEE Southern Ave SE office for background; Office also in Landover

Zenona W. Mally, MD
1634 Eye St NW #402, Washington DC 20006
(202)737-6800
SUBSPECIALTY: cosmetic procedures
MED. DEGREE: Univ. of Toronto '58;
TRAINING: Johns Hopkins Univ. and Univ. of Pennsylvania
BOARD CERT.: Dermatology '69
HOSPITALS: Georgetown, Sibley
LANGUAGES: French (moderate ability)
COMMENTS: My practice is very sensitive to women's concerns, e.g. cosmetic procedures, such as collagen implants, hair loss, sclerotherapy for spider veins, etc.

Cheryl M. Burgess, MD
4119 Connecticut Ave NW, Washington DC 20008
(202)966-3706 SEE Varnum St. NE office for background

Beverly A. Johnson, MD
4119 Conn Ave. NW, Washington DC 20008
(202)966-3706 SEE Varnum St. NE office for background

Ella L. Toombs, MD
Aesthetic Dermatology Dupont Circle
1616 18th St NW #114, Washington DC 20009
(202)483-3376
MED. DEGREE: Ohio State Univ. '81
TRAINING: Medical Coll. of Georgia.; Cleveland Clinic; Howard Univ.; Fellow Derm. National Inst. of Health
BOARD CERT.: Dermatology '87
HOSPITALS: Columbia Hosp. for Women, National Inst. of Health
LANGUAGES: French COMMENTS: We provide complete medical and surgical treatment of disorders involving the skin, hair or fingernails. These services include cosmetic skin procedures.

Mavis B. Marks, MD
3500-14th St. NW #L1, Washington DC 20010
(202)387-4742
MED. DEGREE: Howard Univ. '74
TRAINING: Glen Cove Comm. Hosp., Long Island, NY; Howard Univ. Hosp.; MPH Johns Hopkins Univ.
COMMENTS: Practice is part-time

Lynn McKinley-Grant, MD
Washington Hospital Center
110 Irving St. NW 2B28, Washington DC 20010
(202)877-6654
ASSOCIATES: Drs. Thomas Nigra, Alan Moshell
MED. DEGREE: Harvard Univ. '80
TRAINING: Boston City Hosp., New York Univ.; Dermatology fellow National Inst. of Health; MA counseling Columbia Univ.
BOARD CERT.: Int. med. '83, Dermatology '86
HOSPITALS: Wash. Hosp. Center, George Washington, Children's, National Rehab. Hosp.
LANGUAGES: French and Spanish (little)

Denise Cook, MD
The Washington Clinic
5401 Western Ave NW, Washington DC 20015
(202)244-9100
ASSOCIATES: John Short, MD, derm. (multispecialty clinic)
MED. DEGREE: Washington Univ., St. Louis '82
TRAINING: Sinai Hosp., Baltimore; Howard Univ. Hosp. '88-91 - dermatology
BOARD CERT.: Int. med. '88; Dermatology '92
HOSPITAL: Sibley
LANGUAGES: Spanish (Several others available)
COMMENTS: We are able to treat everything related to the care of the skin including surgical procedures.

Cheryl M. Burgess, MD
1140 Varnum St NE #200, Washington DC 20017
(202)526-4454
SUBSPECIALTY: Cosmetic dermatology, surgery
ASSOCIATES: Beverly Johnson, MD
MED. DEGREE: Howard Univ. '84
TRAINING: Howard Univ. Hospital, Int. med and dermatology; also dermatologic surgery
BAORD CERT.:Dermatology boards '88
HOSPITALS: Providence, Howard, Washington Hosp. Center
LANGUAGES: Spanish (little)
COMMENTS: Cosmetic dermatology, chemical peels, collagen enhancement, comedone extraction, new techniques, tatoo removal, scar revision, sclerotherapy.
SEE office on Conn. Ave. NW also

Beverly A. Johnson, MD
1140 Varnum St NE #200, Washington DC 20017
(202)526-4454
SUBSPECIALTY: skin surgery
ASSOCIATES: Cheryl Burgess, MD
MED. DEGREE: Howard Univ. '79; TRAINING: Staten Island Public Health Hosp., N.Y.
BOARD CERT.: Dermatology '81
HOSPITALS: Providence , Howard
COMMENTS: Skin diseases of adults and children. Dermatologic surgery, dermatologic cosmetic surgery
SEE office on Conn. Ave also

Valerie Callender, MD
Greater SE Skin Care Center
1328 Southern Ave SE #314, Washington DC 20032
(202)561-3747
SUBSPECIALTY: Dermatologic, cosmetic and laser surgery
MED. DEGREE: Howard University '86
TRAINING: Howard Univ.: Int. med. '86-'87, Dermatology '87-'90
BOARD CERT.: Dermatology '90
HOSPITALS: DC General, Howard, Greater SE Comm, Hadley, Prince George's
LANGUAGES: Spanish
See offices on Penn. Ave SE DC and Landover, Md.

Marilyn Berzin, MD
1145 19th St NW #400, Washington DC 20036
(202)822-9591
ASSOCIATES: Drs. Dale Isaacson and Susan Elliott
MED. DEGREE: Albert Einstein Coll. of Med., N.Y. '79
TRAINING: Bronx Municipal Hosp., George Wash. Univ. Med. Ctr.
BOARD CERT.:Dermatology '83
HOSPITALS: George Washington, Sibley, Washington Hosp. Center
LANGUAGES: French
COMMENTS: The practice sees approximately 60-70 patients a day.

Susan Tillman Elliott, MD
1145-19th St. NW #400, Washington DC 20036
(202)822-9591
ASSOCIATES: Drs. Dale Isaacson, Marilyn Berzin
MED. DEGREE: George Washington Univ. '76
TRAINING: Univ. of Oregon '76-'80; MS George Washington Univ.
BOARD CERT.: Dermatology '80
HOSPITALS: George Washington, Sibley, Columbia Hosp. for Women, Washington Hosp. Center
LANGUAGES: Spanish
COMMENTS: With prior call from referral MD or agency, I will see Hispanic speaking patients at no charge if indigent or uninsured.

Deborah Chester Kalter, MD
2440 M St. NW #313, Washington DC 20037
(202)775-1792 SEE Silver Spring Md office for background

Marsha Carol McNeely, MD
George Washington Univ. Med. Center
2150 Penn. Ave. NW, Washington DC 20037
(202)994-4058
ASSOCIATES: Drs. Mervyn Elgart, Bruce Feldman, Pamela Scheinman, Carmen M. Williams
MED. DEGREE:Univ. of Texas Med. Branch '82
TRAINING: Univ. of Texas Med. Branch; also a PhD in human genetics; Fellow Immunodermatology National Inst. of Health
BOARD CERT.: Dermatology '86, Immunoderm. '87
HOSPITALS: George Washington Univ., asst. professor
COMMENTS: Practice is in academic setting. Advantages of many specialists within one setting. Patients sometimes seen with accompanying residents and students.

Michelle A. Rivera, MD
2112 F. St. NW #701, Washington DC 20037
(202)293-1766 SEE Arlington office for background

Pamela L. Scheinman, MD
George Washington Univ. Med. Center
2150 Penn Ave NW, 6th fl. Dermatology, Washington DC 20037
(202)994-4058
ASSOCIATES: Drs. Mervyn Elgart, Bruce Feldman, Marsha McNeely, Carmen M. Williams
HOSPITALS: Mt. Sinai Medical Center, N.Y. '86
TRAINING: St.Luke's/Roosevelt Hosp., N.Y.; Strong Memorial Hosp., Rochester, N.Y. derm.
BOARD CERT.: Dermatology '90
HOSPITALS: George Wash. Univ asst. professor; clin. inst. Univ. of Rochester Med. Ctr. '90 LANGUAGES: Hebrew

Carmen Myrie Williams, MD
George Washington Univ. Med. Center
2150 Pennsylvania Ave NW, Dermatology, Washington DC 20037
(202)994-4058
SUBSPECIALTY: skin cancer
ASSOCIATES: Drs. Carol McNeely, Pamela Scheinman, Mervyn Elgart, Bruce Feldman
MED. DEGREE: New York Univ. '74
TRAINING: New York Univ., anatomical pathology, dermatopathology fellow, clinical derm.
BOARD CERT.: Derm.'78; Anatomical path. '81; dermatopathology certificate '82
HOSPITALS: Dir. Div. of Dermatopathology George Wash. Univ.. assoc. prof. derm., path. LANGUAGES: Spanish (some)

MARYLAND

Lillian Vlalukin, MD
11701 Livingston Rd, Ft. Washington Md 20744
(301)292-6010
MED. DEGREE: Univ. of Belgrade '61
TRAINING: George Wash.-Infectious diseases fellow '65-'67; Georgetown Univ. cardiology fellow; DC General Hosp. '64-'65, Derm., '67-'70
BOARD eligible dermatology LANGUAGES: Slavic

Valerie Callender, MD
Landover Mall, W. bldg #201, Landover, Md 20785
(301)341-7762 SEE Southern Ave SE office for background

Roberta F. Palestine, MD
Wyngate Medical Park, 5606 Shields Dr., Bethesda Md 20817
(301)530-8300
SUBSPECIALTY: Derm. surgery, collagen injections, sclerotherapy
MED. DEGREE: Univ. of Rochester '78
TRAINING: Mayo Graduate Sch. of Medicine, Minnesota
BOARD CERT.: Dermatology '82
HOSPITALS: George Washington, clinical instructor

Mary K. Sopocko, MD
17904 Georgia Ave. #215, Olney Md 20832
(301)924-2912
SUBSPECIALTY: skin surgery
MED. DEGREE: Univ. of Illinois '77
TRAINING: Univ. of Illinois and Walter Reed Army Med. Center
BOARD CERT.: Dermatology COMMENTS: Cosmetic dermatology, spider leg vein injections, collagen injections

Eleanor Ford, MD
Dermatology and Skin Cancer Center
344 University Blvd W #321, Silver Spring Md 20901
(301)681-4233
MED. DEGREE: New Jersey Med. School '80
TRAINING: E. Orange Veterans Admin./NJ Med. School; Howard Univ. Derm. fellow '83-86
BOARD CERT.: Int. med. '83; Derm. '86
HOSPITALS: Washington Adventist, consultant
COMMENTS: I use a contemporary, interactive approach to treating patients. Whenever possible, alternatives are discussed and the best possible treatment is chosen for the individual.

Patricia C. Brown, MD
3925 Ferrara Drive, Silver Spring, Md 20906
(301)933-1547
MED. DEGREE: Yale Univ. '80
TRAINING: New York Univ. surgery intern; Strong Memorial Hosp., Rochester, NY, derm.'87-'90; Continuing medical education award in dermatology, also AMA Physician's Recognition Award
BOARD CERT.: Derm. '90; Dermatopathology '87
HOSPITAL: Washington Adventist
LANGUAGES: French
COMMENTS: My goal is to practice caring, competent dermatology.

Katalin Soltesz Korossy, MD
3925 Ferrara Drive, Silver Spring Md 20906
(301)949-1450
MED. DEGREE: Debrecen Med. School, Hungary, '70
TRAINING: Bethesda Sub. Hosp; George Wash. Univ. - dermatology
BOARD CERT.: Dermatology '80
HOSPITALS: Montgomery General
LANGUAGES: Hungarian COMMENTS: Christian ethics

Deborah Chester Kalter, MD
1104 Spring St. #200, Silver Spring Md 20910
(301)585-1004
SUBSPECIALTY: Immunodermatology, Infectious diseases
ASSOCIATES: Drs. Douglas N. Robins, J. Kevin Poitras
MED. DEGREE: Baylor Coll. of Med., Houston '81
TRAINING: Baylor ; Infectious diseases, London School of Hygiene and Tropical Med.
BOARD CERT.: Derm. '86; Immunoderm. '89
HOSPITALS: Wash. Hosp. Center, National Inst. of Health, Walter Reed Army Med. Ctr.
LANGUAGES: Spanish, Portuguese
COMMENTS: I assume my patients are intelligent and want to understand their medical conditions. I explain the rationale for intended therapy. SEE office M St. NW DC also

VIRGINIA

Julie P. Henry, MD
9004 Fern Park Dr, Burke Va 22015
(703)425-5300
ASSOCIATES: Drs. Paul Kravitz, Alan Moshell
MED. DEGREE: Georgetown Univ. '85
TRAINING: Henry Ford Hosp., Detroit '85- '89
BOARD CERT.: Dermatology '89
HOSPITALS: Fairfax
COMMENTS: We provide care to patients of all ages including children and the elderly. We provide medical and surgical dermatologic care, including vein sclerosing of spider veins.

Alexandra Kazakis, Md
3022 Williams Drive #101, Fairfax, Va 22031
(703)573-5252
MED. DEGREE: U. of Virginia '83; TRAINING: Univ. of Maryland
BOARD CERT.: Dermatology '87
HOSPITALS: Fairfax, Fair Oaks LANGUAGES: Greek

Carol L. Piatt, MD
3028 Javier Rd #410, Fairfax Va 22031
(703)560-3372
MED. DEGREE: Hahnemann Univ. , Philadelphia '81
TRAINING: Medical Coll. of Virginia/Riverside Hosp., Newport News, Va. '81-'84; State Univ. of N.Y. at Buffalo '85-'88; Roswell Park Mem. Inst. in Buffalo fellow derm. oncology and surgery '88-'89
BOARD CERT.: Derm. '88, Family practice '84
HOSPITALS: Fairfax COMMENTS: Do not overbook appointments. 1/2 hour initial patient visit. All treatment possibilities are explained so the patient and I can choose the best modality for that patient. (Practice limited to dermatology and dermatologic surgery.)

Nancy Bruckner, MD
6731 Whittier Ave., Mc Lean Va 22101 (703)790-5850
SUBSPECIALTY: sclerotherapy of spider veins
ASSOCIATES: Max Rubin, MD
MED. DEGREE: George Wash. Univ. '76; TRAINING: Washington Hosp. Center; George Washington Univ.
BOARD CERT.: Dermatology '81
HOSPITALS: Reston, Fairfax, Arlington
LANGUAGES: Fluent Spanish speakers on staff

Inia Irene Yevich, MD
Virginia Med. Associates
5510 Alma Lane, Springfield Va 22151
(703)642-5990
ASSOCIATES: Multi-specialty group
MED. DEGREE: Tulane Univ Med. School '81
TRAINING: Brooke Army Med. Ctr., San Antonio, Texas; MS and PhD in physiology
BOARD CERT.: Dermatology '87
HOSPITALS: Fairfax, Fair Oaks
LANGUAGES: Ukrainian
COMMENTS: Perform minor surgical procedures such as excision of skin cancers, biopsies, cryosurgery. Maintain high level of dermatologic care and a caring attitude for patients.

Linda P. Nims, MD
301 Maple Ave W. Sect. 4, #E, Vienna Va 22180
(703)938-5700
MED. DEGREE: Med. Univ. of S. Carolina '73
TRAINING: Henry Ford Hosp., Detroit, Mi.
BOARD CERT.: Dermatology '77
HOSPITALS: Fairfax COMMENTS: Dr. Nims likes to have her patients become knowledgeable about their diagnoses and therapy, including their medicines, e.g. relative strengths of cortisone creams. The patients are active partners in their care so they understand the nature of their conditions and have realistic expectations.

Michelle A. Rivera, MD
3801 N. Fairfax Drive #53N, Arlington Va 22203
(703)524-7206
MED. DEGREE: Cornell Univ. Med. '80
TRAINING: Children's National Med. Center, pediatric intern./residency; dermatology fellow '83- '86
BOARD CERT.: Dermatology '86
HOSPITALS: Assoc. clinical prof. dermatology George Washington
LANGUAGES: Spanish COMMENTS: Light treatment for psoriasis, dermatologic surgery (mole and cancer removal)
Office also on F St. NW DC

Tina Alster, MD
Washington Institute of Dermatologic Laser Surgery
2311 M St. NW #504, Washington DC 20037
(202)785-8855
MED. DEGREE: Duke Univ. '86
TRAINING: Univ. of Pennsylvania; Yale Univ., derm.; Harvard Univ. fellow laser surgery '89-'90; also BS in nursing, Duke Univ.
BOARD CERT.: Dermatology '90
HOSPITALS: Clinical assoc. prof. pediatrics, Georgetown Univ.
LANGUAGES: French COMMENTS: I specialize in the treatment of benign vascular lesions (portwine stains in children/adults; spider veins in men/women). All work office-based. A make-up/skin care consultant sees all new patients at no extra charge. The office is sleek and was awarded by an architectural magazine. The patients love it!

DISTRICT OF COLUMBIA

Michelle F. Magee, MD
Medlantic Prevention and Research Clinics
650 Penn. Ave SE #050, Washington DC 20003
(202)675-6010
SUBSPECIATLY: Metabolism
ASSOCIATES: Drs. Robert Ratner, David Robbins
MED. DEGREE: Royal Coll. of Surgeons, Ireland '82
TRAINING: George Washington Univ. '85, cert. diabetes educator
BOARD CERT.: Int. med. '85, Endocrinology '87
HOSPITALS: Washington Hospital Center
HOSPITALS: French
COMMENTS: Practice covers all areas of endocrinology and metabolism, including thyroid and diabetes. Interest in diabetic foot disorders, female endocrinology, including excess hair growth and menstrual abnormalities.
SEE also Washington Hosp. Center office, NW DC

Michelle F. Magee, MD
Washington Hospital Center
110 Irving St. NW Rm 2A72, Washington DC 20010
(202)877-6563 SEE SE DC office for background

MARYLAND

Helena W. Rodbard, MD
8218 Wisconsin Ave #114, Bethesda Md 20814
(301)251-0909 SEE Rockville office for background

Helena W. Rodbard, MD
14808 Physicians Ln #111, Rockville Md 20850
(301)251-0909
SUBSPECIALTY: Diabetes
ASSOCIATES: Michael A. Dempsey, MD
MED. DEGREE: Escola Paulista De Medicina, Brazil '72
TRAINING: Washington Hosp. Center; Fellow National Inst. of Health and George Wash. Univ.; yearly post-grad courses
BOARD CERT.: Int. med. '81, Endocrin. '83
HOSPITALS: Georgetown Univ. clinical asst. prof.; Shady Grove, Suburban
LANGUAGES: Portuguese, Spanish
COMMENTS: Active participation in several medical societies and community activities; lecturing in diabetes, thyroid disorders, menopause, osteoporosis etc. Friendly office, responsive to patients' needs and wonderful office personnel. SEE office in Bethesda also

Linda Liu, MD
6246 Montrose Rd, Rockville Md 20852 (301)468-1451
ASSOCIATES: Patricia A. Petrick, MD, partner
MED. DEGREE: Brown Med. School '80
TRAINING: Hahnemann Univ. Hosp., Philadelphia; Memorial Hosp., Worcester, Ma.; Endocrinology fellow National Inst. of Health
BOARD CERT.: Int. med. '83; Endocrin. '85
HOSPITALS: National Inst. of Health, Georgetown faculty, Holy Cross, Shady Grove, Suburban, Psychiatric Inst. Montgomery County
LANGUAGES: French, Chinese
COMMENTS: I believe in preventive medicine (besides therapeutic) and in patient education.

Patricia A. Petrick, MD
6246 Montrose Rd, Rockville Md 20852 (301)468-1451
ASSOCIATES: Linda Liu, MD
MED. DEGREE: Univ. of Pittsburgh '78
TRAINING: Univ. of Pittsburgh; Univ. of California, San Diego; Fellowships: National Inst. of Health, Scripps Clinic, La Jolla, Ca., MS biology '74 Pennsylvania State Univ.
BOARD CERT.: Int. med. '81, Endocrin. '87
HOSPITALS: Georgetown clin. instructor; Shady Grove, Suburban, Holy Cross, Psychiatric Inst. of Montgomery County

VIRGINIA

Suzanne Rogacz, MD
Northern Virginia Endocrinologists
3299 Woodburn Rd #450, Annandale Va 22003
(703)849-8440
ASSOCIATES: Drs. Kathleen Link , Michael Ball, Peter Ross
MED. DEGREE: Univ. of N. Carolina, Chapel Hill '80
TRAINING: Georgetown U.; End., Brigham & Women's Hosp., Boston; med. inst., Harvard Med. Sch. '86-'88
BOARD CERT.: Int. med. '83, Endocrin. '85
HOSPITALS: Fairfax, Fair Oaks, Reston, Arlington; Med. director, International Diabetes Center of Va. SEE office in Fairfax also

Suzanne Rogacz, MD
3650 Joseph Siewick Dr., Fairfax Va 22033
(703)648-1831 SEE Annandale office for background

Alice M. Weisz, MD
1707 Osage St. #401, Alexandria, Va. 22302
(703)998-6511
SUBSPECIALTY: Diabetes
ASSOCIATES: Albert Coo, MD
MED. DEGREE: Catholic Univ. '81
TRAINING: St. Vincent's Med. Center, Bayley Seton Hosp., N.Y. ; Fellow end. George Washington Univ.
BOARD CERT.: Int. med. '86; Endocrin. '91
HOSPITALS: Alexandria, diabetic liaison physician; clin. prof. of med. George Washington Univ.
LANGUAGES: Italian COMMENTS: Treatment of diabetes in a team approach with nurse educator/dietician/patient and physician. Particular interest in gestational diabetes.

DISTRICT OF COLUMBIA

Edna V. Edwards, MD
221-8th St. NE, Washington DC 20002
(202)543-5230
MED. DEGREE: Habana Univ., Cuba '60
TRAINING: Nuevitas Hosp., Cuba; 3 gov't. hosps., Jamaica; Prince George's Gen. '75-'77; Howard U. '77-'79
BOARD eligible Family practice
HOSPITALS: Greater SE Comm., Providence, Wash. Hosp. Center
LANGUAGES: Spanish COMMENTS: My top priority is the interest of the patient, who should be treated with utmost consideration and respect. They should be evaluated thoroughly.

Kathryn A. Vaughn, MD
Community of Hope Health Services
1417 Belmont St. NW, Washington DC 20009
(202)232-9022
ASSOCIATES: Drs. David Hilfiker, Joseph Sherman, Adrian Schultz, Kathy Robinson
MED. DEGREE: Indiana Univ. '79
TRAINING: St. Francis Hosp. Center, Indiana '79-'82
BOARD CERT.: Family practice '82
COMMENTS: Health Services is a part of a multi-faceted service center including homeless shelter, job training, social services, child enrichment program. New patients limited to those in the immediate area. Fees on a sliding scale according to income.

Francyne Anderson, MD
Gerald Family Care Assoc., PC
1160 Varnum St NE#117, Washington DC 20017
(202)832-7007
ASSOCIATES: Drs. Melvin Gerald, Keith Banton, Smita Gondhalekar, Robert Davidson, Allyn Lloyd, Rodderick Edmond, Jonita Conner, Joshua Holloway, Artis T. Atlener
MED. DEGREE: U. of Florida '75; TRAINING: Howard Univ. Hosp.
BOARD CERT.: Family Practice
HOSPITALS: Providence, Washington Hosp. Center, Hadley
COMMENTS: Heavy on patient education and health surveillance, very comprehensive in scope. Health care from cradle to the grave.

Cheryl L. Henson-Everson, MD
1140 Varnum St. NE #105, Washington DC 20017
(202)832-2890
MED. DEGREE: Howard Univ. '85
TRAINING: Georgetown Univ./Providence Hosp.
BOARD CERT.: Family Practice '89
HOSPITALS: Providence, Howard
COMMENTS: We emphasize care for all family members of all ages and stress preventive care with annual physicals, age-appropriate cancer screens and complete blood work.

B. Toloria Braswell, MD
Greater SE Comm. Hospital
1328 Southern Ave #201, Washington DC 20032
(202)574-2244
ASSOCIATES: Stacy Ross, MD
MED. DEGREE: Howard Univ. '82; TRAINING: Howard Univ.
BOARD CERT.: Family Practice '85
HOSPITALS: Greater SE Comm., Prince George's, Howard Univ., Providence, Hadley LANGUAGES: Spanish

MARYLAND

Raman Tuli, MD
3503 Perry St. #B, Mt. Ranier, Md 20712
(301)699-0750 SEE Gaithersburg office for background

Dora M. Mamodesene, MD
4000 Mitchelville Rd #316, Mitchelville Md 20716
(301)262-0030 SEE Greenbelt for background

Robin Bissell, MD
4404 Queensbury Rd, Riverdale Md 20737
(301)277-4400
MED. DEGREE: Univ. of Colorado '83
TRAINING: State Univ. of N.Y. Upstate Medical Ctr., Syracuse, NY; B.S. nursing
HOSPITALS: Leland Memorial, Prince George's, Greater Laurel-Beltsville, Providence
LANGUAGES: Spanish
COMMENTS: Commitment to people from all backgrounds with special attention to Hispanics. Services provided to all ages, pediatrics through geriatrics

Asuncion M. Soriano, MD
119 Capitol Hts. Blvd., Capitol Hts, Md 20743
(301)336-4660
ASSOCIATES: Cesar Soriano, Jr., MD
MED. DEGREE: Univ. of Sto. Thomas, Philippines '65
TRAINING: McKeesport Hosp., St. Francis Gen. Hosp., Pittsburgh, PA; Gen. pathology '69-'72
HOSPITALS: Prince George's Gen.

Cefie S. De la Paz, MD
52 Talbert Dr, Forest Heights Md 20745
(301)839-4727
SUBSPECIALTY: (anesthesiology retired)
MED. DEGREE: Far East Univ., Philippines '61
TRAINING: Michael Reese Hosp., Chicago, Ill.
LANGUAGES: Tagalog
COMMENTS: I tell patients what I am, what I can or cannot do, what may or may not happen involving the medical care afforded them. When patients come, I treat them first, not ask if they have insurance, cash or check. The most important thing is to make them well, have them trust whatever little knowledge and comfort I can provide and be friends. A lot of patients come in not only for medical reasons, but other problems in life, feeling I am part of their families. There is nothing more gratifying and fulfilling in life than to be treated as such.

Leela Krishnamurthy, MD
Till Bergemann & Assoc.
115 Centerway Rd, Greenbelt Md 20770
(301)474-2141
ASSOCIATES: Drs. Till Bergemann, David Granite
MED. DEGREE: Univ. of Delhi, India '67
TRAINING: Univ. of Delhi
BOARD CERT.: Family Practice '87
HOSPITALS: Prince George's General, Doctors
LANGUAGES: Hindi, Tamil

Dora M. Mamodesene, MD
7525 Greenway Ctr Dr #207, Greenbelt Md 20770
(301)345-5828
MED. DEGREE: Georgetown Univ. '82
TRAINING: Johns Hopkins, obstetrics/gyn., family practice '82-'86
BOARD CERT.: Family Practice '86
HOSPITALS: Holy Cross, Prince George's, Doctors, Greater Laurel, Arlington, Providence
LANGUAGES: French, Arabic
COMMENTS: Preventive care, total family care, continuity of care, availability, compassionate SEE office in Mitchelville also

Sandra Robinson-Redway, MD
3311 Toledo Terr #C202, Hyattsville Md 20782
(301)559-0151
MED. DEGREE: Howard Univ. '83
TRAINING: Prince George's Gen. Hosp.; 2 years of general surgery - Sinai Hosp. of Baltimore
BOARD CERT.: Family Practice '90
HOSPITALS: Prince George's, Providence
COMMENTS: All my patients are special to me and I enjoy providing an environment the whole family can feel comfortable in.

Mona Ellis, MD
7505 New Hampshire Ave #320, Langley Park Md 20783
(301)431-2000
ASSOCIATES: Lisa Lilienfield, MD, assoc./owner
MED. DEGREE: Univ. of S. Florida '88
TRAINING: Georgetown Univ./Providence Hosp.
BOARD CERT.: Family Practice '91
HOSPITALS: Providence Hospital; clinical staff Georgetown
LANGUAGES: Spanish (some)
COMMENTS: I love seeing the full spectrum of health and illness, young and old. Special interests include gynecology and pediatrics.

Lisa Lilienfield, MD
7505 New Hampshire Ave #320, Langley Park Md 20783
(301)431-2000
ASSOCIATES: Mona Ellis, MD
MED. DEGREE: Georgetown Univ. '82
TRAINING: Georgetown/Providence Hosp. '82-'85
BOARD CERT.: Family Practice, recertified '91
HOSPITALS: Providence; Georgetown clinical faculty
COMMENTS: Family medicine treats all ages and genders from newborn to elderly

Mary Beck Maloney, MD
4814-71St Ave, Hyattsville Md 20784
(301)577-0555
ASSOCIATES: Thomas G. Maloney, MD
MED. DEGREE: Georgetown '53
TRAINING: Providence Hosp. '54-'55
HOSPITALS: Doctors, Prince George's

Carolyn Baier, MD
Montgomery Medical Group
15225 Shady Grove Rd #105, Rockville Md 20850
(301)926-8500
ASSOCIATES: Drs. Susan Withrow, Charles Karesh, Pasqual Perrino, Steven Dolinsky, Herbert Juarbe, Barbara Bell
MED. DEGREE: Univ. California Los Angeles (UCLA) '83
TRAINING: UCLA '83-'86
BOARD CERT.: Family Practice
HOSPITALS: Shady Grove Adventist SEE office in Mt. Airy also

Barbara L. Bell, MD
15225 Shady Grove Road, Rockville Md 20850
(301)926-8500 SEE Germantown office for background

Frauke Westphal, MD
Rockville Internal Medicine Group
809 Viers Mill Rd, Rockville Md 20851
(301)762-5020
ASSOCIATES: Drs. Stephen Jones, Donald Bucy, Patricia Kellogg, Robert Macon, John Saia, Alan Pollack, Sunita Hanjura
MED. DEGREE: Freiberg Univ., Germany '66
TRAINING: 2 years Germany , 3 years Suburban Hospital, Bethesda
HOSPITALS: Suburban, Shady Grove LANGUAGES: German
COMMENTS: Preventive medicine, good patient-MD relationship

Kamalinee V. Deshpande, MD
6001 Lux Ln, Rockville Md 20852 (301)493-6866
MED. DEGREE: Nagpur Med. College, India '58
TRAINING: Nagpur Med. Coll., Int. med., surgery, obstetrics; All India Inst. of Med. Sciences, pediatrics, surgery; Safdaganj Hosp., New Delhi, surgery; Norton Mem. Infirmary, Kentucky, surgery; Rochester Univ., NY; Wash. Hosp. Center, surgery; basic and advanced cardiac life support; fellow hand surgery
BOARD CERT.: Emergency Med. Part I
HOSPITALS: HolyCross, Shady Grove Adventist, Suburban, Greater Laurel/ Beltsville LANGUAGES:Hindi

Carol W. Garvey, MD
11510 Old Georgetown Rd, Rockville Md 20852
(301)881-3997
ASSOCIATES: Peter Pushkas, MD
MED. DEGREE: Columbia Univ. '69
TRAINING: Wash. Hosp. Center '69-'71, Harvard Fam. Health Care fellow '73-'74; M.P.H. Harvard '75
BOARD CERT.:Family Practice '74, recert. '80, '87; Fellow American College of Preventive Med.
HOSPITALS: Suburban - chair utilization review comm., member quality assurance comm.
COMMENTS: President, Montgomery County Med. Society. My practice is prevention and life-style oriented but includes sick care and terminal care, home visits, hospice care.

Austria Lavigne Hooks, MD
15324 Spencerville Ct #101, Burtonsville Md 20866
(301)421-1884
MED. DEGREE: Georgetown Univ. '87
TRAINING: Georgetown Univ/Providence Hosp. '87-90
BOARD CERT.: Family Practice '90
HOSPITALS: Montgomery General, Holy Cross, Providence
LANGUAGES: Spanish

Barbara L. Bell, MD
Montgomery Medical Group
19530 Doctors Drive, Germantown Md 20874
(301)540-4432
ASSOCIATES: Susan Withrow, MD and other group physicians
MED. DEGREE: Univ. of S. Dakota '81
TRAINING: St. Joseph Hosp., Wichita, Ka.
BOARD CERT.: Family Practice '85
HOSPITALS: Shady Grove Adventist COMMENTS: I am a strong believer in family medicine, from newborns to the elderly.

Susan J. Withrow, MD
Montgomery Medical Group
19530 Doctors Drive, Germantown Md 20874
(301)540-4432
ASSOCIATES: Drs. Carolyn Baier, Charles Karesh, Pasqual Perrino, Steven Dolinsky, Herbert Juarbe, Barbara Bell, Mangala Pandya, Anoma Bandara, A. Frederick North
MED. DEGREE: Med. College of Virginia, Richmond '74; TRAINING: Fairfax Hospital
BOARD CERT.: Family Practice recert. '89
HOSPITALS: Shady Grove Adventist, chair family practice '90-'92

Raman R. Tuli, MD
Maple Spring Med. Center
10810 Darnestown Rd #H2, Gaithersburg, Md 20878
(301)424-1780
SUBSPECIALTY: geriatrics
MED. DEGREE: MLN Med. Coll., India '70
TRAINING: MLN Med. Coll., India; Prince George's Gen. Hosp.; Cardiac life support training
BOARD CERT.: Family Practice '77, recert. '90;
HOSPITALS: Prince George's, Leland Memorial, Shady Grove
LANGUAGES: Hindi, Punjabi COMMENTS: Conservative, more counselling and educating patient on health problems and tailoring the medicine to their need. Office in Mt. Ranier also

Cheryl Winchell, MD
19241 Montgomery Vill. Ave #E10, Gaithersburg Md 20879
(301)926-4222
MED. DEGREE: Case Western Reserve Univ., Cleveland '70
TRAINING: Univ. of Virginia '70-'71; Grady Memorial Hosp., Atlanta '71-'72
BOARD CERT.: Family Practice '76, recert. '90
HOSPITALS: Shady Grove COMMENTS: Comprehensive preventive care and health maintenance

Mary C. Gamez, ND
11141 Georgia Ave, Wheaton Md 20902
(301)929-0112
9801 Georgia Ave #333, Silver Spring Md 20902
(301)681-9857
ASSOCIATES: Alberto Gamez, MD
MED. DEGREE: Univ. Central De Venezuela '64
TRAINING: San Juan, Puerto Rico Sch. of Med.; also training in pathology and occupational health med.
LANGUAGES: Spanish

Mildred G. Eidelman, Md
1602 Dilston Rd, Silver Spring Md 20903
(301)439-1476
MED. DEGREE: Medical Coll. of Pa., Philadelphia '58
TRAINING: Albert Einstein Med. Center, Philadelphia
LANGUAGES: Yiddish and Hebrew

Melissa B. Friedland, MD
Montg. Family Medicine Assoc., P.C.
2415 Musgrove Rd #205, Silver Spring Md 20904
(301)989-0193
ASSOCIATES: Rosie K. Singh, MD
MED. DEGREE: Howard Univ. '84
TRAINING: Univ. of Maryland, Baltimore
BOARD CERT.: Family Practice '87
HOSPITALS: Holy Cross

Rosie K. Singh, MD
Montgomery Family Medicine Assoc., PC
2415 Musgrove Rd #205, Silver Spring Md 20904
(301)989-0193
ASSOCIATES: Melissa B. Friedland, MD
MED. DEGREE: Univ. of New Delhi, India '83
TRAINING: Univ. of Md., Baltimore '86-'89
BOARD CERT.: Family Practice '89
HOSPITALS: Holy Cross; George Wash. clinical instructor
LANGUAGES: Hindi, Burmese COMMENTS: Emphasis on preventive medicine, comprehensive approach

Jean Welsh, MD
1111 Spring St., Silver Spring Md 20910
(301)565-2535
ASSOCIATES: Hector Collison, MD
MED. DEGREE: Univ. of California at Irvine '86
TRAINING: Howard University Hosp.
BOARD CERT.: Family Practice '89
HOSPITALS:Holy Cross, Washington Adventist
COMMENTS: I believe in spending time with my patients and giving all the options available for a particular diagnosis. I believe in the patient being involved in the final decisions.

Carolyn Baier, MD
Montgomery Medical Group
1 N. Main St., Mt. Airy Md 21771
(301)831-0129 SEE Rockville office for background

VIRGINIA

Doreen E. McMahon, MD
3289 Woodburn Rd #325, Annandale Va 22003
(703)573-0092
ASSOCIATES: Edward M. Freidler, MD
MED. DEGREE: U. of Maryland '86; TRAINING: Fairfax '86-'89
BOARD CERT.: Family Practice '89
HOSPITAL: Fairfax

Teresa P. Klansek, DO
Heritage Family Practice Assoc., PC
4001 Fair Ridge Dr #101, Fairfax Va 22033
(703)385-6789
ASSOCIATES: Drs. Eugene Overton, G. Mitchell Edmondson, Michele Romano
MED. DEGREE: Philadelphia Coll. Osteopathic Med. '88
TRAINING: Community Gen. Hosp.; Reading Hosp., Reading, Pa.
BOARD CERT.: Family Practice '92
HOSPITALS: Fair Oaks, Fairfax COMMENTS: I try to emphasize educating my patients to help them understand the causes and treatments of their illnesses. My Christian background has taught me to be sympathetic to my patients' complaints and needs.

Michele A. Romano, MD
Heritage Family Practice Assoc. PC
4001 Fair Ridge Dr #101, Fairfax Va 22033
(703)385-6789
ASSOCIATES: Drs. Eugene W. Overton, G. Mitchell Edmondson, Teresa Klansek
MED. DEGREE: Med. College of Virginia '84
TRAINING: Fairfax Hosp./Med. Coll. of Virginia
BOARD CERT.: Family Practice '87
HOSPITALS: Fairfax , Fair Oaks COMMENTS: Dr. Romano is particularly interested in the health care needs of women and the elderly, not only in treating illness but also in maintaining wellness.

Lora Elise Mackie, MD
108 Elden St. #14, Herndon Va 22070
(703)481-1505
ASSOCIATES: Drs. Deborah Leavens, Robin Shealy, Kevin Weaver, Michael Silverstein
MED. DEGREE: George Washington Univ. '81
TRAINING: Tripler Army Med. Ctr., Hawaii; Eisenhower Army Med. Ctr., Augusta, Ga.
BOARD CERT.: Family Practice '84, recertified '90
HOSPITALS: Reston, Fair Oaks, Fairfax

Janet Avery, MD
1800 Town Center Drive #306, Reston Va 22090
(703)481-5907
SUBSPECIALTY: Internal medicine
MED. DEGREE: Madras Medical, India '70
TRAINING: Brookdale Hosp., Brooklyn, N.Y.
BOARD CERT.: Family Prac.'77, recert. 84, pending '93
HOSPITALS: Reston, Fair Oaks, Fairfax COMMENTS: Preventive medicine with emphasis on emotional wellbeing as well as physical. See all ages and very interested in patients who are trying to recover from any kind of addictions.

Mary E. Braza, MD
380 Maple Ave W. #200, Vienna Va 22180
(703)255-9100
ASSOCIATES: Drs. James Jenkins, Daniel Garfinkle, Alan Dappen, Joseph Gravel
MED. DEGREE: Univ. of Wisconsin at Madison '84
TRAINING: University Hospitals, Cleveland '85; Hennepin County Med. Ctr., Minneapolis '87
BOARD CERT.: Family Practice '87
HOSPITALS: Fairfax, Fair Oaks LANGUAGES: Spanish

Kathryn (Kate) Lemmerman, MD
5275 Lee Highway #200, Arlington Va 22207
(703)532-4892
SUBSPECIALTY: Musculoskeletal problems, acupuncture
ASSOCIATES: Drs. Gary and Anne Kaplan
MED. DEGREE: Rush Medical Coll. '87
TRAINING: U. of Conn. '87-90; Medical acupuncture-UCLA '90-'91
BOARD CERT.: Family Practice '90, certified Virginia acupuncturist
HOSPITALS: Arlington LANGUAGES: Spanish (not fluent)
COMMENTS: All aspects of family medicine with emphasis on prevention, including use of osteopathic manipulative technique and acupuncture.

Darin Schonzeit, MD
Alexandria Family Medicine PC
4600 King St. #6L, Alexandria, Va 22302
(703)671-4141
ASSOCIATES: Drs. Marie Steinmetz, Stephen Cornwell
MED. DEGREE: Rutgers Univ. '86
TRAINING: Fairfax Hosp '86-'89
BOARD CERT.: Family Practice '89
HOSPITALS: Fairfax, Alexandria LANGUAGES: Spanish
COMMENTS: Emphasize preventive medicine and quality care

Marie Steinmetz, MD
Alexandria Family Medicine, P.C.
4600 King St #6L, Alexandria Va 22302
(703)671-4141
ASSOCIATES: Drs. Darin Schonzeit, Stephen Cornwell
MED. DEGREE: Univ. of Pittsburgh '80
TRAINING: Univ. of N. Carolina '83
BOARD CERT.: Family Practice '83 and '89
HOSPITALS: Alexandria, Fairfax.; clinical assoc. prof. Georgetown Univ., Medical Coll. of Virginia

Kazuko K. Price, MD
4701 Kenmore Ave #118, Alexandria Va 22304
(703)751-3344
SUBSPECIALTY: Obstetrics, gynecology, pediatrics
MED. DEGREE: Tokyo Women's Med. College '50
TRAINING: Lutheran Hosp., Cleveland; Baltimore City Hosp.; research asst. Queen's Univ., Canada in colposcopy and colpomicroscopy research.
HOSPITALS: Alexandria
LANGUAGES: Japanese
COMMENTS: Emphasis on preventive medicine, healthy lifestyle, particularly postmenopausal health management.

DISTRICT OF COLUMBIA

Marie L. Borum, Md
George Washington Univ., 5th fl.
2150 Penn Ave NW, MFA bldg, GI Dept. , Washington DC 20037
(202)994-4206
ASSOCIATES: Drs. Hans Fromm, Allen Ginsberg, William Steinberg, Ingram Roberts
MED. DEGREE: Rutgers Medical School, NJ '85
TRAINING: George Wash. Univ., including Gastroenterology fellow
BOARD CERT.: Int. med. '88; Gastroenterology '91
HOSPITALS: Asst. prof. of med., George Washington

MARYLAND

Sheila Levin, MD
10076 Darnestown Rd #201, Rockville Md 20850
(301)340-3252
ASSOCIATES: Drs. Alan Schulman , Robert Eisdorfer
MED. DEGREE: Tufts Univ. '79
TRAINING: New England Med. Ctr., Boston, including fellowship; also MA math education Univ. of Texas '69
BOARD CERT.: Int. med. '83, Gastroenterology '89
HOSPITALS: Shady Grove, Suburban
LANGUAGES: Spanish
COMMENTS: Tender loving care. Take time with patients.

Catherine M. Chura, MD
3801 International Dr #204, Silver Spring Md 20906
(301)598-9770
MED. DEGREE: Med. College of Pennsylvania '63
TRAINING: Guthrie Clinic/Packer Hosp., Sayre, Pa.; Flower Fifth Ave/New York Medical College
BOARD eligible Gastroenterology
HOSPITALS: Montgom. Gen., Suburban, Holy Cross, Shady Grove
COMMENTS: Conservative approach to diseases of the digestive tract and treatment of liver diseases. Full gastrointestinal services available.

VIRGINIA

Carol Susan Schuffler, MD, PhD
8301 Arlington Blvd #308, Fairfax Va 22031
(703)204-1169
MED. DEGREE: Univ. of Colorado '78; TRAINING: Univ. of Colorado; also PhD microbiology, Univ. of Ill.
BOARD CERT.: Internal med. '81, Gastroenterology '87
HOSPITALS: Fairfax, Arlington, Reston, Fair Oaks

Anita M. Wolke, MD
1800 Town Center Dr. #220, Reston Va 22090
(703)435-3366
ASSOCIATES: Alan J. Plotner, MD
MED. DEGREE: Univ. of S. Carolina Medical College '78
TRAINING: Mt. Sinai, N.Y. '78 through fellowship in '84
BOARD CERT.: Gastroenterology '83
HOSPITALS: Reston, Fairfax, Loudoun
COMMENTS: Patient care is our priority. We devote a lot of time to patient education, diet, medications etc.

Myriam Urrutia Eder, MD
2616 Sherwood Hall Lane #203, Alexandria Va 22306
(703)360-2445
MED. DEGREE: Univ. of Panama '77
TRAINING: Georgetown Med. Service, DC General Hosp.
BOARD CERT.: Internal Med. '83, Gastroenterology '85
HOSPITALS: Mt. Vernon, Alexandria , Fairfax
LANGUAGES: Spanish

Kathy S. Brenneman, MD
Washington Hospital Center
110 Irving St. NW #2A38, Washington DC 20010
(202)877-6223
MED. DEGREE: S. Illinois Univ. '85;
TRAINING: Washington Hosp. Center '85-'88
BOARD CERT.: Internal Med. '88, Geriatrics '90
HOSPITALS: Chair, Geriatric medicine, Washington Hosp. Center

DISTRICT OF COLUMBIA

Farah Feri Sadeghian, MD
1328 Southern Ave SE, Washington DC 20032
(202)561-1010 (part-time)
MED. DEGREE: Univ. of Tehran '59
TRAINING: Sibley Hosp., Prince George's Gen. Hosp.; Obst/Gyn. fellow Georgetown Univ. Hosp.
HOSPITALS: Greater Southeast Comm., Hadley Memorial
LANGUAGES: Iranian

MARYLAND

Martha T. Cole, MD
4701 Willard Ave #215, Chevy Chase Md 20815
(301)656-3456
MED. DEGREE: George Washington Univ. '77
TRAINING: George Washington U., yearly cont. educ., laser surgery
BOARD CERT.: Obstetrics/gynecology '83
HOSPITALS: Columbia, Suburban; George Wash., asst. clin. prof.
LANGUAGES: French
COMMENTS: Limits number of patients for compassionate care

Nina Vann Jeanes, MD
9800 Falls Rd #1, Potomac Md 20854
(301)299-2338
MED. DEGREE: Univ. of Maryland '61
TRAINING: Univ. of Maryland '61-'66
BOARD CERT.: Obstetrics/Gyn. '72
HOSPITALS: Suburban, Sibley, Johns Hopkins, Georgetown, Holy Cross, Montgomery Gen., Shady Grove

VIRGINIA

Melissa J. Thiel, MD
6035 Burke Center Pkwy, Burke Va 22015
(703)425-6888 SEE Alexandria office for background

Joanne Herrman, MD, PC
8324 Professional Hill Dr., Fairfax Va 22031
(703)849-9488
MED. DEGREE: Univ. of Pittsburgh '79
TRAINING: George Washington Univ. '83; continuous training
BOARD CERT.: Obstetrics/gynecology '85
HOSPITALS: Fairfax
LANGUAGES: American sign language COMMENTS: Believe patient participation essential to good results. Education important.

Donna G. Hurlock, MD
205 S. Whiting St. #303, Alexandria Va 22304
(703)823-1533
ASSOCIATES: Melissa J. Thiel, MD (share space)
MED. DEGREE: Univ. of Maryland '79
TRAINING: Washington Hosp. Center; training in laser surgery, pelviscopy, LEEP (excision procedure)
BOARD CERT.: Obstetrics/Gynecology '83
HOSPITALS: Alexandria LANGUAGES: minimal French
COMMENTS: Strong supporter of preventive medical care, hormone replacement, healthy living habits.

Melissa J. Thiel, MD
205 S. Whiting St. #303, Alexandria Va 22304
(703)823-1533
2616 Sherwood Hall Lane #203, Alexandria Va 22306
ASSOCIATES: Donna Hurlock, MD (cross coverage)
MED. DEGREE: Cornell Univ. Med. College '79; TRAINING: Walter Reed Army Med. Center '79-83
BOARD CERT.: Obstetrics/Gynecology '85
HOSPITALS: Alexandria COMMENTS: Office hours are regular (not cancelled). Emphasis is on patient education.
SEE also office in Burke

DISTRICT OF COLUMBIA

Belinda Marascalco, MD
Georgetown Univ. Hosp. 3-PHC
3800 Reservoir Rd NW, Washington DC 20007
(202)687-8283
SPECIALTY: Infertility, some gynecology
ASSOCIATES: Drs. Jim Simon, Sanford Markham
MED. DEGREE: Tulane Univ., New Orleans '81
TRAINING: Tulane Univ.; Fellow Infertility & Reproductive Endocrinology Georgetown '88-'90
BOARD CERT.: Obstetrics/Gyn '92; Reprod. End. board eligible
HOSPITALS: Georgetown, Columbia
COMMENTS: I feel that one of the most important traits for a physician to have is to be able to listen well.

MARYLAND

Amy J. Byer, MD
5413 W. Cedar Lane #105C, Bethesda Md 20814
(301)530-6200 SEE Rockville office for background

Rafat Abbasi, MD
Montgomery Fertility Institute
10215 Fernwood Rd #303, Bethesda Md 20817
(301)897-8850 SEE Arlington office for background

Amy J. Byer, MD
9715 Medical Center Dr #414, Rockville Md 20850
(301)840-1893
SUBSPECIALTY: Infertility
ASSOCIATES: Charles I. Schneiderman, MD
MED. DEGREE: Univ. of Maryland '78
TRAINING: Univ. of Tenn. '78-'82; also infertility/pelviscopy and laser surgery
BOARD CERT.: Obstetrics/Gynecology '85
HOSPITALS: Shady Grove; Suburban - sec./treas. Gyn. subsection
COMMENTS: Lectures on menopause and sexuality. A warm, friendly office. I stress explaining the patient's problem, how and why to follow treatment. Also emphasize preventive medicine and the need for regular mammograms, paps, etc.
SEE Bethesda office also

Victoria Diaz, MD
11120 New Hampshire Ave. #407, Silver Spring Md 20904
(301)593-7136
SUBSPECIALTY: Infertility
MED. DEGREE: San Marcos Univ., Peru '72
TRAINING: Washington Hosp. Center '73-'77
BOARD CERT.: Obstetrics/gynecology '79
HOSPITALS: Washington Adventist, Holy Cross
LANGUAGES: Spanish

VIRGINIA

Melinda S. Hall, MD
6400 Arlington Blvd #640, Falls Church Va 22042
(703)532-3630
SUBSPECIALTY: infertility, laser surgery
MED. DEGREE: Louisiana State Univ. '81
TRAINING: Charity Hosp., New Orleans; George Washington Univ.; also laser, colposcopy, infertility
BOARD CERT.: Obstetrics/gynecology '89
HOSPITALS: Fairfax, Alexandria

Rafat Abbasi, MD
3801 N. Fairfax Drive #12N, Arlington Va 22203
(703)525-4776
SPECIALTY: Infertility, reproductive endocrinology
ASSOCIATES: Drs. Oscar Dodek, Herb Kotz, Jay Grodin, Frank Chang, Bill Meyer, Sherilynn Hummel, Chuck Boice
MED. DEGREE: Dow Med. College, Pakistan '70;
TRAINING: St. Joseph's Hosp., Towson, Md.; also laser preceptorship, pelviscopy training
BOARD CERT.: Obstetrics/Gyn '83; Reproductive end.'89
HOSPITALS: Georgetown, Arlington, Suburban
LANGUAGES: Urdu, French
COMMENTS: Caring attitude, state of the art technology, good nursing and support staff. SEE Bethesda office also

Nirmala S. Limaye, MD PC
1715 N George Mason Dr #301, Arlington Va 22205
(703)528-1771
SUBSPECIALTY: Infertility, menopause
MED. DEGREE:Univ. of Bombay, India '62
TRAINING: Georgetown Univ. '72-'74; also laser and microsurgery, Norplant, cervical cap, adolescent gyn.
BOARD CERT.: Obstetrics/Gyn '91;
HOSPITALS: Fairfax, Northern Virginia, Arlington, Georgetown
LANGUAGES: Indian COMMENTS: Try to have human touch and adequate time for each patient.

Emine Cay, MD
8301 Arlington Blvd #302, Fairfax Va 22031
(703)573-6770
SUBSPECIALTY: menopause, laser surgery
Founder, dir., The Menopause Center;
ASSOCIATES: Alison Ansher, MD
MED. DEGREE: Georgetown Univ. '83
TRAINING: Washington Hosp. Ctr., 2 years surgery, 4 years gyn.
BOARD CERT.: Obstetrics/gynecology '91
HOSPITALS:Fairfax, Arlington
LANGUAGES: Turkish COMMENTS: An empathetic and educational approach with patients helps us understand their gynecological concerns. Preventive gynecological care, pro-choice.

Sherilynn Hummel, MD
10215 Fernwood Rd #303, Bethesda Md 20817
(301)897-8850
ASSOCIATES: Drs. Oscar Dodek, Herb Kotz, Chuck Boice, Frank Chang, Jay Grodin, Bill Meyer, Rafat Abbasi
MED. DEGREE: Univ. of Illinois, '77
TRAINING: Univ. of Louisville '77-'81; Gynecologic Oncology Anderson Hosp., Houston; Georgetown Univ. fellow gynecologic oncology '81-'83; fellow American Cancer Society '82-'83
BOARD CERT.: Obstetrics/Gyn '84; Gynecologic Oncology '87
HOSPITALS: Columbia Hosp. for Women, Washington Hosp. Center, member Cancer Comm.; Holy Cross, Georgetown, George Washington, Sibley
COMMENTS: I am board certified in Gyn Oncology (cancer surgery and chemotherapy). I also do about 50% general gynecology. No obstetrics.

DISTRICT OF COLUMBIA

Margo A. Smith, MD
Washington Hospital Center
110 Irving St. NW, #2A-56, Washington DC 20010
(202)877-7164
ASSOCIATES: Charles S. Levy, MD
MED. DEGREE: Univ. of Mass. '82; TRAINING: Washington Hosp. Ctr. '85, fellow infectious diseases '87
TRAINING: Internal med. '85; Infectious Diseases '88
HOSPITALS: Washington Hosp. Center, assoc. program dir., Attending Infectious diseases. COMMENTS: Want patients to be active participants in their care as much as possible.

MARYLAND

Jeanne R. Spellman, MD
8630 Fenton St. #230, Silver Spring Md 20910
(301)588-2525
SUBSPECIALTY: Internal med.
ASSOCIATES: Drs. Phuong D. Trinh, Hubert Alpert
MED. DEGREE: Johns Hopkins Univ. '80
TRAINING: Georgetown Univ.; Georgetown/Washington Hosp. Center fellow inf. diseases
BOARD CERT.: Internal med. '84; Infect. Diseases '86
HOSPITALS: Holy Cross, Suburban, Washington Adventist
COMMENTS: 80% of my practice hours are involved in infectious disease consultations on hospitalized patients. I maintain a small internal medicine practice. Appointment priority is given to physician referrals, follow-up of hospital consults and patients already in the practice.

VIRGINIA

Mary E. Schmidt, MD
3289 Woodburn Rd #200, Annandale Va 22003
(703)560-7900
ASSOCIATES: Drs. Donald M. Poretz, Lawrence J. Eron, Robin I. Goldenberg, Allan J. Morrison
MED. DEGREE: Medical College of Pennsylvania '84
TRAINING: Albany Med. Ctr., NY; Inf. Dis.:George Wash. Univ./ Wash. Hosp. Center and Veterans Hospitals
BOARD CERT.: Internal med.'88; Pediatrics '89; board eligible infectious diseases
HOSPITALS: Fairfax, Fair Oaks and Reston
LANGUAGES: some Spanish COMMENTS: A caring practioner. Has patients involved in understanding the diagnosis and treatment options/decisions. Very personable. Will see adults and children.

Maria Regina Alivisatos, MD
Infectious Diseases Associates, PC
7910 Andrus Rd #6, Alexandria Va 22306
(703)799-1644
ASSOCIATES: John Symington, MD
MED. DEGREE: Univ. of Athens '80
TRAINING: Elmhurst City Hosp., N.Y.
BOARD CERT.: Internal med. '87, Infectious Diseases '90
HOSPITALS: Mt. Vernon, Alexandria, Potomac, Fairfax
LANGUAGES: Greek

Deborah Arbit, MD
George Washington Univ. Medical Center
2150 Penn Ave. NW, Ob/Gyn Dept., Washington DC 20037
(202)994-4614
ASSOCIATES: Drs. Robert Stillman, Paul Gindoff, Gilbert Mottla
MED. DEGREE: Sackler Sch. of Med. Tel Aviv Univ. '87
TRAINING: State Univ. of NY/Kings County Hosp. Center '87-'91; fellow, Reprod. Endocrin./Infert. '91-'93
BOARD CERT.: Obstetrics/gyn boards '91; board eligible reproductive endocrinology
HOSPITALS: George Washington, adjunct asst. prof.
COMMENTS: I see patients for reprod. end. disorders or infertility

Maria Bustillo, MD
Genetics & IVF Institute, 3020 Javier Rd, Fairfax Va 22031
(703)698-7355
ASSOCIATES: Institute physicians; Joseph Shulman, MD, founder
MED. DEGREE: Medical College of Wisconsin '75
TRAINING: Harbor-UCLA Med. Center, Torrance, Ca.; fellow reproductive endocrinology /infertilty
BOARD CERT.: Obstetrics/gyn '82, Reproductive End. '83
HOSPITALS: Fairfax Hosp.; Medical Coll. Virginia, clin. asst. prof.
LANGUAGES: Spanish, French
COMMENTS: Innovative, state of the art rep. endocrinology practice, full service infertility treatment.

DISTRICT OF COLUMBIA

Mary Alice Johnson-Crockett MD
1827 First St. NW, Washington DC 20001
(202)462-1559
SUBSPECIALTY: geriatrics
ASSOCIATES: Margaret Akpan, MD; Sheldon Weissmeyer, DPM
MED. DEGREE: Howard Univ. '62
TRAINING: Howard Univ./Freedman's Hosp., DC General Hosp, Veterans Admin. Hosp.
BOARD eligible Internal medicine
HOSPITALS: Providence and Wash. Hospital Center arranged

SOUTHEAST

Deborah Edge, MD
666 Pennsylvania Ave SE #100, Washington DC 20003
(202)546-4504
ASSOCIATES: Drs. Robert Berenson, Peter Basch, Dawn Reed Jones, Daniel Waterman
MED. DEGREE: Northwestern Univ. '74
TRAINING: George Washington Univ.; Rush-Presbyterian-St. Luke's Med. Ctr., Chicago
BOARD CERT.: Int. med. '78; AMA continuing education certificate
HOSPITALS: George Washington asst. clin. prof. of health care sciences and medicine; Washington Hosp. Center, Columbia
COMMENTS: Emphasize communication, working with patient as partner with goal of helping them stay or become as well as possible.

Dawn Reed Jones, MD
666 Pennsylvania Ave SE #100, Washington DC 20003
(202)546-4504
ASSOCIATES: Drs. Robert Berenson, Deborah Edge, Peter Basch, Daniel Waterman
MED. DEGREE: Stanford Univ. '82
TRAINING: George Washington Univ. '82-'85
BOARD CERT.: Internal medicine '85
HOSPITALS: George Washington Univ., asst. prof.; Washington Hosp. Center
COMMENTS: I practice with an emphasis on prevention of the major diseases which afflict a great number of Americans. I stress education and more natural approaches to treatment when possible and I am open to combining traditional medicine with alternative modes of therapy when appropriate. I do birth control counseling and routine gynecological care for women.

Amy Kossoff, MD
DC Gen. Hosp., Georgetown Dept. of Medicine
19th and Mass Ave. SE, Washington DC 20003
(202)675-5677
MED. DEGREE: George Wash. Univ. '83; TRAINING: Washington Hospital Center
BOARD CERT.: Internal medicine '86
HOSPITALS: DC Gen.; medical co-dir. of Washington Free Clinic
COMMENTS: Interested in caring for underserved populations, indigents.

NORTHWEST

Randi Abramson, MD
Zaccheus Free Medical Clinic, staff physician
1329 N St. NW, Washington DC 20005
(202)265-2400
SUBSPECIALTY: primary care
MED. DEGREE: Rush Medical College '86
TRAINING: Northwestern Univ. '86-'88; Washington Hosp. Center '89; fellow primary care George Washington Univ. '89-'91
BOARD CERT.: Int. med. '90
HOSPITALS: George Washington Univ.
LANGUAGES:Spanish COMMENTS: Free medical clinic, serving low income people with dignity & respect. No income qualifications.

Darcy Jeanne Hansen, MD
2021 K St. NW #310, Washington DC 20006
(202)429-2401
MED. DEGREE:Columbia Univ. '78
TRAINING: Georgetown Univ. Hosp. '78-'81; chief resident Creighton Univ., Omaha '81-'82
BOARD CERT.: Internal medicine '82
HOSPITALS: Sibley; Georgetown Univ., clinical inst.
COMMENTS: Preventive orientation

Prudence Kline, MD
2021 K St. NW #512, Washington DC 20006
(202)293-3636
SUBSPECIALTY: Eating disorders
ASSOCIATES: Drs. Matthew Parker, Mitchell Dunn
MED. DEGREE: Rutgers Univ. , NJ '78; TRAINING: George Washington Univ. '81
BOARD CERT.: Internal medicine '81; Emergency med. '86
HOSPITALS: George Washington, Sibley, Georgetown, Columbia COMMENTS: I run on time!

Marilee C. S. Cole, MD
Georgetown Univ. Hosp. IMA, PHC-6
3800 Reservoir Rd NW, Washington DC 20007
(202)687-8124
ASSOCIATES: Drs. Jerry Earll, Dominick Memoli, David Lambert, Keith Muccino, Daniel Sulmasy, Donald Lyons, Joan St. Onge, Karen Myers, Z.C. Roulidis
MED. DEGREE: Johns Hopkins Sch. of Med. '72
TRAINING: Francis Scott Key Med. Center., Baltimore '72-'74, Georgetown Univ. primary care fellow. '82-'84
BOARD CERT.: Internal medicine '83
HOSPITALS: Georgetown LANGUAGES: French
COMMENTS: I encourage patients' involvement and participation at all levels of decision-making. I promote patients to assumption of responsibility throughout management of illness.

Karen R. Myers, MD
Georgetown Univ. Hospital
3800 Reservoir Rd NW, 6 PHC , Washington DC 20007
(202)687-8124
SUBSPECIALTY: Eating disorders, weight loss
ASSOCIATES: Joan St. Onge, Keith Muccino, David Lambert, Dominick Memoli, Daniel Sulmasy, Marilee Cole, Jerry Earll, Donald Lyons, Z.C. Roulidis
MED. DEGREE: Ohio State Univ. '85
TRAINING: Metropolitan Hosp.Ctr. (New York Medical Coll/Univ. Hosp.) '85-'88
BOARD CERT.: Internal medicine '90
HOSPITALS: Asst. prof. Georgetown; asst. medical dir. Georgetown diet management and eating disorders

Joan St. Onge, MD
Georgetown Univ. Hospital, 6 PHC
3800 Reservoir Rd NW, Washington DC 20007
(202)687-6403
ASSOCIATES: Drs. Jerry Earll, Dominick Memoli, David Lambert, Keith Muccino, Donald Sulmasy, Donald Lyons, Marilee Cole, Karen Myers, Z.C. Roulidis
MED. DEGREE: Georgetown Univ.; TRAINING: Georgetown Univ.
BOARD CERT.: Internal medicine '89
HOSPITALS: Georgetown COMMENTS: Private practice within academic medical center. Only half-time spent with my own practice, the other half with residents and students.

Ann Barber, MD
Zaccheus Medical Clinic
1329 N St. NW, Washington DC 20009
(202)265-2400
ASSOCIATES: Physicians at Zaccheus, a free medical clinic.
Dr. Barber is one of many volunteer physicians.
MED. DEGREE: Northwestern Univ. '81
TRAINING: Northwestern Univ. '81-'84; MS Math Stanford '74
BOARD CERT.: Internal medicine '82
HOSPITALS: National Inst. of health, med. staff fellow '84-'87; Providence Hosp. emergency room only
LANGUAGES: Spanish
COMMENTS: AMA physician recognition awards, '85, '88. At Zaccheus, we use volunteer physicians for no-cost medical care. The clinic specializes in the care of patients with chronic diseases, such as hypertension and diabetes. Many of the physicians are women.

Helene C. Freeman, MD
Spring Valley Primary Care P.C
4910 Mass Ave NW #312, Washington DC 20016
(202)686-0813
SUBSPECIALTY: Gynecology
ASSOCIATES: Drs. Michael Grady, Theodore Li and Daniel Young
MED. DEGREE: Hahnemann Med., Philadelphia '85; TRAINING: Georgetown Univ. '85-'88
BOARD CERT.: Internal medicine '88
HOSPITALS: Sibley; Georgetown, clinical instructor of medicine
COMMENTS: Practice started in 1989 by 4 physicians on staff at Georgetown. We designed our office for the convenience of our patients. It is ideally situated for patients from DC, MD and VA. We perform lab work, x-rays, treadmill tests, flexible sigmoidoscopy in the office. We provide evening and Saturday hours. As a primary care provider, I find it very important to focus on health maintenance issues, instructing my female patients in current recommendations for mammogram screening, paps, sigmoidoscopies.

Marta A. Schneider, MD
5401 Macarthur Blvd NW, Washington DC 20016
(202)362-3905
MED. DEGREE: George Wash. Univ. '77
TRAINING: St. Francis Hosp. Med. Center, Hartford, Conn.
BOARD CERT.: Internal medicine '80
HOSPITALS: Sibley, Providence
LANGUAGES: German COMMENTS: I feel thorough history and physical exam are where emphasis of care should be placed. Frequently obviates need for multitude of tests.

Carole Horn, MD
1145-19th St. NW #605, Washington DC 20036
(202)296-0670
ASSOCIATES: Drs. James Ramey, Richard Kaufman, Gilbert Eisner, Maurice Sislen, Morton Kavalier
MED. DEGREE: George Washington Univ. '78
TRAINING: George Washington U. '78-81; MA English Columbia U.
BOARD CERT.: Internal medicine '81
HOSPITALS: George Washington, assoc. clinical prof. of med.; Georgetown, Washington Hosp. Center

Devra C. Marcus, MD
1145-19th St. NW #600, Washington DC 20036
(202)728-9630
ASSOCIATES: Drs. Richard Perry, David Lawrenz, Richard Schubert, Cathryn McAlpine, William Battle and W. Tabb Moore
MED. DEGREE: Stanford Univ. '66
TRAINING: Stanford '66-'68; infectious diseases fellow also
BOARD CERT.: Internal medicine '76
HOSPITALS: Georgetown, George Washington - asst. clinical prof.
LANGUAGES: Spanish (a little) COMMENTS: Dr. Marcus advises seeing a new physician for a minor problem first. If rapport is good, then schedule a physical. Interviewing formally results in stiffness.

Eve Bargmann, MD
George Washington Univ. Med. Center
2150 Penn. Ave NW, Washington DC 20037
(202)994-7700
SUBSPECIALTY: Primary Care
ASSOCIATES: George Washington Univ. faculty
MED. DEGREE: Univ. of N. Carolina '77
TRAINING: State Univ. of NY at Buffalo '77-'78; George Washington Univ. Hosp. '78-'80
BOARD CERT.: Internal medicine '81
HOSPITALS: George Washington Univ, asst. prof., director Primary Care Medicine Residency

Barbara Basuk, MD
George Washington Univ. Medical Center
2150 Pennsylvania Ave NW, Washington DC 20037
(202)994-7700
ASSOCIATES: George Washington faculty associates
MED. DEGREE: Duke Univ. '79; TRAINING: Duke Univ. '80-'83
BOARD CERT.: Internal Medicine '83
HOSPITALS: Washington Hosp. Center, George Washington

Lucy Chang, MD
George Washington Univ. Medical Center
2150 Penn. Ave NW, Washington DC 20037
(202)994-4669
ASSOCIATES: George Washington Univ. Medical faculty
MED. DEGREE: Univ. of Maryland '86
TRAINING: George Washington Univ.; also fellow internal medicine
BOARD CERT.: Internal Medicine '89;
HOSPITALS: George Washington Univ., asst. clinical prof. of medicine
LANGUAGES: Chinese

Nancy E. Falk, MD
2440 M St NW #422, Washington DC 20037
(202)659-4257
ASSOCIATES: Shares office and coverage with 3 other doctors
MED. DEGREE: St. Univ. of New York '71
TRAINING: George Washington Univ.
BOARD CERT.: Internal medicine '74
HOSPITALS: George Washington, assoc. clin. prof; Sibley, Columbia
LANGUAGES: Spanish (some)
COMMENTS: I practice conservative non-invasive medicine as much as possible, treating the whole patient with much emphasis on mental health as well.

Barbara Fenton, MD
George Washington Univ. Medical Center
2150 Penn. Ave NW, Washington DC 20037
(202)994-7200
ASSOCIATES: Drs. Gail Povar, Robert Sherrick, affiliated with GWU Health Plan
MED. DEGREE: George Washington Univ. '81
TRAINING: George Washington Univ.
BOARD CERT.: Internal medicine
HOSPITALS: George Washington Univ., clin. asst. prof. of Med. and Health Care Sciences
LANGUAGES: Spanish (minimal) COMMENTS: Prevention

MARYLAND

BELTSVILLE

Eva L. Myers, MD
11615 Beltsville Drive, Beltsville Md 20705
(301)572-4344
SUBSPECIALTY: Primary care
MED. DEGREE: National Univ. of Mexico '57
TRAINING: Providence Hosp; St. Agnes Hosp., Baltimore; Graduate course in endocrinology/diabetes
BOARD eligible Internal medicine
HOSPITALS: Suburban Hosp. staff LANGUAGES: Spanish
COMMENTS: Preventive medicine SEE Bethesda office also

GREENBELT

Stephanie Trifoglio, MD
7500 Greenway Center Dr. #430, Greenbelt Md 20770
(301)345-5857
SUBSPECIALTY: geriatrics
ASSOCIATES: Drs. Peter Schissler and Stuart Turkewitz
MED. DEGREE: U. Autonoma de Guadalajara '84
TRAINING: Prince George's Hosp. Ctr., Univ. of Maryland
BOARD CERT.: Internal medicine '89
HOSPITALS: Prince George's, teaching staff; Doctors, Holy Cross
LANGUAGES: Spanish

BETHESDA

Loreto S. Albiol, MD
8218 Wisconsin Ave. #105, Bethesda Md 20814
(301)907-8624
MED. DEGREE: National Univ., Paraguay '80; TRAINING: Franklin Square Hosp., Baltimore '83-'86
BOARD eligible Internal medicine
HOSPITALS: Suburban, Shady Grove
LANGUAGES: Spanish COMMENTS: I spend more time with patients trying to provide full medical care.

Eva L. Myers, MD
4300 Montgomery Ave #101, Bethesda Md 20814
(301)656-3222 SEE Beltsville office for background

CHEVY CHASE

Irene G. Tamagna, MD
7101 Connecticut Ave, Chevy Chase Md 20815
(301)652-2274
MED. DEGREE: Women's Med. Coll. of Pa. '43
TRAINING: Columbia Univ. '43-'44; Goldwater Memorial Hosp., '44-'46; cardiology fellow Columbia '46-'47
BOARD eligible Internal medicine
HOSPITALS: George Washington Univ., prof. emeritus
LANGUAGES: German, French, Italian

ROCKVILLE

Melinda Wolf, MD
14820 Physicians Ln #241, Rockville Md 20850
(301)217-0333
MED. DEGREE: Georgetown Univ. '80
TRAINING: Montefiore Hosp., Pittsburgh '81-'84, Internal med.; Psychiatry intern. Charlestown, S.C. '80-'81
BOARD CERT.: Internal medicine '85
HOSPITALS: Shady Grove LANGUAGES: French; Spanish (a little)
COMMENTS: I loot at the whole patient, not just the parts - comprehensive, preventive care.

Sunita Hanjura, MD
Rockville Internal Medicine Group
809 Viers Mill Rd. Rockville Md 20851
(301) 762- 5019
SUBSPECIALTY: Geriatrics
ASSOCIATES: Drs. Stephen Jones, Donald Bucy, Patricia Kellogg, Robert Macon, John Saia, Alan Pollack, Frauke Westphal
MED. DEGREE: Univ. of Pittsburgh '87
TRAINING: Case Western Reserve Univ., Cleveland. '87-'90
BOARD eligible Internal medicine and geriatrics
HOSPITALS: Suburban, Shady Grove; George Washington (clinical preceptor)
LANGUAGES: Hindi COMMENTS: I strongly believe in preventive medicine. We have facilities in our office for all general medicine needs, including Paps/pelvics. We have 3 women in our group, so you always have a woman doctor available.

Patricia Deal Kellogg MD
Rockville Internal Medicine Group
809 Veirs Mill Rd, Rockville Md 20851
(301)762-5010
ASSOCIATES: Drs. Stephen Jones, Donald Bucy, John Saia, Robert Macon, Frauke Westphal, Alan Pollack, Sunita Hanjura
MED. DEGREE: U. of Maryland '76; TRAINING: George Wash. U.
BOARD CERT.: Internal medicine '79
HOSPITALS: Suburban, Shady Grove
LANGUAGES: Spanish (a little)
COMMENTS: Generally non-authoritarian, trying to involve patient in decision-making. Believe my job is to educate patient to help themselves and help them understand medical treatment options.

Carol L. Bender, MD
11510 Old Georgetown Rd, Rockville Md 20852
(301)770-4950
MED. DEGREE: State Univ. of NY Upstate Med. Center '72
TRAINING: George Washington Univ. '72-'73; Washington Hosp. Ctr. '73-'75; MA teaching Columbia U. '66; attend annual review courses in internal medicine
BOARD eligible Internal medicine
HOSPITALS: George Washington instructor; assoc. attending at Suburban Hosp.
COMMENTS: We provide excellent medical care in a very pleasant office setting. Usually same day appointments are available. Staff very courteous and helpful.

Irina Krayterman MD
807G Rockville Pike, Rockville Md 20852
(301)762-1700
ASSOCIATES: Drs. John B. K. Allotey, Koranteng Addo
MED. DEGREE: USSR Medical School '62
TRAINING: Prince George's Gen. Hosp. '83-'86
BOARD eligible Internal medicine
LANGUAGES: Russian, Ukrainian, some German

Donna Rinis, MD
11510 Old Georgetown Rd, Rockville Md 20852
(301)881-2644
MED. DEGREE: U. of Maryland '81
TRAINING: Washington Hosp. Ctr.
BOARD CERT.: Internal medicine '84
HOSPITALS: Suburban

GAITHERSBURG

Maryam Y. Mizrahi, MD
902 Wind River Ln, Gaithersburg Md 20878
(301)840-0005
SUBSPECIALTY: Family practice
ASSOCIATES: Allen Vinitsky, MD
MED. DEGREE: Univ. of Medicine, Iran '75
TRAINING: 2 internships in Iran; Int., residency Georgetown program at Veterans Admin. Med. Center, DC
BOARD eligible Internal medicine
HOSPITALS: Doctors, Shady Grove LANGUAGES: Farsi
COMMENTS: Practice offers many different types of services. I see a lot of emergencies, including stitches. We do EKGs, cardiac stress tests, Halter monitors (cardiac) and much more.

Suhair Abulfarag, MD
19261 Montgomery Village Ave #G10, Gaithersburg Md 20879
(301)330-4414
MED. DEGREE: Univ. of Cairo, Egypt '77
TRAINING: Georgetown Univ; DC General Hosp.
BOARD eligible Internal medicine
HOSPITALS: Suburban, Shady Grove, Montgomery Gen.
LANGUAGES: Arabic, French, Spanish

Marilyn E. Giles, MD
19642 Club House Drive #615, Gaithersburg, Md 20879
(301)963-0040
ASSOCIATES: Drs. Michael Greene, Jay Morrow
MED. DEGREE: Univ. of Missouri, Columbia '81
TRAINING: Univ. of Mass. Medical Center '81-84; M. Ed. counseling; MS biochemistry
BOARD CERT.: Internal medicine '85
HOSPITALS: Shady Grove COMMENTS: The patients' involvement in their own care is of paramount importance. I spend a lot of time teaching my patients about health maintenance, the basis behind their individual disease processes and how I plan and execute any necessary diagnostic evaluations.

KENSINGTON

Jeanne P. Asher, MD
3720 Farragut Ave, Kensington Md 20895
(301)949-4242
ASSOCIATES: Drs. Barry N. Rosenbaum , Martin C. Shargel
MED. DEGREE: New Jersey Med. Sch., Newark '81
TRAINING: Naval Hosp., Bethesda
BOARD CERT.: Internal medicine '85
HOSPITALS: Holy Cross

SILVER SPRING

Penny Bisk, MD
10313 Georgia Ave., Silver Spring Md 20902
(301)681-8000
ASSOCIATES: Drs. Julie Fox, Robert Kramer
MED. DEGREE: Cornell Univ. '77
TRAINING: George Washington Univ., chief resident in medicine; training in infectious diseases
BOARD CERT.: Internal Medicine '80
HOSPITALS: Holy Cross, Suburban
COMMENTS: Patient, responsive, good bedside manner.

Julie Kramer Fox, MD
10313 Georgia Ave, Silver Spring Md 20902
(301)681-8000
ASSOCIATES: Drs. Penny Bisk and Robert Kramer
MED. DEGREE: Mt. Sinai Sch. of Med., NY '88
TRAINING: George Washington Univ. '88-91
BOARD CERT.: Internal medicine '92
HOSPITALS: Holy Cross, Suburban
COMMENTS: The patient always comes first.

Merlyn Vemury, MD
9801 Georgia Ave #227, Silver Spring Md 20902
(301)593-7792
SUBSPECIALTY: Geriatrics
MED. DEGREE: Univ. of Juarez Medical School, Mexico '84
TRAINING: Franklin Square. Hosp., Baltimore; PhD nutrition
HOSPITALS: Suburban, Holy Cross, Shady Grove, Montgom. Gen.
LANGUAGES: Some Spanish and Asian Indian languages
COMMENTS: General medicine, extensive geriatrics experience. Spends time with patients in understanding problems and explaining disease process and treatments. Involves patient in problem solving.

Kathleen K. Davis, MD
Cameron Medical Group
8700 Georgia Ave #400, Silver Spring Md 20910
(301)585-6049
ASSOCIATES: Drs. Deborah Goldberg, Ruth Kevess-Cohen, Theresa McLaughlin
MED. DEGREE: George Washington Univ. '77; TRAINING: George Washington Univ. Med. Center '77-'80
BOARD CERT.: Internal medicine '80
HOSPITALS: Holy Cross; teaching affiliation George Washington
COMMENTS: We emphasize care of the whole patient in health and disease. We emphasize prevention of disease, including smoking and dietary counseling and the psychosocial aspects of disease.

Deborah B. Goldberg, MD
Cameron Medical Group
8700 Georgia Ave #400, Silver Spring Md 20910
(301)585-6049
SUBSPECIALTY: Medical hypnosis
ASSOCIATES: Drs. Ruth Kevess-Cohen, Kathleen Davis, Theresa McLaughlin
MED. DEGREE: Harvard Univ. '68
TRAINING: Cambridge Hosp; Georgetown Univ., chief resident Georgetown Service/DC General Hosp.
BOARD CERT.: Internal med.'72, recert. '80, oncology '79
HOSPITALS: Holy Cross, med. exec. comm.; Wash. Adventist, Suburban, clin. asst. prof. George Washington
LANGUAGES: French (some) COMMENTS: I (we) feel that illness has to be considered not just as abnormal somatic physiology, but in a psychosocial context. Illness is shaped and generated often by social and psychological factors. We support patients who need to feel control over the management of their illness.

Ruth Kevess-Cohen, MD
Cameron Medical Group
8700 Georgia Ave. #400, Silver Spring Md 20910
(301)585-6049
SUBSPECIALTY: Women's health, geriatrics
ASSOCIATES: Drs. Deborah Goldberg, Kathleen Davis, Theresa McLaughlin
MED. DEGREE: Johns Hopkins Univ. '83
TRAINING: George Washington Univ.
BOARD CERT.: Internal medicine '87
HOSPITALS: Holy Cross; clin. inst. George Washington
LANGUAGES: French
COMMENTS: In my practice I emphasize preventive health care and a comprehensive approach to each patient.

Theresa G. McLaughlin
Cameron Medical Group
8700 Georgia Ave. #400, Silver Spring Md 20910
(301)585-6049
ASSOCIATES: Drs. Deborah Goldberg, Ruth Kevess-Cohen, Kathleen Davis
MED. DEGREE: Penn State Univ. '89
TRAINING: George Washington Univ. '89-'92
BOARD CERT.: Internal medicine '92
HOSPITALS: Holy Cross LANGUAGES: Spanish by staff

VIRGINIA

ANNANDALE

Ann Rose Eapen, MD
Woodburn Internal Medicine Assoc., Ltd.
3299 Woodburn Rd #300, Annandale Va 22003
(703)698-9000
ASSOCIATES: Drs. Michael Hattwick, Samuel Shor, Steven Voss, Ava Kaufman
MED. DEGREE: Cornell Univ. Med. Coll. '87
TRAINING: N. Shore U. Hosp./ Sloan Kettering Cancer Ctr., N.Y.
BOARD CERT.: Internal medicine '90
HOSPITAL: Fairfax COMMENTS: Stress preventive health/medicine; Special interest in cardiology

Robin B. Merlino, MD
3289 Woodburn Rd #330, Annandale Va 22003
(703)641-0333
ASSOCIATES: Joanne Crantz, MD
MED. DEGREE: Univ. of Michigan '80
TRAINING: George Washington Univ. '80-'83
BOARD CERT.: Internal medicine '83
HOSPITALS: Fairfax COMMENTS: Named one of the top primary care physicians "Washingtonian" 1987

Ilene Robeck, MD
3299 Woodburn Rd, Annandale Va 22003
(703)573-4015
MED. DEGREE: State Univ. of N.Y. at Buffalo
TRAINING: Fairfax Hosp.; Georgetown Univ.
BOARD CERT.: Internal medicine '80
HOSPITALS: Fairfax

BURKE

Karen Bloxom White, MD
Potomac Internal Medicine Assoc.,PC
9289 Old Keene Mill Rd, Burke Va. 22015
(703)866-4144
ASSOCIATES: Robert B. Posner, MD
MED. DEGREE: Eastern Virginia Medical School, Norfolk '84; TRAINING: Georgetown Univ. '84-'87
BOARD CERT.: Internal medicine '88
HOSPITALS: Fairfax, Alexandria COMMENTS: Focus on patient education, preventive health awareness. Courteous, warm, quality medical care provided at all times.

FAIRFAX

Judith Mechanick, MD
Access of Fairfax, 4315 Chain Bridge Rd, Fairfax Va 22030
(703)591-9322
ASSOCIATES: Drs. Stephen Wills, George Jastrzebski
MED. DEGREE: Univ. of Pennsylvania '82
TRAINING: George Washington Univ. '82-'85
BOARD CERT.: Internal medicine '85
HOSPITALS: Med. dir. Access of Fairfax; Fair Oaks
LANGUAGES: French
COMMENTS: Available for emergencies, short-term treatment of problems with referrals to local practioners.

Barbara A. Carson, MD
9926 Main Street, Fairfax Va 22031
(703)352-1182
ASSOCIATES: Fran DuRocher, MD
MED. DEGREE: Woman's Medical College of Pennsylvania '70
TRAINING: Medical Coll. of Pa. Hosp.; Philadelphia Veterans Admin. Hosp.; cont. educ. courses
BOARD CERT.: Internal Medicine '77
HOSPITALS: Fairfax COMMENTS: Warm, caring, competent.

Donna S. Cheng, MD
8316 Arlington Blvd #232, Fairfax Va 22031
(703)560-8834
MED. DEGREE: The American Univ.of the Carribean '85; TRAINING: St. John's Hosp., Detroit
BOARD eligible Internal medicine
HOSPITALS: Fairfax
LANGUAGES: Chinese COMMENTS: We care about our patients. We listen. We also emphasize the importance of prevention.

Fran DuRocher, MD
9926 Main St, Fairfax Va 22031
(703)352-1182
ASSOCIATES: Barbara Carson, MD
MED. DEGREE: Woman's Medical College of Pennsylvania '70
TRAINING: Medical Coll. of Pennsylvania Hosp.; Philadelphia Veterans Admin. Hosp.; MS dev. biology; continuing educ. courses
BOARD CERT.: Internal medicine '73
HOSPITALS: Fairfax COMMENTS: Warm, homey, friendly, caring, thorough, competent. Take time for patients.

Carol E. Kennedy, MD
8316 Arlington Blvd #222, Fairfax Va 22031
(703)560-6566
MED. DEGREE: Georgetown Univ. '70
TRAINING: Washington Hosp. Center
BOARD CERT.: Internal medicine '73
HOSPITALS: Fairfax, Arlington

FALLS CHURCH

Carolyn D. Blair, MD
311 Park Ave, Falls Church Va 22046
(703)536-2626
ASSOCIATES: Drs. Michael Davidov, Margie Akbari, Lillian Gavrillovich
MED. DEGREE: Univ. of Louisville '86
TRAINING: Georgetown Univ. '86-'89; continuing educ. courses
BOARD CERT.: Internal medicine '89
HOSPITALS: Fairfax, Fair Oaks, Arlington
LANGUAGES: German, Serbian
COMMENTS: I feel I have two roles - help care for acute health problems, educate patients so they can better keep themselves healthy.

RESTON

Tessa M. Cholmondeley, MD
1800 Town Center Drive #212, Reston Va 22090
(703)435-2227
ASSOCIATES: Drs. Lynne Fagan, Gwilym Parry
MED. DEGREE: Univ. of Connecticut '88
TRAINING: George Washington Univ. '88-'91; Fellow George Washington '91-'92
BOARD CERT.: Internal medicine '91
HOSPITALS: Reston
COMMENTS: Comprehensive care and patient education are the primary goals of my practice. I want my patients to feel comfortable discussing all their health concerns with me. Special interest in prevention and cancer screening.

Lynne L. Fagan, MD
Medical Assoc. of Reston
1800 Town Center Dr., Reston Va 22090
(703)435-2227
ASSOCIATES: Drs. Gwilym Parry, Tessa Cholmondeley
MED. DEGREE: Albert Einstein Coll. of Med. , NY '84
TRAINING: Washington Hospital Center
BOARD CERT.: Internal medicine '88
HOSPITALS: Reston, Fairfax, Sibley
COMMENTS: Particular interest in women's health issues, preventive medicine.

MCLEAN

Lois C. Bartis, MD
6888 Elm St #2D, Mc Lean Va 22101 (703)847-9800
MED. DEGREE: State Univ. of NY, Brooklyn '74
TRAINING: Brookdale Hosp. Medical Center, Brooklyn
BOARD CERT.: Internal medicine '79
HOSPITALS: Fairfax, Arlington

SPRINGFIELD

Barbara Whayne, MD
Internal Medicine Assoc of N. Va., Ltd.
6807 Springfield Plaza #201, Springfield Va 22150
(703)451-4524
SUBSPECIALTY: Diabetes management
ASSOCIATES: Drs. Scheldon Kress, Allen Gardner, Maxwell Maillis, Raymond Murrow, Ernest Katz
MED. DEGREE: Southwestern Medical, Dallas '84
TRAINING: Univ. of Texas, San Antonio '84-'87; also diabetes management training
BOARD CERT.: Internal medicine '88
HOSPITALS: Fairfax COMMENTS: Former chief of diabetes clinic Dallas VA Hosp. Stress patient education, encourage questions, provide support with therapeutic guidelines. Also maintain active interest in general internal medicine.

VIENNA

Surjit K. Singh, MD
301 Maple Ave W., Elm bldg #C, Vienna Va 22180
(703)938-0700
SUBSPECIALTY: hypertension
MED. DEGREE: Univ. of Delhi, India '67
TRAINING: Prince George's Gen.Hosp.; fellow hypertension Veterans Admin. Med. Center (Georgetown program) '83-'85
BOARD CERT.: Internal Med. board equivalent India '71
HOSPITALS: Fairfax, Fair Oaks
LANGUAGES: Hindi, Punjabi, Urdu COMMENTS: Multi-lingual staff. Female physician with extensive general internal medicine experience. Initial evaluation always thorough and complete.

Laurel D. Tschirgi, MD
301 Maple Ave., W., Vienna Va 22180
(703)938-8588
MED. DEGREE: Univ. of Virginia, Charlottesville '78
TRAINING: Christ Hosp., Cincinnati
BOARD CERT.: Internal medicine '82
HOSPITALS: Fairfax, Arlington COMMENTS: I emphasize the responsibility of the individual to maintain her own health. My role is to advise but I expect patients to participate in decision-making.

ARLINGTON

Sanda Costescu, MD
3801 N Fairfax Dr #64, Arlington Va 22203
(703)527-0333
MED. DEGREE: MD Bucharest, Hung. '57: MD Univ. of Illinois '78
TRAINING: Univ. of Illinois, Chicago; geriatrics training also
BOARD CERT.: Internal medicine '79
HOSPITALS: Arlington, No. Va. Doctors, Fairfax
LANGUAGES: Spanish, French, German, Romanian

Jane Hoyme, MD
3801 N.Fairfax Drive #45, Arlington Va 22203
(703)522-0092
MED. DEGREE: Univ. of Virginia '79
TRAINING: Georgetown Univ. Hosp. '81
BOARD CERT.: Internal medicine '87
HOSPITALS: Arlington, Fairfax

Girja R. Jalla, MD
611 S. Carlin Springs Rd #509, Arlington Va 22204
(703)820-6060
MED. DEGREE: Univ. of Kashmir, India '74
TRAINING: Georgetown Univ. '82-'84
BOARD eligible Internal medicine
HOSPITALS: No. Va. Doctors, Arlington, Fairfax, Fair Oaks
LANGUAGES: Hindi, Urdu, Punjabi, Kashmiri

Martha Maturi, MD
611 S. Carlin Springs Rd #411, Arlington Va 22204
(703)379-7110
ASSOCIATES: Working part-time for Dr. Alan Terlinsky
MED. DEGREE: Boston Univ. Med. Sch. '80
TRAINING: Washington Hospital Center '80-'83
BOARD CERT.: Internal medicine '84
HOSPITALS: Fairfax, Arlington, No. Va. Doctors
LANGUAGES: French (some)

Mary Jane Major, MD
1715 N. George Mason Dr #204, Arlington Va 22205
(703)525-8863
ASSOCIATES: Drs. Nina Selvaggi, Gary Fender, Arthur Rubin, David Weingarten
MED. DEGREE: Albany Med. Coll., Union Univ. '77
TRAINING: George Washington Univ.
BOARD CERT.: Internal medicine '81
HOSPITALS: Arlington, Fairfax
COMMENTS: We supply brochures to our patients outlining our practice goals and our recommendations for good health maintenance. Communication comes first and the rest will follow naturally.

ALEXANDRIA

Esther Matias, MD
1707 Belleview Blvd, Alexandria Va 22307
(703)765-3520
MED. DEGREE: Univ. of Sto. Tomas, Philippines '72
TRAINING: Univ. of Sto. Tomas Hosp.; Doctors Hosp., DC; Prince George's Gen. Hosp.
HOSPITALS: Mt. Vernon, Alexandria
LANGUAGES: Spanish (a little) and Tagalog
COMMENTS: Personal, small sized practice

Mary A. Vorachek, MD
923 Cameron St., Alexandria Va 22314
(703)548-5414
SUBSPECIALTY: Hypnosis
MED. DEGREE: George Washington Univ. '74; TRAINING: Univ. of Illinois; also hypnosis training
BOARD CERT.: Internal medicine '79
HOSPITALS: Alexandria, Mt. Vernon
COMMENTS: Offer Medifast weight loss program

Ava Curtis, MD
8720 Georgia Ave #802, Silver Spring Md 20910
(301)588-0202
SUBSPECIALTY: Allergy/immunology
MED. DEGREE: Univ. of Texas, San Antonio '78
TRAINING: Danbury Hosp./Yale Univ., Danbury, Ct.; fellow Allergy and immunology Howard Univ.
BOARD eligible Internal medicine
HOSPITALS: Howard Univ., Holy Cross
COMMENTS: God has blessed me to be able to study medicine and therefore I treat it as a ministry.
Office also at Ong Medical and Health Care Center
6357 Oxon Hill Rd, Oxon Hill Md 20745
(301)839-2700 Allergy only

Patricia Davidson, MD
7733 Alaska Ave. NW, Washington DC 20012
(202)882-5300
SUBSPECIALTY: Cardiology, hypertension
ASSOCIATES: Danny Mamodesene, MD
MED. DEGREE: Univ. of Louisville '78
TRAINING: Howard Univ. Hosp.; MS in chemistry
BOARD CERT.: Internal medicine '82
HOSPITALS: Wash. Hosp. Ctr., Holy Cross, Providence, Doctors, Prince George's, Howard, Greater SE, Hadley
COMMENTS: Preventive health with a concentration on diet.

Mary Restifo, MD
3301 New Mexico Ave NW #348, Washington DC 20016
(202)362-4467
SUBSPECIALTY: Cardiovascular disease
ASSOCIATES: Drs. Wesley Oler, Frank MacMurray, Oscar Mann, Charles Duvall, Alexander Chester, Lawrence Klein, Saulius Naujokaitis, Andrew Umhau
MED. DEGREE: Case Western Reserve Univ., Cleveland'67
TRAINING: Univ. of N. Carolina, Chapel Hill; card. - Georgetown
BOARD CERT.: Internal medicine '74, Cardiology '74
HOSPITALS: Sibley, Georgetown

Faranak F. Sotoudeh, MD
7525 Greenway Center Dr #209, Greenbelt Md 20770
(301)474-0400
SUBSPECIALTY: Endocrinology
MED. DEGREE: Tehran Univ., Iran '67
TRAINING: Henry Ford Hosp., Detroit; Washington Hosp. Ctr.
BOARD CERT.: Internal med. '75; Endocrinology '77
HOSPITALS: Chief endocrinologist Prince George's Gen. Hosp.
LANGUAGES: Farsi, some Spanish
COMMENTS: I believe in total patient care and prevention.

Nina Selvaggi, MD
1715 N. George Mason Dr #204, Arlington Va 22205
(703)525-8863
SUBSPECIALTY: Endocrinology
ASSOCIATES: Drs. Mary Jane Major, Arthur Rubin, Gary Fender, David Weingarten
MED. DEGREE: McGill Univ., Montreal '70
TRAINING: McGill Univ. '71-75, int. med., endocrin./metabolism
BOARD CERT.: Int. med.'78, (Canada '77); board elig. endocrin.
HOSPITALS: Arlington, Fairfax
LANGUAGES: French, Italian and little Spanish
COMMENTS: Our group believes in preventive measures for good health maintenance. We supply our patients with brochures outlining our philosophy and recommendations. Good lines of communication between MD and patient paramount.

Tahira Habib, MD
2616 Sherwood Hall Lane #203, Alexandria Va 22306
(703)360-2445
SUBSPECIALTY: Endocrinology
ASSOCIATES: Myriam Eder, MD (gastroenterologist)
MED. DEGREE: Dow Med. Coll., Pakistan '67
TRAINING: National Health Service Hospitals, United Kingdom '68-'77; Endocrinology George Washington Univ '78-'80
BOARD CERT.: Internal med.; Adv. Cardiac Life Support '92
HOSPITALS: Fairfax, Alexandria, Mt. Vernon and DeWitt Army

Lucy Beck, MD
Washington Internal Med. Group, P.C.
730 24th Street NW #7, Washington DC 20037
(202)338-5050
SUBSPECIALTY: Gastroenterology
ASSOCIATES: Drs. Raymond Scalettar, Robert Fischer, Lowell Weiss, Harold Mirsky, Lawrence McDonald, Paul Rudolf, Anthony Felice
MED. DEGREE: Northwestern Univ. '80
TRAINING: George Washington Univ.
BOARD CERT.: Internal med. '83; Gastroenterology '87
HOSPITALS: George Washington, Sibley
LANGUAGES: Vietnamese and Spanish (spoken by staff)

Mary H. Fang, MD
121 Congressional La #310, Rockville Md 20852
(301)340-8989
SUBSPECIALTY: Gastroenterology
MED. DEGREE: Med. Coll. of Virginia '74
TRAINING: George Washington Univ.; fellow in gastroenterology
BOARD CERT.: Internal med. '77, Gastroenterology '84
HOSPITALS: Shady Grove
LANGUAGES: Chinese (Mandarin), French

Lila T. McConnell, MD
5530 Wisconsin Ave #915, Chevy Chase Md 20815
(301)907-9757
SUBSPECIALTY:Geriatrics
MED. DEGREE: Georgetown Univ. '76
TRAINING: St. Vincent's Hosp. N.Y.; also fellow in geriatrics, Duke Univ. '83-85
BOARD CERT.: Internal medicine; Geriatrics
HOSPITALS: Sibley Mem.; asst. clin. prof George Washington Univ.
COMMENTS: I practice with an holistic attitude and am interested in preventive care for men and women.

Joanne Gittleson Crantz, MD
3289 Woodburn Rd, Annandale Va 22003
(703)641-0333
SUBCPECIALTY: Geriatrics
ASSOCIATES: Robin Merlino, MD
MED. DEGREE: George Washington Univ. '79
TRAINING: Beth Israel Hosp., Boston
BOARD CERT: Internal medicine '82; Geriatrics '89
HOSPITALS: Fairfax
COMMENTS: A personal approach to the patient.

Ava Kaufman, MD, MPH
Woodburn Internal Medicine Assoc.
3299 Woodburn Rd #300, Annandale VA 22003
(703)698-9000
SUBSPECIALTY: Geriatrics
ASSOCIATES: Drs. Anne Rose Eapen, Michael Hattwick, Samuel Shor, Steven Voss
MED. DEGREE: Case Western Reserve Univ., Cleveland'79
TRAINING: George Washington Univ.; MPH Health Services Administration Univ. of Mich.'84
BOARD CERT.: Internal med. '83; Geriatrics '92
HOSPITALS: Fairfax, Georgetown
COMMENTS: Interest in medical complications during pregnancy, general health care of women, strong preventive medicine bias.

Carol C. Jagdeo, MD
4000 16th St NW, Washington DC 20011 (202)882-9763
SUBSPECIALTY: Gynecology
ASSOCIATES: Jerome J. Canady, MD
MED. DEGREE: Univ. of Pennsylvania '81
TRAINING: Georgetown Univ. '81-'84
BOARD CERT.: Internal medicine '91
HOSPITALS: Georgetown clinical inst.; Wash. Hospital Center, Providence
COMMENTS: Interested in total patient care concept. Strong emphasis on preventive medicine and patient education.

Grace E. Sagayadan
Yater Medical Group
1780 Massachusetts Ave NW, Washington DC 20036
(202)785-2400
SUBSPECIALTY: Hematology/oncology
ASSOCIATES: Yater Medical Group multi-specialty physicians
MED. DEGREE: Univ. of the East, Philippines '81
TRAINING: St. Barnabas Hosp./Cornell Univ., NY
BOARD CERT.: Internal med. '89; Hem/Oncology board eligible
HOSPITALS: Washington Hosp. Center, Sibley
LANGUAGES: Spanish, Filipino, some French

Margaret Eka Akpan
6128 Landover Road, Cheverly Md 20785
(301)772-1112, also (202)462-1559
SUBSPECIALTY: Hematology/oncology
MED. DEGREE: St. George's Univ., West Indies '82
TRAINING: DC General Hosp. (Howard Univ. Med. Service, DC); also fellowship
BOARD CERT.: Int. Med. '88; Hematology/Oncology board eligible
HOSPITALS: DC General, assoc. prof.; Providence, Prince George's, Doctor's, Lanham.

Elisa J. Martinez, MD
8808 Hidden Hill Lane, Potomac Md 20854
(301)299-7200
SUBSPECIALTY: Hematology/Oncology
MED. DEGREE: Univ. of Puerto Rico '59
TRAINING: Harrisburg Hosp., Pa.; Jefferson Med. Coll., Philadelphia - hematology
BOARD CERT.: Internal medicine '73;
HOSPITALS: Holy Cross, Suburban, Shady Grove, Washington Adventist
LANGUAGES: Spanish COMMENTS: Patient contact. one on one. Personal care. Comprehensive one stop.

Kathryn Siena Kirwin, MD
10400 Conn Ave #606, Kensington Md 20895
(301)942-2212
SUBSPECIALTY: Hematology/oncology
ASSOCIATES: Drs. Daniel Rosenblum, Eugene Libre, Richard Pollen, Jeremy Cooke
MED. DEGREE: Univ. of Maryland '81
TRAINING: Univ. of N. Carolina '81-'84; fellow hematology Univ. of N.C.'84; fellow hematology/oncology George Washington U. '85-'87; MS biochemistry Univ. of Pennsylvania
BOARD CERT.: Int. med. '84, Hematology '86, oncology '89
HOSPITALS: Suburban, Holy Cross
LANGUAGES: German, American sign language
COMMENTS: Medical dir., Jewish Social Services Hospice Program. Teach at George Washington Medical School and teaching attending for med. students and fellows in hematology at V.A. Medical Center.

Thonia H. Gab-Allah, MD
6408G Seven Corners Pl., Falls Church Va 22044
(703)237-1084
SUBSPECIALTY: Hematology/oncology
MED. DEGREE: Ain-Shams Univ. Cairo, Egypt '71
TRAINING: DC Gen. Hosp. '80-'84; hematol./oncol. '84-'86
BOARD eligible Internal med. and Hematology/Oncology
HOSPITALS: Arlington, Fairfax LANGUAGES: Arabic

Carol Salzman, MD, PhD
5530 Wisconsin Ave #530, Chevy Chase Md 20815
(301)657-9424
SUBSPECIALTY: Infectious Diseases
ASSOCIATES: Neil Ravin, MD
MED. DEGREE: Georgetown Univ. '81
TRAINING: George Washington Univ.; PhD Georgetown, physiology
BOARD CERT.: Internal med. '84; Infectious Dis. '88
HOSPITALS: Sibley, George Washington, Georgetown

Susan M. Ginsburg, MD
106 Irving St. NW #419, Washington DC 20010
(202)723-4015
SUBSPECIALTY: Nephrology
MED. DEGREE: Jefferson Coll., Philadelphia '78
TRAINING: Washington Hospital Center; fellow nephrology at Washington Hospital Center '81-'83
BOARD CERT.: Internal medicine '81; Nephrology '84
HOSPITALS: Washington Hosp. Ctr., Providence, National Rehab.
COMMENTS: We have a very one on one practice, informed and helpful staff, comfortable office, dialysis, general medicine. We see a lot of eating disorder patients, diabetes. Handicapped exam room. Dr. Ginsburg can be reached by patients in a very timely fashion.

Wilhelmina M. Cruz MD
7700 Old Branch Ave. #D205, Clinton Md 20735
(301)868-3858
SUBSPECIALTY: Nephrology/critical care medicine
MED. DEGREE: Univ. of Sto. Tomas, Philippines '65
TRAINING: Memorial Hosp, Albany, NY; Maimonides Med. Ctr./Coney Island division, Brooklyn, NY
BOARD CERT.: Internal medicine '75; Nephrology '76
HOSPITALS: Doctors Comm, Southern Maryland
LANGUAGES: Filippino

Pamela Gallagher Guha MD
Heritage Med. Park
8926 Woodyard Rd #501, Clinton Md 20735
(301)856-2810
SUBSPECIALTY: Nephrology
MED. DEGREE: Univ. of Sydney, Australia '59
TRAINING: St. Vincent's Hosp., Prince Henry Hosp., Sydney
BOARD CERT.: Internal medicine '76; Nephrology '80

Alison Norris, MD
1450 Research Blvd #220, Rockville Md 20850
(301)424-4011
SUBSPECIALTY: Nephrology
MED. DEGREE: Medical Coll. of Pennsylvania '80
TRAINING: Univ. Hospitals Cleveland/Case Western Reserve '80-'83; Cornell Univ/NY Hosp. Nephrology fellow '83-'85
BOARD CERT.: Internal med. '83; Board eligible Nephrology
HOSPITALS: Holy Cross; Med. dir. Renal Treatment Ctr. Dialysis Unit, Rockville; Suburban, chair quality assurance comm., sec. Dept. of Med.; Shady Grove, med. review comm.
COMMENTS: We are here to serve the patients.

Melanie J. Blank, MD
301 Maple Ave W., Elm Bldg, #B, Vienna Va 22180
(703)281-5100
SUBSPECIALTY: Nephrology
MED. DEGREE: New York Medical Coll. '85
TRAINING: Lenox Hill Hosp., NY; also MA degree
BOARD CERT.: Internal med.'88; Nephrology board eligible
HOSPITALS: Fairfax, Arlington, Fair Oaks, No. Virginia Doctors
LANGUAGES: French COMMENTS: Professional and friendly atmosphere. Patient oriented practice interested in acute and chronic care, as well as preventive medicine.

Pamela M. Peeke MD, MPH
911 Russell Ave, Gaithersburg Md 20879
(301)258-0944
SUBSPECIALTY: Nutrition, eating disorders, obesity, sports med.
ASSOCIATES: Drs. John Melnick, Byrl Johnson
MED. DEGREE: Michigan State Univ. '80
TRAINING: George Washington Univ. '80-'83; MPH Univ. of California Berkeley Sch. of Public Health; Post doctoral scholar Univ. California at Davis - clinical nutrition/metabolism; National Institutes of Health - sports medicine, nutrition, obesity, eating disorders.
BOARD CERT.: Int. med. '89; Clinical nutrition/metab. board eligible
HOSPITALS: National Inst. of Health, Shady Grove, George Washington
LANGUAGES: French
COMMENTS: Basic internal medicine and primary care gynecology as a practice foundation; also consulting in the area of nutrition, obesity, eating disorders and sports medicine, especially geared to women patients. I combine my practice with medical research at NIH. I encourage patients to contact me with questions.

Marjorie A. Voith, MD
5530 Wisconsin Ave #830, Chevy Chase Md 20815
(301)652-4220
MED. DEGREE: Univ. of Maryland '72
TRAINING: U. of Maryland; fellow oncology National Cancer Inst.
BOARD CERT.: Int. med. '88; Addictionology '91; onc. board elig.
HOSPITALS: Sibley, Holy Cross, Wash. Hosp. Center, George Washington
COMMENTS: Practice is time intensive and comprehensive. First visits average 1.5 hours, follow-ups a half hour. Patients are virtually never kept waiting as the schedule will not be overbooked.

Marsha Seidelman, MD
10301 Georgia Ave #304, Silver Spring Md 20902
(301)681-7200
SUBSPECIALTY: Pulmonary and Critical Care medicine
ASSOCIATES: Drs. Carol Mahoney, Irnest Oser, Ira Tauber
MED. DEGREE: Albert Einstein NY
TRAINING: Jacobi/Albert Einstein '83-'86; Pulmonary med. Montefiore/Albert Einstein '87-'88
BOARD CERT.: Int. med.'86; Pulm. med.'90; Critical care
HOSPITALS: Holy Cross

Deborah L. Gofreed, MD
Pulmonary & Medical Assoc. of No. Virginia, Ltd.
1400 S Joyce St., Arlington Va 22202
(703)521-6662
SUBSPECIALTY: Pulmonary Care
ASSOCIATES: Drs. Philip Rodilosso, Stephen Zimmet, Wilson Coudon, M. Anthony Casolaro, Lawrence Stein
MED. DEGREE: Univ. of Maryland '80
TRAINING: George Washington Univ.; fellow in pulmonary diseases
BOARD CERT.: Int. med. '83; Pulmonary diseases '88
HOSPITALS: Arlington, National Hosp. for Orthopedics & Rehab., No. Virginia Doctors
COMMENTS: Preventive health care. I take care of many women patients, PAPs etc. Special interest in asthma.

DISTRICT OF COLUMBIA

Patricia G. Roberts, MD
106 Irving St. NW #408, Washington DC 20010
(202)291-1704
SUBSPECIALTY: Hypertension, Internal Medicine
MED. DEGREE: George Washington Univ. '87
TRAINING: George Washington Univ. '87-'88; Sinai Hosp. Baltimore '88-'90; Washington Hosp. Center fellow nephrology '90-'92; MA Political Science Univ. of Pittsburgh '70
BOARD CERT.: Internal med. '91; Nephrology board eligible
HOSPITALS: Washington Hosp. Center, George Washington, Sibley

Violet Habwe, MD
The Nephrology Center
730-24th St. NW #17, Washington DC 20037
(202)337-7660
ASSOCIATES: Drs. Stefan Dosa, Edward Dudek, Bruce Garrett, Anne Thompson
MED. DEGREE: Howard Univ. '81
TRAINING: Henry Ford Hosp., Detroit; also MS microbiology, Medical College of Virginia
BOARD CERT.: Internal med. '88, Nephrology '90
HOSPITALS: George Washington, Washington Hosp. Center

Susie Lew, MD
George Washington Univ. Med. Center
2150 Penn Ave NW #4-425, Washington DC 20037
(202)994-4244
ASSOCIATES: Drs. Juan Bosch, Paul Kimmel, Manuel Velasquez, Sandy Gibson, Beat von Albertini
MED. DEGREE: State Univ. NY Downstate '79; TRAINING: Brookdale Hosp., NY; fellow Mount Sinai, NY
BOARD CERT.: Internal med. '83, Neph. '86
HOSPITALS: George Washington Univ., asst. prof. of med.
LANGUAGES:Cantonese
COMMENTS: Hospital-based nephrology practice. All aspects of nephrology. Dialysis and transplantation

Anne M. Thompson, MD
The Nephrology Center
730-24th St NW #17, Washington DC 20037
(202)337-7660
ASSOCIATES: Drs. Stefan Dosa, Edward Dudek, Bruce Garrett, Violet Habwe
MED. DEGREE: Thomas Jefferson Univ., Philadelphia '67
TRAINING: Univ. of Southern Cal. '67-'68; George Washington Univ. '68-71, also neph. fellow
BOARD CERT.: Internal med. '73, Neph. '74
HOSPITALS: George Washington , Washington Hosp. Center
LANGUAGES: Spanish, Czech and Hungarian avail.
COMMENTS: Practice limited to kidney disease, including dialysis, transplantation and hypertension

VIRGINIA

Marietta F. Grundlehner, MD
8316 Arlington Blvd, Fairfax Va 22031
(703)560-1313
ASSOCIATES: Drs. Barry Strauch, Kenneth Geoly, Nabil Yakub, David Tietjen
MED. DEGREE: Thomas Jefferson Med. College, Philadelphia '74
TRAINING: St. Vincent's, NY; Thomas Jefferson Med. Coll.; fellow neph. Lankeman Hosp., Philadephia
BOARD CERT.: Internal med. '80, Neph. '86
HOSPITALS: Fairfax LANGUAGES: Arabic
COMMENTS: We only see patients with kidney problems. We work closely with primary care doctors.

NEPHROLOGY / INTERNAL MEDICINE

Margarita E. Nazdin, MD
1140 Varnum St. NE #203, Washington DC 20017
(202)832-7774
MED. DEGREE: Univ. Autonoma Nuevo Leon, Mexico '74
TRAINING: Georgetown Univ. Hosp. '76-'80, DC Gen. Hosp.; Fellow clinical neph. Georgetown Univ. and National Inst. of Health
BOARD CERT.: Internal med.'83; board eligible nephrology
HOSPITALS: Providence, Washington Hosp. Center
LANGUAGES: Spanish

DISTRICT OF COLUMBIA

Adrienne Smith, MD
650 Penn Ave SE #210, Washington DC 20003
(202)546-5122
SUBSPECIALTY: Aids, epilepsy
MED. DEGREE: Medical College of Pennsylvania '76
TRAINING: Children's National Med Ctr., George Washington Univ.
HOSPITALS: Washington Hosp. Ctr., Children's, Sibley, Holy Cross
COMMENTS: Women and children and their health issues - important. Large and varied practice, with expertise in AIDS related illnesses, post-trauma, epilepsy, neurobehavioral
SEE office on Conn. Ave. NW DC also

Marianne Schuelein, MD
Georgetown Univ. Hospital
3800 Reservoir Rd NW #307 Kober Cogan, Washington DC 20007
(202)687-4947
SUBSPECIALTY: Child neurology
ASSOCIATES: Faculty of Georgetown Univ. Med. Center
MED. DEGREE: New York Univ. '59
TRAINING: Yale Univ.; Michael Reese, Chicago (pediatric resid.); Fellow neurology Children's, DC '62-'63; neurology resid. Georgetown Univ. 63-'67
BOARD CERT.: Neur. '69; Ped.'64; Special qualifications in child neurology '69
HOSPITALS: Georgetown LANGUAGES: German
COMMENTS: I see children and adults with neurological disorders, including epilepsy, learning and behavior disorders, migraine, stroke, Parkinson's disease, muscular dystrophy, multiple sclerosis, etc.

Adrienne Smith, MD
4530 Conn Ave NW #101, Washington DC 20008
(202)244-4444 SEE Penn Ave SE for background

MARYLAND

Nirmala Khot Fernbach, MD
7726 Finns Ln, Lanham Md 20706 (301)577-5155
SUBSPECIALTY: adult and pediatric
MED. DEGREE: Maulana Azad Coll; Univ. of New Delhi '65; Univ. of Bombay '66-'67
TRAINING: St. Mary's Hosp., N.J.; Maimonides Med. Center, N.Y.; NY Medical Coll.; Kingsbrook Jewish Medical Center, NY '72-'74
BOARD eligible Neurolgy, Pediatrics
HOSPITALS: So. Maryland, Doctors, Prince George's
LANGUAGES: Hindi COMMENTS: Practice is done on one to one basis. Time given to patient.

Helene A. Emsellem, MD
Neurology Center
5454 Wisconsin Ave #1720, Chevy Chase Md 20815
(301)652-1617
MED. DEGREE: George Washington Univ. '77
TRAINING: George Washington Univ.
BOARD CERT.: Neur. '83, Clinical neurophysiology '85, sleep disorders med. (clin. polysomnographer) '89
HOSPITALS: George Washington Univ., Sibley, Suburban, Holy Cross, Shady Grove LANGUAGES: French

Rosita Dee, MD
8830 Cameron St. #207, Silver Spring Md 20910
(301)587-2257
SUBSPECIALTY: Neurophysiology
MED. DEGREE: Univ. of Sto. Tomas, Philippines '72
TRAINING: Univ. of Louisville '75; Medical Coll. of Virginia '76-'80
BOARD eligible neurology
HOSPITALS: Holy Cross, Washington Adventist
LANGUAGES: Mandarin, Fookien, Spanish, Filipino
COMMENTS: Patient just before anything else.

VIRGINIA

Jody E. Green, MD
Virginia Neurologic Center, Ltd.
3299 Woodburn Rd #300, Annandale Va 22003
(703)849-0930
SUBSPECIALTY: behavioral, geriatric neurology, headaches
ASSOCIATES: Virginia Neurologic Center specializes in neurologic surgery, adult and pediatric neurology, neuropsychiatry. Offices also in Alexandria, Annandale, Reston, Mt. Vernon, Fairfax
MED. DEGREE: Temple Univ. , Pa. '83
TRAINING: Rutgers Univ., NJ; Washington Univ., St. Louis '84-'87, chief res. '86-'87; Mass. Gen. Hosp.- behavioral and geriatric neurology, fellow in Alzheimer's disease '87-'89; fellow Massachusetts Inst. of Technology '87-'89
BOARD CERT.: Psychiatry/Neurology '89
HOSPITALS: Fairfax, Dominion; clinical instr. Georgetown
LANGUAGES: Some Spanish COMMENTS: I want my patients to take responsibility for their health care and not be passive. I enjoy playing the role of medical educator.

Kathleen Brelsford French, MD
3020 Hamaker Ct B104, Fairfax Va 22031 (703)641-4877
SPECIALTY: Neurosurgery
MED. DEGREE: Boston Univ. '80
TRAINING: Johns Hopkins Univ., general and neurosurgery
BOARD eligible Neurology
HOSPITALS: Fairfax, Reston, Fair Oaks

Linda S. Sigmund, MD
Neurology Center of Fairfax Ltd.
3020 Hamaker Ct, Fairfax Va 22031 (703)876-0800
SUBSPECIALTY: Parkinson's disease, movement disorders
ASSOCIATES: Drs. James Simsarian, David Grass, James Grim, Larry Zarchin, Robert Kurtzke, Lewis Eberly
MED. DEGREE: Georgetown Univ. '81
TRAINING: Letterman Army Med. Center, San Francisco
BOARD CERT.: Psychiatry/Neurology '87
HOSPITALS: Fairfax, Fair Oaks, Reston
LANGUAGES:Spanish available COMMENTS: We do our own diagnostic testing, believe in holistic medicine.

Aysegul Soyer, MD
2296 Opitz Blvd #360, Woodbridge Va 22191
(703)690-0049
ASSOCIATES: Drs. Peter Bernad, Kim Yang, Andrew Becker, Richard Leschek
MED. DEGREE: Istanbul Faculty of Medicine '80
TRAINING: Medical Coll. of Pennsylvania '81-'85
BOARD CERT.: Psychiatry/Neurology '87
HOSPITALS: Alexandria, Potomac, Fairfax
LANGUAGES: Turkish, German
SEE Alexandria office also

Faye Rosenbaum, Md
611 S. Carlin Springs Rd #208, Arlington Va 22204
(703)671-5400
ASSOCIATES: Drs. Archie McPherson, Alberto Chalmeta, Jerry Mikszewski
MED. DEGREE: Rush Univ., Chicago '84
TRAINING: Univ. of Southern California; Baylor Coll. of Medicine
BOARD CERT.: Psychiatry/Neurology '89
HOSPITALS: Arlington, Fairfax, Northern Virginia Doctors

Aysegul Soyer, MD
2616 Sherwood Hall La #201, Alexandria Va 22306
(703)360-8200 SEE Woodbridge office for background

DISTRICT OF COLUMBIA

NORTHEAST

April Rubin, MD
636 A St NE, Washington DC 20002
(202)547-4604
MED. DEGREE: St. Louis U. '77; TRAINING: U. of Chicago '77-'81
BOARD CERT.: Obstetrics/gynecology '83
HOSPITALS: Columbia Hosp., chair Utilization management comm., credentials comm, managed care task force; Georgetown Univ.

SOUTHEAST

Marciana W. Wilkerson, MD
650 Penn Ave SE #340, Washington DC 20003
(202)675-4616 SEE M. St. NW for background

NORTHWEST

Maureen Y. Chua MD
106 Irving St NW #403, Washington DC 20010
(202)723-0552 SEE F St. NW for background

Dorothy B. Gaither, MD
106 Irving St. NW, Washington DC 20010
(202)723-9100 SEE Penn. Ave. SE for background

Carin Kleiman, MD
106 Irving St. NW #403, Washington DC 20010
(202)723-0552 SEE F St. NW for background

Peggy J.B. Scurry, MD, PhD
6323 Georgia Ave. NW #206, Washington DC 20011
(202)291-0045
MED. DEGREE: Howard Univ. '77
TRAINING: Howard Univ. '77-'82; also Howard Univ. M.S., PhD in analytical chemistry
BOARD CERT.: Obstetrics/gynecology '84
HOSPITALS:Howard Univ., Providence, Washington Hosp. Center, Columbia Hosp. for Women
COMMENTS: Quality and caring health care for women.

Sandra Caskie, MD
Foxhall Ob/Gyn Assoc., P.C.
3301 New Mexico Ave NW #340, Washington DC 20016
(202)244-3523
ASSOCIATES: Drs. Marilyn Jerome, Achim Heintze, Richard Beckerman, Sharon Malone
MED. DEGREE: George Washington Univ. '82
TRAINING: Georgetown Univ. '82-'86
BOARD CERT.: Obstetrics/gynecology '88
HOSPITALS: George Washington Univ., asst. clin. prof.; Sibley and Columbia
LANGUAGES: German speaking physician in office
COMMENTS: We are a group practice, although each doctor has his or her own primary patients. If a woman wants to see exclusively a woman under all circumstances, it is important to know that in an emergency this would not be possible in our practice.

Marilyn C. Jerome, Md
Foxhall Ob/Gyn Assoc., P.C.
3301 New Mexico Ave NW #340, Washington DC 20016
(202)244-3523
ASSOCIATES: Drs. Sandra Caskie, Achim Heintze, Richard Beckerman, Sharon Malone
MED. DEGREE: Univ. of Cincinnati '78
TRAINING: George Washington Univ. '78-'82; training in gynecological laser and laparascopic surgery, hysteroscopy
BOARD CERT.: Obstetrics/gynecology '84
HOSPITALS: George Washington Univ., asst. clin. prof.

Sharon Denise Malone
Foxhall OB/GYN Associates, P.C.
3301 New Mexico Ave #340, Washington DC 20016
(202)244-3523
ASSOCIATES: Drs. Achim Heintze, Marilyn Jerome, Sandra Caskie, Richard Beckerman
MED. DEGREE: Columbia Univ. '88
TRAINING: George Washington Univ. '88-'92
BOARD eligible obstetrics/gynecology
HOSPITALS: George Washington, Sibley
LANGUAGES: Spanish

SOUTHEAST

Dorothy B. Gaither, MD
3230 Pennsylvania Ave SE, Washington DC 20020
(202)583-3626
MED. DEGREE: Howard Univ. '70
TRAINING: Howard Univ. '70-'75; annual conferences
BOARD CERT.: Obstetrics/gynecology '81
HOSPITALS:Washington Hosp. Center, Providence, Alexandria
COMMENTS: I give personal attention to the patients so they are informed about their problems. The staff does not do counseling. We want patients to be pleased with services received.
SEE office also on Irving St. NW

NORTHWEST

Constance J. Bohon, MD
Women Physicians Assoc.
1140-19th St. NW #500, Washington DC 20036
(202)887-0660
ASSOCIATES: Drs. Janet Schaffel, Nancy Ripp, Heather Johnson, Nancy Sanders, Gloria Grover
MED. DEGREE: George Washington Univ. '78
TRAINING: George Washington Univ. '78-'82
BOARD CERT.: Obstetrics/gynecology '85
HOSPITALS: Columbia Hospital for Women, attending faculty
SEE Gaithersburg office also

Gloria A. Grover, MD
Women Physicians Assoc.
1140-19th St. NW #500, Washington DC 20036
(202)887-0660
ASSOCIATES: Drs. Constance Bohon, Janet Schaffel, Nancy Ripp, Heather Johnson, Nancy Sanders
MED. DEGREE: Univ. of Virginia '88; TRAINING: Univ. of Virginia
BOARD eligible obstetrics - oral exam summer '93
HOSPITALS: Columbia Hosp. for Women LANGUAGES: German

Theressa Loretta James
1145-19th St. NW #410, Washington DC 20036
(202)331-1740
ASSOCIATES: Drs. Mark Reiter, Charles Hill, Eva Olah
MED. DEGREE: Georgetown Univ. '87; TRAINING: Georgetown U.
BOARD eligible obstetrics/gynecology
HOSPITALS: Georgetown Univ., assoc. clinical professor
LANGUAGES: Spanish SEE Arlington, Chevy Chase offices also

Heather L. Johnson, MD
Women Physicians Assoc.
1140-19th St. NW #500, Washington DC 20036
(202)887-0660
ASSOCIATES: Drs. Constance Bohon, Janet Schaffel, Nancy Ripp, Nancy Sanders, Gloria Grover
MED. DEGREE: Yale Univ. '79; TRAINING: Walter Reed Army Med. Center '79-'83
BOARD CERT.: Obstetrics/gynecology '85
HOSPITALS: Columbia Hosp. for Women, attending faculty
SEE Gaithersburg office also

Deena A. Kleinerman, MD
Yater Medical Group, 1780 Mass Ave NW, Washington DC 20036
(202)785-2400
ASSOCIATES: Howard Smith, Md, and Yater Med. Group multi-specialty physicians
MED. DEGREE: George Washington Univ. '80
TRAINING: Sinai Hosp. of Baltimore '84
BOARD CERT.: Obstetrics/gynecology '87
HOSPITALS: Columbia, clin. faculty; George Wash., asst clin. prof.
LANGUAGES: Spanish available COMMENTS: Obst./Gyn practice independently except for cross coverage as necessary.

Eva A. Olah, MD
1145-19th St. NW #410, Washington DC 20036
(202)331-1740
ASSOCIATES: Drs. Mark Reiter, Charles Hill, Theressa James
MED. DEGREE: Georgetown Univ. '87
TRAINING: Washington Hosp. Ctr. '87-'88, Georgetown '88-'91
BOARD eligible Obstetrics/gynecology
HOSPITALS: Arlington Hosp., Georgetown Univ, asst. clin. faculty
LANGUAGES: Spanish, Hungarian
SEE offices in Arlington and Chevy Chase

Nancy M. Ripp, MD
Women Physicians Assoc.
1140-19Th St NW #500, Washington DC 20036
(202)887-0660
ASSOCIATES: Drs. Constance Bohon, Janet Schaffel, Heather Johnson, Nancy Sanders, Gloria Grover
MED. DEGREE: Georgetown Univ. '81
TRAINING: Washington Hosp. Center '81-'85, chief resident, '84-'85
BOARD CERT.: Obstetrics/gynecology '87
HOSPITALS: Columbia Hosp. for Women, attending faculty
SEE office in Gaithersburg also

Nancy L. Sanders, MD
Women Physicians Assoc.
1140-19th St. NW #500, Washington DC 20036
(202)887-0660
ASSOCIATES: Drs. Constance Bohon, Janet Schaffel, Nancy Ripp, Heather Johnson, Gloria Grover
MED. DEGREE: New York Univ. '83
TRAINING: Cedars Sinai Med. Center Los Angeles '83-'87
BOARD CERT.: Obstetrics/gynecology '89
HOSPITALS: Columbia Hosp. for Women, assoc. faculty
LANGUAGES: Spanish (conversant) SEE Gaithersburg office also

Janet Schaffel, MD
Women Physicians Assoc., 1140-19th St. NW #500, Wash.DC 20036
(202)887-0660
ASSOCIATES: Drs. Constance Bohon, Nancy Ripp, Heather Johnson, Nancy Sanders, Gloria Grover
MED. DEGREE: Brown Univ. '79
TRAINING: Prentice Women's Hosp./ Northwestern U., Chicago '83
BOARD CERT.: Obstetrics/gynecology '86
HOSPITALS: Columbia Hosp. for Women, Georgetown
SEE office in Gaithersburg also

Kathleen Bis, MD
Foggy Bottom Ob/Gyn, Inc.
2112 F St NW #509, Washington DC 20037
(202)298-8322
ASSOCIATES: Morton Roberts, MD
MED. DEGREE: George Washington Univ. '72
TRAINING: George Washington Univ. affiliated hospitals
BOARD CERT.: Obstetrics/gynecology '77
HOSPITALS: Columbia Hosp. for Women, Sibley

Rebecca Busch, MD
2141 K St NW #808, Washington DC 20037
(202)331-9293
ASSOCIATES: Drs. Julian Safran, Stephen Horwitz, Richard Newman, Kenneth Blank
MED. DEGREE: Louisiana State Univ. '85
TRAINING: Georgetown Univ. Hosp. '89
BOARD CERT.: Obstetrics/gynecology '91
HOSPITALS: Columbia Hosp. for Women

Maureen Y. Chua, MD
2112 F St. NW #504, Washington DC 20037
(202)293-6455
ASSOCIATES: Carin Kleiman, MD
MED. DEGREE: Univ. of the East, Philippines '67
TRAINING: Washington Hosp. Center; also fellow clinical sonography
BOARD CERT.: Obstetrics/gynecology '76
HOSPITALS: Washington Hosp. Ctr., sr attending; Providence
SEE office on Irving St. NW also

Christine F. Colie
2424 Pennsylvania Ave #201, Washington DC 20037
(202)296-4062
ASSOCIATES: Drs. Patricia Hoyne, Anthony Scialli, Dessouky Dessouky
MED. DEGREE: Georgetown Univ. '87
TRAINING: Georgetown Univ. '87-'91; MPH candidate George Washington U.; training in occupational medicine, teratology fellow.
BOARD eligible obstetrics/gyn. Oral exam 11/93
HOSPITALS: Georgetown, full-time faculty

Rebecca A. Douglas, MD
2440 M Street NW #320, Washington DC 20037
(202)223-4540
MED. DEGREE: Univ. of Louisville '85
TRAINING: Washington Hosp. Center '85-'89; additional training laser surgery, hysteroscopy '90
BOARD CERT.: Obstetrics/gynecology '89
HOSPITALS: Columbia Hosp. for Women, attending faculty
LANGUAGES: German, Spanish available
COMMENTS: Solo women's practice devoted to women's improvement through holistic women's health care.

Elizabeth Ann Garreau, MD
2112 F St. NW #305, Washington DC 20037
(202)625-1166 SEE Falls Church for background

Florie Hirsch, MD
2440 M St. NW, Washington DC 20037 (202)457-0764
MED. DEGREE: George Washington Univ. '74
TRAINING: George Washington Univ.
BOARD CERT.: Obstetrics/gynecology '79
HOSPITALS: Columbia Hosp. for Women

Nicolette Horbach, MD
George Washington Univ. Med. Center
2150 Penn Ave NW, Dept. Ob/Gyn, Washington DC 20037
(202)994-4357
SUBSPECIALTY: Urogynecology (female bladder abnormalities)
ASSOCIATES: Obstetrics/gyn. faculty at George Washington (10 associates with specialization in maternal-fetal medicine)
MED. DEGREE: Washington Univ., St. Louis, '82
TRAINING: Univ. of Cal. San Francisco '82-'86; Univ. of Cal. Irvine, fellow female urology and laser surgery
BOARD CERT.: Obstetrics/gynecology '89
HOSPITALS: George Washington Univ., dir. division of Gynecology and Urogynecology, asst. prof. of obstetrics/gynecology.

Patricia M. Hoyne, MD
2424 Penn Ave. NW #201, Washington DC 20037
(202)296-4062
ASSOCIATES: Drs. Anthony Scialli, Dessouky A. Dessouky, Christine Colie
MED. DEGREE: Georgetown Univ. '83
TRAINING: Georgetown Univ. '83-'87
BOARD CERT.: Obstetrics/gynecology '90
HOSPITALS: Georgetown Univ., full-time instructor. See patients in a satellite facility at above address

Carin Kleiman, MD
2112 F St. NW #504, Washington DC 20037
(202)293-6455
ASSOCIATES: Maureen Chua, MD
MED. DEGREE: George Washington Univ. '79;
TRAINING: Long Beach Veterans Admin. Hosp., CA; Washington Hosp. Center
BOARD CERT.: Obstetrics/gynecology '87
HOSPITALS: Washington Hosp. Ctr.
LANGUAGES: Spanish-speaking nurse
SEE office on Irving St. NW also

Caryl G. Mussenden, MD
2112 F St. NW #305, Washington DC 20037
(202)625-1166 SEE Falls Church office for background

Joan Redfearn, MD
2440 M St NW #411, Washington DC 20037
(202)223-6030
SUBSPECIALTY: Infertility
MED. DEGREE: Emory Univ., Atlanta '83
TRAINING: Georgetown Univ.; also nursing degree
BOARD eligible obstetrics/gynecology
HOSPITALS: Columbia, Prince George's
LANGUAGES: Spanish SEE Oxon Hill office also

Marciana W. Wilkerson, MD
2440 M St. NW #710, Washington DC 20037
(202)835-8363
MED. DEGREE: State Univ. NY at Buffalo '77
TRAINING: Univ. of Maryland '77-'81
BOARD CERT.: Obstetrics/gynecology '86
HOSPITALS: Columbia Hosp. for Women, sec.-treas. of medical staff 4 yrs.; med. dir. Planned Parenthood Washington metropolitan area
LANGUAGES: Spanish SEE also Penn Ave SE office

MARYLAND

LANHAM

Cynthia Sadler, MD
Metropolitan Health Care Plus
10300 Greenbelt Rd #202, Lanham Md 20706
(301)262-2229
MED. DEGREE: Howard Univ. '82; TRAINING: Howard Univ.
BOARD eligible Obstetrics/gynecology
HOSPITALS: Columbia Hosp. for Women, Prince George's, Greater Laurel/ Beltsville

Elliece S. Smith, MD
9470 Annapolis Rd #316, Lanham Md 20706
(301)459-5744
MED. DEGREE: Howard Univ. '75
TRAINING: Howard Univ. Hosp. '75-'80
BOARD CERT.: Obstetrics/gynecology '82
HOSPITALS: Doctors Comm., Prince George's Gen. (chair Ob/gyn Dept.), Howard Univ., Greater SE Comm. COMMENTS: Very warm environment. Spend a lot of time with patients.

OXON HILL

Joan Redfearn, MD
6196 Oxon Hill Rd #610, Oxon Hill Md 20745
(301) 839-5804 SEE M St. NW, D.C. for background

GREENBELT

Ann B. Burke, MD
7500 Greenway Center Dr #1120, Greenbelt Md 20770
(301)220-2380
ASSOCIATES: Drs. C. K. Travers, Robert Levitt, Allan Lazarus
MED. DEGREE: Univ. of Mississippi '84
TRAINING: Wash. Hospital Center
BOARD CERT.: Obstetrics/gynecology '90
HOSPITALS: Holy Cross (medical exec. comm.), Washington Adventist, Montgomery General COMMENTS: Strong interest in preventive medicine. Expect patient participation. Not paternalistic. Focus on education of patient. SEE office in Silver Spring also

CHEVERLY

Nirmala K. Narla, MD
6005 Landover Rd #6, Cheverly Md 20785 (301)341-1666
MED. DEGREE: Guntur Med. College, India '71
TRAINING: Prince George's Hosp.; psychiatry and pathology training, '73-'75
BOARD CERT.: Obstetrics/gynecology '82
HOSPITALS: Prince George's, Holy Cross, Doctors
LANGUAGES: Hindi, Telugu
COMMENTS: Friendly and caring atmosphere. Treat with empathy.

LANDOVER

Shanaz H. Quaraishi, MD
6130 Landover Rd, Landover Md 20785 (301)322-5353
MED. DEGREE: Dow Med. College, Pakistan
TRAINING: Prince George's Gen. Hospital
BOARD CERT.: Obstetrics/gynecology '78
HOSPITALS: Prince George's, Doctors, Leland, Southern Maryland
LANGUAGES: Urdu

BETHESDA

Susan G. Board, MD
Women's Healthcare Specialists
4550 Montgomery Ave. #833N, Bethesda Md 20814
(301)654-5756
ASSOCIATES: Lori M. Kaler, MD
MED. DEGREE: Univ. of Illinois, Chicago '84
TRAINING: Loyola Univ. Med. Center, Ill. '84-'85; Rush Presbyterian St. Luke's Med. Center, Ill. '85-'89
BOARD CERT.: Obstetrics/gynecology '91
HOSPITALS: Columbia Hosp. for Women, Washington Hosp. Center
COMMENTS: Our practice strives to be sensitive to each patient's medical needs and emotional concerns. We schedule 60 minutes for new patient visits and encourage questions from patients, spouses.

Dianne C. Cinnamon, Md
8218 Wisconsin Ave #401, Bethesda Md 20814
(301)656-3013
MED. DEGREE: George Washington Univ. '73
TRAINING: George Washington Univ.
BOARD CERT.: Obstetrics/gynecology '80
HOSPITALS: Columbia, George Washington

Lori M. Kaler, MD
Women's Healthcare Specialists
4550 Montgomery Ave #833N, Bethesda Md 20814
(301)654-5756
ASSOCIATES: Susan G. Board, MD
MED. DEGREE: Univ. of Illinois '85
TRAINING: St. Francis Hosp., Evanston, Ill. '85-'86; Rush Presbyterian St. Luke's Med. Center, Ill. '86-'89
BOARD CERT.: Obstetrics/gynecology '91
HOSPITALS: Columbia, Washington Hosp. Center
COMMENTS: We plan to limit the size of practice so that we will be able to spend additional time with our patients. Patient education is an important aspect of our practice.

CHEVY CHASE

Theressa Loretta James
5530 Wisconsin Ave, Chevy Chase Md 20815
(301)654-5700 SEE 19th St. NW DC office for background

Eva A. Olah, MD
5530 Wisconsin Ave, Chevy Chase Md 20815
(301)654-5700 SEE 19th St. NW DC office for background

ROCKVILLE

Zidi Berger, MD
9715 Medical Center Dr #435, Rockville Md 20850
(301)279-0488
SUBSPECIALTY: Infertility
MED. DEGREE: Sch. of Medical Sciences, Argentina '77
TRAINING: Stanford Univ.'79; Washington Hosp. Center,'81-'84; fellow Stanford Univ. '78; pelviscopy and laser surgery training; also former primary school teacher
BOARD CERT.: Obstetrics/gynecology '90
HOSPITALS: Shady Grove, Suburban LANGUAGES: Spanish

Lesley A. Furlong, MD
14915 Broschart Rd #104, Rockville Md 20850
(301)762-5501
ASSOCIATES: Drs. Helena Kirkpatrick, Judith Gurdian
MED. DEGREE: McGill Univ., Canada '75
TRAINING: Univ. of Iowa; MS - genetics
BOARD CERT.: Obstetrics/gynecology '87
HOSPITALS: Shady Grove
LANGUAGES: French

Judith Gurdian, MD
14915 Broschart Rd #104, Rockville Md 20850
(301)762-5501
ASSOCIATES: Drs. Helena Kirkpatrick, Lesley Furlong
MED. DEGREE: Georgetown Univ. '79; TRAINING: Georgetown U.
BOARD CERT.: Obstetrics/gynecology '85
HOSPITALS: Shady Grove COMMENTS: We have a physician assistant who sees the majority of teenage patients. She is capable and qualified to do all procedures except surgery and delivery of babies.

Helena P. Kirkpatrick, MD
14915 Broschart Rd. #104, Rockville Md 20850
(301)762-5501
ASSOCIATES: Drs. Judith A. Gurdian, Lesley Furlong
MED. DEGREE: Univ. of Cal. '81; TRAINING: Georgetown Univ.
BOARD CERT.: Obstetrics/gynecology '87
HOSPITALS: Shady Grove
COMMENTS: We strive to offer our patients complete care and to develop positive, caring relationships.

Jill Ladd, MD
15215 Shady Grove Rd #300, Rockville Md 20850
(301)424-3444
SUBSPECIALTY: Infertility, menstrual disorders, menopause
ASSOCIATES: Drs. Craig Dickman, Claudia Taubman
MED. DEGREE: Georgetown '77
TRAINING: Washington Hosp. Center '77-'81
BOARD CERT.: Obstetrics/gynecology '83
HOSPITALS: Holy Cross, Suburban, Shady Grove, Washington Hosp. Center
COMMENTS: Interested in "wellness" care and concentrate on open communication and participation of patient in health care decisions. SEE also Silver Spring office

Claudia Taubman, MD
15215 Shady Grove Rd #300, Rockville Md 20850
(301)424-3444
ASSOCIATES: Drs. Jill Ladd, Craig Dickman
MED. DEGREE: Georgetown Univ. '82
TRAINING: Washington Hosp. Center; also masters in educ.
BOARD CERT.: Obstetrics/gynecology '89
HOSPITALS: Holy Cross, Suburban, Shady Grove, Washington Hosp. Center
SEE also Silver Spring office

GAITHERSBURG

Constance J Bohon, MD
Women Physicians Assoc.
16220 Frederick Road #419, Gaithersburg Md 20877
(301)258-0680 SEE NW DC office for background

Gloria A. Grover, MD
Women Physicians Assoc.
16220 Frederick Rd #419, Gaithersburg, Md 20877
(301)258-0680 SEE NW DC office for background

Heather L. Johnson, MD
Women Physicians Assoc.
16220 Frederick Road #419, Gaithersburg Md 20877
(301)258-0680 SEE NW DC office for background

Janice D. Johnson, MD
507 N. FrederickAve. Gaithersburg Md 20877
(301)840- 1200
ASSOCIATES: Mark S. Seigel, MD
MED. DEGREE: Duke Univ. '86; TRAINING: Univ. of Maryland
BOARD CERT.: Obstetrics/gynecology '92
HOSPITALS: Shady Grove, Suburban

Nancy M. Ripp. MD
Women Physicians Assoc.
16220 Frederick Rd #419, Gaithersburg Md 20877
(301)258-0680 SEE NW DC office for background

Nancy L. Sanders, MD
Women Physicians Assoc.
16220 Frederick Road #419. Gaithersburg, Md 20877
(301)258-0680 SEE NW DC office for background

Janet Schaffel, MD
Women Physicians Assoc.
16220 Frederick Rd, Gaithersburg Md 20877
(301)258-0680 SEE NW DC office for background

Joanne S. Hinson. MD
19261 Montgomery Village Ave., Gaithersburg, Md 20879
(301)977-3301 SEE Silver Spring office for background

Nancy Neuren Kator
19261 Montgomery Village Ave, Gaithersburg Md 20879
(301)977-3301 SEE Silver Spring office for background

SILVER SPRING

Ann B. Burke, MD
10801 Lockwood Dr #320, Silver Spring Md 20901
(301)681-3400 SEE Greenbelt office for background

Jill Ladd, MD
10801 Lockwood Drive, Silver Spring Md 20901
(301)593-5595 SEE Rockville office for background

Claudia Taubman, MD
10801 Lockwood Dr, Silver Spring Md 20901
(301)593-5595 See Rockville office for background

Joanne S. Hinson, MD
10313 Georgia Ave. #202, Silver Spring Md 20902
(301)681-9101
ASSOCIATES: Drs. Bernard Band, Robert Badwey, Thomas Goodridge, Rolando Perez, Nancy Kator
MED. DEGREE: Univ. of N. Carolina, Chapel Hill '83
TRAINING: George Washington Univ. '83-'87
BOARD CERT.: Obstetrics/gynecology '89
HOSPITALS: Holy Cross, Suburban, Shady Grove
COMMENTS: I encourage patient participation in their health care and emphasize patient education. SEE also Gaithersburg office

Nancy Neuren Kator
10313 Georgia Ave, Silver Spring Md 20902
(301)681-9101
ASSOCIATES: Drs. Bernard Band, Robert Badwey, Thomas Goodridge, Rolando Perez, Joanne Hinson
MED. DEGREE: Medical Coll. of Georgia '85
TRAINING: Sinai Hosp. Baltimore; George Washington Univ.
BOARD CERT.: Obstetrics/gynecology '91
HOSPITALS: Holy Cross, Suburban, Shady Grove; resident instructor George Washington Univ.
COMMENTS: Discussion of preventive medicine as well as treatment options. Patient education is encouraged. We do some infertility and laser surgery, up to date technologic pelviscopy, and high risk obstetrics. I enjoy treating teenagers and post-menopausal patients. We have one of the largest obstetrical practices in the area. SEE also Gaithersburg office

Susan G. Smigocki, MD
10301 Georgia Ave #301, Silver Spring Md 20902
(301)681-5900
SUBSPECIALTY: Infertility
ASSOCIATES: Drs. Paul McCauley, John Bruchalski
MED. DEGREE: Univ. of Maryland '82
TRAINING: St. Agnes Hosp., Baltimore
BOARD CERT.: Obstetrics/gynecology '88
HOSPITALS: Holy Cross, Suburban

Donna W. Wemple, MD
12200 Tech Rd #340, Silver Spring Md 20904
(301)622-0777
MED. DEGREE: George Washington Univ. '78; TRAINING: Washington Hosp. Center
BOARD CERT.: Obstetrics/gynecology '85
HOSPITALS: Washington Adventist, Holy Cross
COMMENTS: We have a small, family-oriented, friendly practice with a warm and enthusiastic attitude towards our patients. We can provide sonography, colposcopy, cryosurgery and LLETZ (large loop excision of the transformation zone) in the office.

VIRGINIA

ANNANDALE

Mary Campbell, MD, MPH
7501 Little River Tpke #203, Annandale Va 22003
(703)642-6610
MED. DEGREE: Johns Hopkins '77
TRAINING: Children's Hosp., Oakland, Cal.; Georgetown Univ.; also MPH Johns Hopkins '79
BOARD CERT.: Obstetrics/gynecology '87
HOSPITALS: Alexandria
COMMENTS: Calm, quiet, low key office

BURKE

Felicia L. Donald, MD
8990 Fern Park Dr., Burke, Va 22015
(703)978-0700 SEE Fairfax office for background

Janice J. Emery
9004 Crownwood Ct., Burke Va 22015
(703)978-5553 SEE Fairfax office for background

Kathleen M. Griffis, MD
8991 Cotswold Dr, Burke Va 22015 (703)425-5100
SUBPSECIALTY: Infertility
ASSOCIATES: Drs. Jan P. Fruiterman, J. John Raviotta
MED. DEGREE: Univ. of Florida '84
TRAINING: Univ. of Florida '84-'88
BOARD CERT.: Obstetrics/gynecology '90
HOSPITALS: Fair Oaks, Fairfax COMMENTS: Evenings and weekends available. Interactive, educational style.

FAIRFAX

Kathleen M. Matalone, MD
Women Physicians of No. Virginia PC
3613A Chain Bridge Rd, Fairfax Va 22030 (703)352-3910
ASSOCIATES: Drs. Susan L. Rattner, Kathleen A. Rausch
MED. DEGREE: Univ. of Arizona '81; TRAINING: Univ. of Arizona
BOARD CERT.: Obstetrics/gynecology '89
HOSPITALS: Fair Oaks, Reston
COMMENTS: I like to provide comprehensive preventive medical care for women. I also like to involve my patients in the decision-making process as it pertains to their health care and lifestyle.

Susan L. Rattner, MD
Women Physicians of No. Virginia PC
3613A Chain Bridge Rd, Fairfax Va 22030 (703)352-3910
ASSOCIATES: Kathleen Matalone, Kathleen Rausch
MED. DEGREE: George Washington Univ. '82
TRAINING: George Washington Univ. '82-'86
BOARD CERT.: Obstetrics/gynecology'88
HOSPITALS: Reston, Fair Oaks LANGUAGES: Spanish
COMMENTS: Our practice specializes in open communication between women. We believe that to give good health care, we need to explain all the options to our patients.

Kathleen A. Rausch, MD
Women Physicians of No. Virginia PC
3613A Chain Bridge Road, Fairfax Va 22030 (703)352-3910
SUBSPECIALTY: Infertility
ASSOCIATES: Drs. Susan L. Rattner, Kathleen M. Matalone
MED. DEGREE: Univ. of Texas at San Antonio '88
TRAINING: Albany Med. Center, N.Y.; laser and laparoscopy also
BOARD CERT.: Obstetrics/Gyn. board elig '93
HOSPITALS: Reston, Fair Oaks COMMENTS: We are a practice of women who treat women. We have the expertise, experience, empathy to effectively treat our patients.

Alison Ansher
8301 Arlington Blvd #302, Fairfax Va 22031 (703)573-6770
ASSOCIATE: Emine Cay, MD
MED. DEGREE: Univ. of Maryland '84
TRAINING: Washington Hospital Center, '84-'88, chief resident '88; infectious disease research, microbiology honor society
BOARD eligible Obstetrics/gynecology
HOSPITALS: Shady Grove; Fairfax
COMMENTS: Accepted to medical school after three years of undergraduate work. Born DC 1959, grew up in Montgomery County.

Nancy Lynn Asarkof Hafner, MD
8316 Arlington Blvd #420, Fairfax Va 22031 (703)698-8060
ASSOCIATES: Drs. David Carlson, John Maddox, David Berry
MED. DEGREE: George Washington Univ. '84
TRAINING: Tufts-New England Med. Center '84-'85; George Washington Univ. '85-'89
BOARD CERT.: Obst./gyn. '91 HOSPITALS: Fairfax, Fair Oaks

Felicia L. Donald, MD
Fairfax Ob/Gyn Associates
3650 Joseph Siewick Dr, Fairfax, Va 22033 (703)391-1500
SUBSPECIALTY: Infertility
ASSOCIATES: Drs. Leonard A. Rosen, Robert C. Castle
MED. DEGREE: Eastern Va. Med. Sch. '82
TRAINING: U. of Maryland '82-'84; U. of Arizona '84-'85; East Carolina U. '85-'87; also MS physiology
BOARD CERT.: Obstetrics/gynecology '90
HOSPITALS: Fairfax, Fair Oaks, Potomac
LANGUAGES: some Spanish SEE offices in Burke and Woodbridge

Janice J. Emery, MD
4001 Fair Ridge Dr #202, Fairfax Va 22033 (703)385-2015
ASSOCIATES: Drs. Robert Bettini, Gary Melnick
MED. DEGREE: Univ. of Iowa '75
TRAINING: Maimonides Med. Center, N.Y. '75-'79; AMA recognition award for cont. educ. credits
BOARD CERT.: Obstetrics/gynecology '81
HOSPITALS: Fairfax, Fair Oaks
COMMENTS: Adequate time discussing patient's history and concerns. Patients are provided information for self education and preventive health care. Patients are actively involved in health decision-making matters. SEE office in Burke also

FALLS CHURCH

Elizabeth Ann Garreau, MD
5201 Leesburg Pike #301, Falls Church Va 22041
(703)845-8686
ASSOCIATES: Caryl Mussenden, MD
MED. DEGREE: Robert Wood Johnson Med. School (formerly Rutgers U. NJ)
TRAINING: Washington Hosp.Center '86-'90, chief resident '89-'90
BOARD CERT.: Obstetrics/gynecology '92
HOSPITALS: Arlington, Columbia
LANGUAGES: French COMMENTS: We are two young energetic, friendly women physicians, dedicated to educating our patients and delivering quality care in a warm, supportive female environment. SEE F St. NW office also

Jennifer Kilmer, MD
5109 Leesburg Pike #914, Falls Church Va 22041
(703)845-4955
ASSOCIATES: Linda MacDonald, MD; Drs. Carol Ciofalo and Jeffrey Elliott (cross coverage)
MED. DEGREE: Pennsylvania State Univ. '78
TRAINING: Georgetown Univ.; training in laser surgery, laparoscopy, LEEP (Loop electrosurgical excision procedure)
BOARD CERT. : Obstetrics/gynecology
HOSPITALS: Arlington, Quality Assurance Comm.

Linda MacDonald, MD
5109 Leesburg Pike #914, Falls Church Va 22041
(703)845-4955
ASSOCIATES: Jennifer Kilmer, MD; Drs. Carol Ciofalo, Jeffrey Elliot (cross coverage)
MED. DEGREE: U. of Arizona '79; TRAINING: Providence Hosp.
BOARD CERT.: Obstetrics/gynecology '85
HOSPITALS: Arlington, Alexandria

Caryl G. Mussenden, MD
5201 Leesburg Pike #301, Falls Church Va 22041
(703)845-8686
ASSOCIATES: Elizabeth Ann Garreau, MD
MED. DEGREE: Howard Univ. '75
TRAINING: Howard Univ., Georgetown Univ. '79
BOARD CERT.: Obstetrics/gynecology '82
HOSPITALS: Columbia, Arlington
LANGUAGES: French by Dr. Garreau
SEE office on F St. NW DC also

HERNDON

H. Sharon Sethi, MD
13350 Franklin Farm Rd, Herndon Va 22071
(703)435-5700
MED. DEGREE: Osmania Univ., India '78
TRAINING: New York Med. Coll./Metropolitan Hosp.
BOARD CERT.: Obstetrics/gynecology '87
HOSPITALS: Arlington, Fair Oaks
LANGUAGES: Indian dialects COMMENTS: Dedicated to taking care of women-teens, infertility, pregnancies, menopause.

RESTON

Margaret H. Loewith, MD
1760 Reston Ave #200, Reston Va 22090
(703)787-3300 SEE Arlington office for background

Eveline B. Marquardt, MD
Reston Women's Group PC
1800 Town Center Dr #319, Reston Va 22090 (703)481-5100
ASSOCIATES: Susan Sigleo, MD
MED. DEGREE: George Washington Univ. '85
TRAINING: Georgetown Univ. '89
BOARD CERT.: Obstetrics/gynecology '91
HOSPITALS: Reston
LANGUAGES: French, German, Swiss German, Spanish
COMMENTS: My partner and I restrict the number of patients we see to ensure that we spend plenty of time with each. We emphasize preventive health, active patient participation in her health care and welcome patients' questions and insights.

Maureen O'Regan MD
1760 Reston Pkwy #511, Reston Va 22090
(703)437-8080 SEE Arlington office for background

Jane E. Piness, MD
1760 Reston Pkwy #200, Reston Va 22090
(703)787-3300 SEE Arlington office for background

Susan Sigleo, MD
Reston Women's Group, PC.
1800 Town Center Dr. #319, Reston Va 22090 (703)481-5100
SUBSPECIALTY: High-risk obstetrics, infertility, PMS
ASSOCIATES: Eveline Marquardt
MED. DEGREE: George Washington Univ. '85
TRAINING: Georgetown Univ. '85-'89; MS biochemistry
BOARD CERT.: Obstetrics/gynecology '92
HOSPITALS: Reston
LANGUAGES: German
COMMENTS: Prefer to treat the whole patient, incorporate assessment of stress, nutrition and lifestyle in evaluation. Strong background in high-risk obstetrics.

SPRINGFIELD

Viviane Fonteyn, MD
Northern Virginia Gynecologists
6807 Old Springfield Pl #206, Springfield Va 22150
(703)451-4311
SUBSPECIALTY: Infertility
ASSOCIATES: Drs. Leonard Levine, H. Eric Stern, Vincent Policelli, Peter Rothschild, Samuel Belinsky
MED. DEGREE: Boston Univ. '84; TRAINING: George Washington
BOARD CERT.: Obstetrics/gynecology '90
HOSPITALS: Fairfax
COMMENTS: Complete care in gynecology, obstetrics and infertility

VIENNA

Denita Faye Speyer, MD
246 Maple Ave. East, Vienna Va 22180
(703)281-2215
ASSOCIATES: Drs. James E. Anderson; Paul Tudder (cross coverage)
MED. DEGREE: Loma Linda Univ., Cal. '86
TRAINING: Loma Linda Med. Center '86-'90
BOARD CERT.: Obstetrics/gynecology '92
HOSPITALS: Reston, Fair Oaks

WOODBRIDGE

Valarie L. Carter, MD
Potomac OB/GYN Associates
2296 Opitz Blvd #320, Woodbridge Va 22191 (703)670-1800
ASSOCIATES: Barbara DiPietro, MD
MED. DEGREE: New York Univ. '85
TRAINING: Univ. of Cincinnati '85-'89
BOARD eligible Obstetrics/gynecology
HOSPITALS: Potomac LANGUAGES: Spanish available
COMMENTS: We involve our patients in their care. Preventive medicine is an important aspect of our practice.

Barbara DiPietro, MD
Potomac OB/GYN Associates
2296 Opitz Blvd #320, Woodbridge Va 22191
(703)670-1800
ASSOCIATES: Valarie Carter, MD
MED. DEGREE: Univ. of Virginia '87
TRAINING: Hershey Med. Center/Pennsylvania State Univ. '87-'91
BOARD eligible Obstetrics/gynecology
HOSPITALS: Potomac
LANGUAGES: Spanish available
COMMENTS: Preventive medicine is an important aspect of my practice. Patient education is emphasized to enable patients to make informed decisions and be active participants in planning their care.

Felicia L. Donald, MD
2028 Opitz Blvd, Woodbridge, Va 22191
(703)491-7181 SEE Fairfax office for background

ARLINGTON

Carol E. Ciofalo, MD
3803 N Fairfax Dr #406, Arlington Va 22203
(703)522-4448
MED. DEGREE: Georgetown Univ. '78
TRAINING: Georgetown Univ.
BOARD CERT.: Obstetrics/gynecology '85
HOSPITALS: Arlington, Alexandria; clin. inst. Georgetown Univ.
COMMENTS: Small practice. Personal care. Only 6-7 obstetrics patients per month.

Sanda DiPaolo, MD
(As of summer '93) 3803 N. Fairfax Dr. #404, Arlington Va. 22203
(703)351-9700
SUBSPECIALTY: Infertility
ASSOCIATES: Nicolae Filipescu, MD, PhD
MED. DEGREE: Georgetown Univ. '89
TRAINING: George Washington Univ., Georgetown Univ.
BOARD eligible Obstetrics/gynecology '94
HOSPITALS: Fairfax, Sibley, No. Virginia Doctors
LANGUAGES: French, Spanish
COMMENTS: Additional time for kindness, discussion, and concern, so that women will be more comfortable.

Margaret H. Loewith, MD
3801 N Fairfax Dr. #33, Arlington Va 22203
(703)516-9600
SUBPSECIALTY: Adol., pediatric gyn., infertility, sonography
ASSOCIATES: Drs. Jane Piness, Gustavo A. Rossi
MED. DEGREE: Temple Univ. '82
TRAINING: Georgetown Univ. Hosp. '82-'86; MPH Harvard '86
BOARD CERT.: Obstetrics/gynecology '88
HOSPITALS: Arlington, asst. dir. Ob/Gyn residency; Reston, Fairfax
LANGUAGES: Spanish SEE Reston office also

Jane E. Piness, MD
3801 N. Fairfax Drive #33, Arlington Va 22203
(703)516-9600
ASSOCIATES: Drs. Margaret Loewith and Gustavo Rossi
MED. DEGREE: Georgetown Univ. '86
TRAINING: Georgetown Univ. '86-'90; MS physiology
BOARD CERT.: Obstetrics/gynecology '92
HOSPITALS: Arlington, asst. dir. of Ob/Gyn educ.; Reston, Fairfax
LANGUAGES: Spanish, some French SEE also Reston office

Maureen O'Regan, MD
1715 N George Mason Dr #207, Arlington Va 22205
(703)528-6500
ASSOCIATES: Drs. Pablo A. Falo, Michele Wylen
MED. DEGREE: Georgetown Univ. '72
TRAINING: Georgetown Univ. '72-'75; continuing educ. updates
HOSPITALS: Georgetown, asst. prof. Ob/Gyn; Arlington, Reston
LANGUAGES: Spanish COMMENTS: Pro-life
SEE also Reston office

Michele Wylen, MD
1715 N. George Mason Dr #207, Arlington Va 22205
(703)528-6300
ASSOCIATES: Drs. Pablo Falo, Maureen O'Regan
MED. DEGREE: Georgetown Univ. '88
TRAINING: Georgetown Univ. '88-'92; also MS physiology Georgetown Univ.
BOARD eligible Obs./gyn.; Passed written boards, orals pending '94
HOSPITALS: Georgetown LANGUAGES: Spanish
COMMENTS: Special interest in adolescents. Patient education/communication is of primary importance.

Marion Bissell, MD
4820A South 31St., Arlington Va 22206
(703)578-3100 SEE Alexandria office for background

Theressa Loretta James
5015 Lee Highway, Arlington Va 22207
(703)527-0725 SEE NW DC for background

Eva A. Olah, MD
5015 Lee Highway, Arlington Va 22207
(703)527-0725 SEE NW DC office for background

ALEXANDRIA

Mary Elizabeth Cutting, MD
Alexandria WomenCare
4660 Kenmore Ave #902, Alexandria Va 22304
(703)370-4300
MED. DEGREE: Univ. of Virginia '80
TRAINING: Georgetown Univ. '80-'84; training in laser endoscopy
BOARD CERT.: Obstetrics/gynecology '86
HOSPITALS: Alexandria Hosp.; clin. asst. prof. Ob/Gyn George Washington

Fern L. Grapin, MD
4660 Kenmore Ave #604, Alexandria Va 22304
(703)370-0400
ASSOCIATES: Drs. Barry Rothman, Alice McKnight
MED. DEGREE: George Washington Univ. '83
TRAINING: George Washington Univ. '83-'87
BOARD CERT.: Obstetrics/gynecology '89
HOSPITALS: Alexandria
COMMENTS: Patient education about ailments, pregnancy guidance for real life experiences etc.

Alice M. McKnight, MD
4660 Kenmore Ave #604, Alexandria, Va 22304
(703)370-0400
ASSOCIATES: Drs. Barry Rothman, Fern Grapin
MED. DEGREE: Medical College of Pennsylvania '81
TRAINING: Howard Univ. Hosp.; laser surgery
BOARD CERT.: Obstetrics/gynecology '89
HOSPITALS: Alexandria

H. Evangeline Tomlinson, MD
5249 Duke St. #300, Alexandria Va 22304 (703)751-7750
MED. DEGREE: Ohio State '71
TRAINING: Riverside Hosp., St. Ann's Hosp. for Women, Columbus, O. '71-'75; surg. fellow Wash. Hosp. Ctr.
BOARD eligible Obstetrics/gynecology
HOSPITALS: Alexandria LANGUAGES: German
COMMENTS: Very personalized obstetrical and surgical care.

Marion Bissell, MD
OB-GYN Assoc. of N. Va., Ltd
1451 Belle Haven Rd, Alexandria Va 22307
(703)765-2120
ASSOCIATES: Drs. Jerome Stein, David Axelrod, Norman Tacktill
MED. DEGREE: New York Medical College '84
TRAINING: North Shore Univ. Hosp., Manhasset, NY
BOARD CERT.: Obstetrics/gynecology '90
HOSPITALS: Alexandria COMMENTS: Specializing in all aspects of women's care. SEE Arlington office also

Stefani J. Filak, MD
6418 Grovedale Dr. #102A, Alexandria Va 22310
(703)719-7808
MED. DEGREE: Baylor Coll. of Med. '82
TRAINING: George Washington Univ.; AMA recognition award for continuing med. education
BOARD CERT.: Obstetrics/gynecology '88
HOSPITALS: Alexandria
COMMENTS: Personable. Education of the patient. Spend time with patient.

Julie Okkema, MD
Women's Healthcare Associates
5115 Franconia Rd, #G, Alexandria Va 22310
(703)922-3434
ASSOCIATES: Mark R. Fracasso, MD
MED. DEGREE: George Wash. Univ. '81
TRAINING: Washington Hosp. Center '81-85
BOARD CERT.: Obstetrics/gynecology '88
HOSPITALS: Alexandria
COMMENTS: Stress wellness, weight control, sensitive to PMS. Encourage discussion of habits/home life. Take time with patients. No double booking. Accessible.

Cheryl A. Mason, MD
6462 Little River Turnpike #A, Alexandria Va 22312
(703)354-0074
SUBSPECIALTY: PMS, Infertility, menopause, laser surg., adol. gyn.
MED. DEGREE: Howard Univ. '81
TRAINING: Georgetown Univ. ; San Pedro & Peninsula Hosp., Ca.
BOARD CERT.: Obstetrics/gynecology '89
HOSPITALS: Alexandria, Columbia

Tobie Beckerman, MD
315 S. Patrick St., 2nd fl., Alexandria Va 22314
(703)684-1177
ASSOCIATES: Andrea M. Jackson, MD
MED. DEGREE: George Washington Univ. '84
TRAINING: George Washington Univ. '84-'88
BOARD CERT.: Obstetrics/gynecology '90
HOSPITALS: Fairfax, Alexandria
LANGUAGES: moderate Spanish and Hebrew

Andrea M. Jackson, MD
315 S. Patrick St., 2nd fl., Alexandria Va 22314 (703)684-1177
ASSOCIATES: Tobie Beckerman, MD
MED. DEGREE: Duke Univ. '84
TRAINING: George Washington Univ. '88
BOARD CERT.: Obstetrics/gynecology '90
HOSPITALS: Alexandria, Fairfax

Vanessa M. Barnabei, MD, PhD
George Washington Univ., Ob/Gyn. Dept.
2150 Pennsylvania Ave NW, Washington DC 20037
(202)994-4357
SUBSPECIALTY: Adolescent gynecology, genetics
ASSOCIATES: full-time faculty, Dept. Ob/Gyn, George Washington
MED. DEGREE: Univ. of Virginia '85
TRAINING: Northwestern U., Chicago; PhD Genetics, U. of Virginia
BOARD CERT.: Obstetrics/gynecology
HOSPITALS: George Washington Univ., asst. prof.; Children's

Susan L. Bathgate, MD
George Washington Univ., Dept. of Ob/Gyn
2150 Penn. Ave NW, Washington DC 20037
(202)994-4331
ASSOCIATES: faculty of George Washington Ob/gyn. Dept.
MED. DEGREE: George Washington Univ. '86
TRAINING: George Washington Univ.
BOARD CERT.: Obs/gyn; BOARD eligible maternal/fetal medicine
HOSPITALS: George Washington, Holy Cross
LANGUAGES: some Spanish
COMMENTS: I am a member of the GWU Ob/Gyn Dept. Maternal-fetal division, which specializes in high risk pregnancies, preconceptional counseling and prenatal diagnosis. The department provides comprehensive ob/gyn services, including an active in-vitro fertilization program, specialized menopausal care clinic, gynecologic urologic evaluation, gynecologic oncology and general ob/gyn care.

Jean C. Bolan MD
2440 M St. NW #712, Washington DC 20037 (202)293-6086
SPECIALTY: Maternal-fetal med. High risk obstetric cases only
ASSOCIATES: Drs. George F. Bronsky, Jon Katz
MED. DEGREE: Univ. of N. Carolina '76
TRAINING: Georgetown Univ. '76-'80; fellow George Washington Univ. '80-'82
BOARD CERT.: Obs/gyn'83; maternal/fetal med. '85
HOSPITALS: Columbia Hosp. for Women, co-dir. matern.-fetal med.
COMMENTS: Practice is a division of Columbia Hospital. Satellite office at 14801 Physicians Lane, Rockville

Rosemary Sokas, MD, MOH, MPH
2300 K St. NW #201, Washington DC 20037 (202)994-1734
ASSOCIATES: Laura S. Welch, MD, div. director
MED. DEGREE: Boston Univ. '74
TRAINING: Boston City Hosp.; Brigham & Women's Hosp./Harvard; MOH, MPH Harvard Sch. of Public Health
BOARD CERT.: Int. med. '77; Occ. med. '85
HOSPITALS: George Washington LANGUAGES: Spanish
COMMENTS: We see patients in referral from their primary care physicians to evaluate the presence of work-related disease and to help prevent future illness through workplace control recommendations.

Ellen Kessler, MD, MPH
Virginia Medical Associates
5510 Alma Lane, Springfield Va 22151 (703)642-5990
ASSOCIATES: Drs. John Mamana, Lewis Suskiewicz, Michael Price, Peter Francis, Linda Coleman, Elizabeth Ettinger
MED. DEGREE: Georgetown Univ.
TRAINING: Thomas Jefferson Univ.; Georgetown Univ.; Johns Hopkins Univ. Occ. med. and MPH
BOARD CERT.: Int. Med. '84, Occ. Med. '89
HOSPITALS: Fairfax COMMENTS: Occupational and environmental medicine - a preventive medical specialty.

Pamela Jo Harris, MD
1810 Calvert St. NW #5, Washington DC 20009 (202)265-4060
ASSOCIATES: Angela Manns, MD
MED. DEGREE: Ohio St. Univ. '76; honors
TRAINING: Washington Hosp. Center '76-'79; fellow: Immunobiology, Sloan Kettering Inst.; Immuno-Oncology, Georgetown Univ.; Hematology/Oncology, George Washington Univ. '81-'83; Oncology/Human genetics, Univ. of Miami '83-'84
BOARD CERT.: Int. Med. '80; Med. Oncology '87
HOSPITALS: Sibley, Suburban, Washington Adventist, Columbia; director The AIDS Clinical Research Center
LANGUAGES: Spanish

Alison Martin, MD
The Washington Clinic
5401 Western Ave NW, Washington DC 20015 (202)244-9270
ASSOCIATES: Multi-specialty group. Fred Smith, MD, oncology
MED. DEGREE: George Washington Univ. '80
TRAINING: Univ. of Pittsburgh;
Fellow in oncology National Cancer Inst. '84-'87
BOARD CERT.: Int. Med. '84, Oncology '87
HOSPITALS: Georgetown , Sibley, Suburban
LANGUAGES AVAILABLE: Spanish, Chinese, French, Italian, Romanian
COMMENTS: I think the oncology patient is best served by a team approach. I am happy to work with physicians and caregivers outside the clinic or within. Diagnostic radiology, laboratory, physical therapy, nutritional counselling, a support group for the patient and/or family, chemotherapy available.

DISTRICT OF COLUMBIA

NORTHWEST

Shirley P. Middleton, MD
2101 16th St NW, Washington DC 20009 (202)265-1811
MED. DEGREE: Howard Univ. '71; TRAINING: Howard Univ.
BOARD CERT.: Ophthalmology '82
HOSPITALS: Providence, Howard
LANGUAGES: some Spanish
COMMENTS: Handicapped accessible.

H. Jane Blackman, MD
3301 New Mexico Ave NW #326, Washington DC 20016
(202)966-7805
SUBSPECIALTY: Contact lenses, cataract, uveitis (inflammation)
ASSOCIATES: Drs. Christina Braun, Steven Bernstein
MED. DEGREE: Indiana Univ. '69
TRAINING: Kaiser Foundation Hosp., San Francisco; Univ. of Wisconsin '70-'73; Proctor Foundation , San Francisco '74-'76; National Eye Inst. fellow '76-'78
BOARD CERT.: Ophthalmology '75
HOSPITALS: Sibley, Georgetown; Washington Hosp. Center/Pres. of Foundation, Wash. National Eye Center

Christina Braun, MD
3301New Mexico Ave NW #326, Washington DC 20016
(202)966-7805
SUBSPECIALTY: Cataract surgery, glaucoma, contact lens
ASSOCIATES: H. Jane Blackman, MD
MED. DEGREE: Univ. of Virginia '85
TRAINING: Georgetown Univ.; Univ. of Virginia; MPH Harvard
BOARD CERT.: Ophthalmology '92
HOSPITALS: Sibley

Nancy Eve Thomas, MD
4301 48th St NW, Washington DC 20016 (202)363-4300
SUBSPECIALTY: Retinal surgery
MED. DEGREE: Univ. of Pennsylvania '68
TRAINING: Wake Forrest Univ.'68-'69; Univ. of Pennsylvania Scheie Eye Inst. '69-'74, retina fellow '75-76
BOARD CERT.: Ophthalmology '75
HOSPITALS: Sibley, Georgetown Univ., clin. asst. prof.; Wash. Hosp. Center, treasurer of Retina Society
LANGUAGES: Spanish

MARYLAND

Mary L. Scott, MD
12164 Central Ave #220, Mitchelville Md 20721
(301)390-4300
ASSOCIATES: Melvin Gaskin, MD
MED. DEGREE: Howard Univ. '82
TRAINING: White Mem. Med. Center; Howard Univ.
BOARD CERT.: Ophthalmology '87
HOSPITALS: Providence, Howard Univ.

Kathleen Haas Miller, MD
14458-101 Old Mill Road, Upper Marlboro Md 20772
(301)627-8404
ASSOCIATES: Drs. Michael J. Dodd, Nancy J. Surig
MED. DEGREE: Univ. of Maryland '79
TRAINING: Mercy Hosp., Balt.; Univ. of Maryland Hosp.
BOARD CERT.: Ophthalmology '85
HOSPITALS: Calvert Memorial, Prince Frederick, Md.; Univ. of Maryland Hosp., Baltimore
COMMENTS: Caring, personalized, comprehensive medical and surgical eye care. Offices also in Annapolis and Prince Frederick.

Arlene L. Murray, MD
Landover Mall W. Off.Bldg #206, Landover Md 20785
(301)386-3700
MED. DEGREE: Howard Univ. '84
TRAINING: Highland Gen. Alameda County Hosp., Cal. '84-'85; Howard Univ. '85-'88
BOARD CERT.: Ophthalmology '89
HOSPITALS: Providence, Howard
LANGUAGES: some Spanish COMMENTS: I strive to promote an educational approach, to encourage understanding of eye diseases, their prevention and treatment. Offer comprehensive eye care, surgical and medical. No contact lens dispensing.

Mary Ann Duke, MD
10000 Falls Rd #208, Potomac Md 20854 (301)299-7107
SUBSPECIALTY: Cataracts, laser surgery, retinal pathology, glaucoma
MED. DEGREE: Albany Medical College '85
TRAINING: Hackensack Med. Ctr., NJ; Albany Med. Coll., NY
BOARD CERT.: Ophthalmology '92
HOSPITALS: Holy Cross, Shady Grove, Suburban
COMMENTS: All eyelid surgeries, including cosmetic. Contact lenses and general ophthalmology.

VIRGINIA

Kimberly Ann Lucey, MD
3301 Woodburn Rd #201, Annandale Va 22003
(703)560-7300
MED. DEGREE: Georgetown Univ. '85
TRAINING: Mercy Hosp., Sinai Hosp., Baltimore; residency also at Wilmer Eye Inst., Johns Hopkins
BOARD CERT.: Ophthalmology '91
HOSPITALS: Fairfax, Alexandria
COMMENTS: Selected for Who's Who Among Rising Young Americans 1991

Linda Dressler, MD
12011 Lee Jackson Hwy #305, Fairfax Va 22033
(703)273-2398
MED. DEGREE: Harvard Univ. '82
TRAINING: St. Vincent's Hosp. NY; Manhattan Eye, Ear & Throat .
BOARD CERT.: Ophthalmology '88
HOSPITALS: Fairfax, Reston, Fair Oaks
LANGUAGES: some Spanish
COMMENTS: Personal and explanatory. I believe patients have a right to understand their health and participate in clinical decisions.

Heidi Lisker, MD
1830 Town Center Drive #307, Reston Va 22090
(703)471-8490
SUBSPECIALTY: retinal diseaes, diabetic retinopathy
MED. DEGREE: Boston Univ. '81
TRAINING: New England Deaconess Hosp., Boston; Washington Hosp. Ctr. - Oph., fellow retinal diseases
BOARD CERT.: Ophthalmology '87 HOSPITALS: Reston, Fairfax
LANGUAGES: Spanish
COMMENTS: I practice on a highly personal, one-on-one low volume and high quality basis. I do not use technicians. I do every part of the exam myself. I do not believe in mass-marketed high volume practice.

Lisa Framm Sklar, MD
302 Maple Ave West, Vienna Va 22180 (703)938-1201
SUBSPECIALTY: Glaucoma, cataract surgery
ASSOCIATES: Share space with Dr. Daniel Framm
MED. DEGREE: Eastern Virginia. Med. Sch. '84
TRAINING: Boston Univ., Georgetown Univ.; fellow glaucoma, cataracts, Mt. Sinai Hosp., NY '88
BOARD eligible Ophthalmology
HOSPITALS: Fairfax (teach hospital glaucoma clinic)
COMMENTS: I have made a strong commitment to provide excellent, high quality ophthalmologic care. We care a great deal about our patients. We do not overbook and almost always stay on schedule so patients do not need to wait. We do all the work ourselves. We do not have the patients seen by technicians first.

Geraldine Kelleher Richter, MD
3301 Woodburn Rd #104, Annandale Va 22003
(703)631-0139
SUBSPECIALTY: Sports medicine
MED. DEGREE: Georgetown Univ. '73
TRAINING: Georgetown Univ. '73-78; AMA recognition awards for continuing educ. BOARD CERT.: Orthopedic Surgery '79
HOSPITALS: Fairfax, Prince William, Fair Oaks, Reston Hosp.; clincial asst. prof. Georgetown Univ. Hosp.

Laura L. Tosi, MD
Children's National Medical Center
111 Michigan Ave NW, Washington DC 20010
(202)745-4063
SPECIALTY: Pediatric Orthopedic surgery
ASSOCIATES: Drs. William Robertson, Michael Thomas, Peter Sturm, Steven Buckley
MED. DEGREE: Harvard Univ. '77
TRAINING: Columbia Presbyterian Med. Center NY: intern, general surg.'77-'80; NY Orthopedic Hosp.'80-'83; fellow Ped. Orthopedics, Hospital for Sick Children, Toronto '83-'84
BOARD CERT.: Orthopedic Surgery '86
HOSPITALS: Children's, full-time staff surgeon; asst. prof. George Washington
LANGUAGES: little Spanish
COMMENTS: Special interest in birth defects, cerebral palsy, hip dysplasia, and club foot deformities.

Catherine Picken, MD
Georgetown Univ. Hosp.
3800 Reservoir Rd NW, Washington DC 20007
(202)687-8186
SUBSPECIALTY: Head/Neck Surgery
ASSOCIATES: Drs. Roy Sessions, Thomas Troost, Julya Gulya, Michael Morris
MED. DEGREE: Northwestern Univ. '79
TRAINING: Northwestern Univ.; Georgetown Univ.
BOARD CERT.: Otolaryngology '89
HOSPITALS: Georgetown, asst. prof.; Veterans Admin. Med. Center, chief Ear Nose Throat Division
COMMENTS: Special interests - head and neck cancer, sinus problems, sleep disorders, facial trauma.

DISTRICT OF COLUMBIA

SOUTHEAST

Michele Berman, MD
650 Pennsylvania Ave SE #220, Washington DC 20003
(202)546-4540
ASSOCIATES: Drs. Milton Werthmann, Richard Jones
MED. DEGREE: Washington Univ., St. Louis '81
TRAINING: St. Louis Children's Hosp.
BOARD CERT.: Pediatrics '87
HOSPITALS: George Washington and Georgetown clin. faculty; Shady Grove, Holy Cross, Sibley, Columbia, Washington Hosp. Center, Children's
COMMENTS: Adolescents welcome. Partners with specialty training in neonatology, sports medicine.
SEE Chevy Chase office also

NORTHWEST

Ioana Razi, MD
3537 R St NW, Washington DC 20007 (202)337-1774
SUBSPECIALTY: Homeopathy
MED. DEGREE: Univ. of Paris '78
TRAINING: Washington Hosp. Center; Georgetown Univ. Hosp.
BOARD CERT.: Pediatrics '84
HOSPITALS: Arlington, Fairfax
LANGUAGES: French, some Greek, some spanish

Dorothy A. Richmond, MD
Georgetown Univ. Hosp.
3800 Reservoir Rd NW, Washington DC 20007
(202)687-5437
ASSOCIATES: Drs. David Nelson, Janie Cox, Miriam Toporowicz, Alan Zuckerman
MED. DEGREE: Harvard Univ. '75
TRAINING: Boston City Hosp.; Georgetown Univ. ; also MA biology
BOARD CERT.: Pediatrics '80
HOSPITALS: Georgetown Univ., assoc. prof. of Pediatrics
COMMENTS: My group of pediatricians is very academically oriented. We try to treat the patient first, with emphasis on maintaining health.

Nina Scribanu, MD
Georgetown Univ. Hosp., Dept. of Ped., Child development center
3800 Reservoir Rd NW, Washington DC 20007
(202)687-8669
SUBSPECIALTY: clinical genetics
MED. DEGREE: Bucharest Med. School '57
TRAINING: Bellevue NYU Med. School '66-'69; continuing medical education courses
BOARD CERT.: Pediatrics '69, Genetics (clinical) '87;
HOSPITALS: Georgetown Univ., assoc. prof. Pediatrics and Obstetrics/gynecology
LANGUAGES: French, Russian, German, Hebrew, Romanian
COMMENTS: Our practice is family oriented. We have the objective to improve the lives of the children with developmental disabilities and their families.

Rumana Kazmi, MD
106 Irving St NW #212, Washington DC 20010 (202)726-5800
ASSOCIATES: Fisseha Tekle-Wold, MD
MED. DEGREE: Dhaka Med. Coll. '70
TRAINING: Evanston Hosp., Ill.; Wyler Children's Hosp., Chicago; fellow in neonatology BOARD CERT.: Pediatrics '79
HOSPITALS: Children's, Columbia, Washington Hosp. Center
LANGUAGES: Urdu, Bengali

Fisseha Tekle-Wold, MD
106 Irving St. NW #212, Washington DC 20010 (202)726-5800
ASSOCIATES: Rumana Kazmi
MED. DEGREE: American Univ. of Beirut; Haile Selassie Univ. '68
TRAINING: Brookdale Hosp. NY; New York Univ. '73-'77, ambulatory pediatrics BOARD CERT.: Pediatrics '81
HOSPITALS: Washington Hosp. Center, Children's
LANGUAGES: Ethiopian

Lillian Mclean Beard, MD
5505 5th St. NW #401, Washington DC 20011 (202)882-5437
ASSOCIATES: Bette L. Catoe, MD
MED. DEGREE: Howard Univ. '70
TRAINING: Children's National Med. Center '70-'73
BOARD CERT.: Pediatrics '76
HOSPITALS: George Washington Univ., assoc. clin. prof.; Children's, Howard, Columbia, Providence, Washington Hosp. Center
COMMENTS: Individual comprehensive care provided in a child friendly environment with parent friendly professionalism.

Bette L. Catoe MD
5505 5th St. NW #401, Washington DC 20011
(202)882-3362
SUBSPECIALTY: Adolescent medicine
ASSOCIATES: Lillian M. Beard, MD
MED. DEGREE: Howard Univ. '51
TRAINING: Howard Univ.; AMA continuing med. educ. certificate, post-grad. programs at least twice yearly
BOARD eligible Pediatrics
HOSPITALS: Howard, clin. inst.
COMMENTS: Interested in long term pediatric and adolescent care, including mental, physical and school development, as well as family interaction and relationships. Quality care as a necessity and reality.

NORTHEAST

Esther G. Pinder, MD
1201 Franklin St NE, Washington DC 20017 (202)635-7985
MED. DEGREE: Howard Univ. '69
TRAINING: Wm. Beaumont Hosp., El Paso, Texas; Children's National Med. Center
BOARD CERT.: Pediatrics '75
HOSPITALS: Children's, Providence, Washington Hosp. Center, Holy Cross, Columbia

Smita S. Gondhalekar, MD
5000 Nannie Burroughs Ave NE, Washington DC 20019
(202)397-2650
ASSOCIATES: Gerald Family Care Assoc. physicians
MED. DEGREE: B.J. Med. College, India '76
TRAINING: Ochsner Med. Hospital Foundation, New Orleans
BOARD CERT.: Pediatrics '92
HOSPITALS: Prince George's, Howard
LANGUAGES: Marathi, Hindi SEE office in Glenarden, Md also

SOUTHEAST

Janet L. Adams, MD
555 Newcomb St. SE, Washington DC 20032 (202)574-3322
MED. DEGREE: Howard Univ. '79; TRAINING: Howard Univ.
BOARD CERT.: Pediatrics '86
HOSPITALS: Greater SE Comm., Columbia Hosp. for Women

Minaxi N. Shah, MD
747 Alabama Ave SE, Washington DC 20032
(202)563-0100
ASSOCIATES: B.D. Absalon, MD
MED. DEGREE: Bombay Univ., India '72
TRAINING: Monmouth Med. Center, Long Branch, NJ
BOARD eligible Pediatrics
HOSPITALS: Greater SE Comm. LANGUAGES: Hindi

NORTHWEST

Agnes E. Schweitzer, MD
Yater Medical Group
1780 Massachusetts Ave NW, Washington DC 20036
(202)785-2400
ASSOCIATES: Ronald Bashian, MD and Yater multi-specialty physicians
MED. DEGREE: McGill Univ., Canada '59
TRAINING: Ottawa Civic Hosp.; Children's National Medical Center; also MS McGill
BOARD CERT.: Pediatrics '65
HOSPITALS: Georgetown Univ., clin. assoc. prof.; George Washington Univ., clin. asst. prof.; Sibley, Columbia, Children's
LANGUAGES: Hungarian, German

Ellie Hamburger, MD
George Washington Univ., Pediatrics
2150 Pennsylvania Ave NW, Washington DC 20037
(202)994-4661
ASSOCIATES: George Washington pediatrics faculty
MED. DEGREE: Univ. of Pennsylvania '81
TRAINING: Children's National Medical Center
BOARD CERT.: Pediatrics '85
HOSPITALS: George Washington Univ., asst. prof.; Children's
LANGUAGES: French

MARYLAND

GLENARDEN

Smita Gondhalekar, MD
Gerald Family Care Associates
7940 Johnson Ave, Glenarden Md 20706
(301)341-5450
SEE NE DC office for background

BOWIE

Azar M. Dashti, MD
4379 Northview Dr, Bowie Md 20716 (301)262-2627
ASSOCIATES: John H. Moling, MD
MED. DEGREE: Pahlavi Univ., Iran '70
TRAINING: Philadelphia Gen. Hosp.; Akron Children's Hosp.; Shohada Medical Center, Iran
BOARD CERT.: Passed written boards Pediatrics '78
HOSPITALS: Prince George's, Holy Cross
LANGUAGES: Farsi
COMMENTS: Very friendly office crew, children oriented.

FORT WASHINGTON

Rosario G. Dancel, MD
9401 Indian Head Highway #335, Fort Washington, Md. 20744
(301)248-1500 SEE Alexandria office for background

HYATTSVILLE

Jolan Rhodes, MD
3311 Toledo Terrace C204, Hyattsville Md 20782
(301)559-6356
MED. DEGREE: Howard Univ. '83; TRAINING: Howard Univ.
BOARD CERT.: Pediatrics '91
HOSPITALS: Providence, chair, Ped. Dept.; Columbia, Prince George's, Wash. Adventist, Children's, Holy Cross, Washington Hosp. Center
LANGUAGES: some Spanish

LANDOVER

Janet A. Gingold, MD
Promenade and Landover Mall, Landover Md 20785
(301)386-5900
ASSOCIATES: Drs. Brenda Bellamy, Marilyn McPherson Corder, Frederick Corder
MED. DEGREE: Univ. of Michigan '77
TRAINING: Univ. of Rochester, NY
BOARD CERT.: Pediatrics '82
HOSPITALS: Children's, Greater SE Comm.
COMMENTS: Group practice providing general pediatric care to a wide variety of families. I have a particular interest in treating asthma, as well as feeding and sleep disorders of infants and children.

BETHESDA

Amy J Meltzer, MD
10401 Old Georgetown Rd, Bethesda Md 20814
(301)530-2203
SUBSPECIALTY: Adolescent Med.
ASSOCIATES: Drs. Donald Wiczer, George Korengold, William Sterling
MED. DEGREE: New York Med. College '81
TRAINING: Georgetown Univ. '87-'90; Johns Hopkins Sch. of Hygiene and Public Health, '82-'84, MPH '83
BOARD CERT.: Preventive Med. '86, BOARD eligible Pediatrics
HOSPITALS: Georgetown, Sibley, Shady Grove, Holy Cross

CHEVY CHASE

Leah Brasch, MD
Elizabeth Arcade, 4601 N. Park Ave, Chevy Chase, Md 20815
(301)656-2745
ASSOCIATES: Drs. Linda Goldstein, Flavia Mercado
MED. DEGREE: Univ. of Col. '80
TRAINING: Children's National Medical Center '80-'83, chief resident '84
BOARD CERT.: Pediatrics '86
HOSPITALS: Children's, Holy Cross, Sibley, Columbia, George Washington Univ. - asst. prof. Ped.
COMMENTS: Relatively small, intimate practice where we can get to know the families and individualize care to meet their needs.

Michelle Berman, MD
5530 Wisconsin Ave. #1125, Chevy Chase, Md 20815
(301)907-3960 SEE SE DC office for background

Linda Goldstein, MD
The Elizabeth Arcade, 4601 N. Park Ave, Chevy Chase Md 20815
(301)656-2745
ASSOCIATES: Drs. Leah Brasch, Flavia Mercado
MED. DEGREE: New York Univ. '80
TRAINING: Children's National Medical Center '80-'83
BOARD CERT.: Pediatrics '85
HOSPITALS: Children's, clinical asst. prof.; Holy Cross, Sibley, Columbia, George Washington LANGUAGES: Spanish, Greek

BETHESDA

Anna Erdman, MD
10215 Fernwood Rd #103, Bethesda Md 20817
(301)530-8400
ASSOCIATES: Drs. J.B. D'Albora, Judith Osha, C. Coggeshall, T. Botsford
MED. DEGREE: Medical Academy, Warsaw '76
TRAINING: Georgetown Univ. Hosp. '79-'82
BOARD CERT.: Pediatrics '85
HOSPITALS: Georgetown clin. faculty; Sibley, Shady Grove
LANGUAGES: Polish

Judith Osha, MD
10215 Fernwood Rd, Bethesda Md 20817
(301)530-8400
SUBSPECIALTY: Adolescents only - ages 11-21
ASSOCIATES: Drs. James D'Albora, Charles Coggeshall, Thomas Botsford, Anna Erdman, Mark Melzer
MED. DEGREE: Georgetown Univ. '71
TRAINING: Georgetown Univ. '74
BOARD CERT.: Pediatrics '77
HOSPITALS: Georgetown, asst. clin. prof.

ROCKVILLE

Carol A. Plotsky, MD
Shady Grove Pediatrics Assoc.
14804 Physicians Lane, Rockville Md 20850 (301)294-9242
ASSOCIATES: Marinda Schwartz, MD
MED. DEGREE: George Washington Univ. '86
TRAINING: Children's Hosp. of Pittsburgh '86-'89; Fellow Ped. Hematology/ Oncology, National Inst. of Health '89-'91; also law degree Univ. of Conn. '74
BOARD CERT.: Pediatrics '89
HOSPITALS: Shady Grove

Marinda Schwartz, MD
Shady Grove Pediatrics Assoc.
14804 Physicians Lane #222, Rockville Md 20850 (301)294-9242
SUBSPECIALTY: School, developmental problems
ASSOCIATES: Carol A. Plotsky, MD
MED. DEGREE: Johns Hopkins Univ. '63
TRAINING: Johns Hopkins U.; Children's National Medical Center
BOARD CERT.: Pediatrics '72
HOSPITALS: Shady Grove
COMMENTS: Emphasis on teaching parenting and safety.

Deborah E. Lindsey, MD
121 Congressional Lane #204, Rockville Md 20852
(301)984-8940
ASSOCIATES: Drs. Mary Margaret Dugan, David L. Kettl
MED. DEGREE: Tufts Univ. '87
TRAINING: Georgetown Univ. '87-'90
BOARD CERT.: Pediatrics '90
HOSPITALS: Sibley, Holy Cross, Shady Grove, Children's, Georgetown
LANGUAGES: French

Hari Cheryl Sachs, MD
11119 Rockville Pike, Rockville Md 20852 (301)468-9225
ASSOCIATES: Drs. Raymond H. Coleman, Allan B. Coleman
MED. DEGREE: Univ. of Maryland '85
TRAINING: Children's National Med. Ctr.'86-'88; continuing education courses
BOARD CERT.: Pediatrics '90
HOSPITALS: Children's, clinical assoc.; George Washington, Holy Cross, Shady Grove, Sibley, Columbia

GERMANTOWN

Earlene Jordan MD
19501 Doctor's Drive, Germantown MD 20874
(301)540-0555 SEE Gaithersburg office for background

Mangala Pandya, MD
Montgomery Medical Group
19530 Doctors Drive, Germantown Md 20874 (301)540-4432
SUBSPECIALTY: young adults
ASSOCIATES: Drs. Susan J. Withrow, Carolyn Baier, Charles Karesh, Herbert Juarbe, Pasqual Perrino, Anoma Bandara, Steven Dolinsky, A Frederick North, Barbara Bell
MED. DEGREE: Bombay Univ., India '70
TRAINING: Baltimore City Hospital; St. Agnes Hosp., Baltimore '81-82, chief resident
BOARD eligible Pediatrics
HOSPITALS: Shady Grove Adventist LANGUAGES: Hindi

Sandra Takai, MD
19501 Doctors Dr, Germantown Md 20874 (301)540-0555
ASSOCIATES: Drs. Edward Feroli, Frank Pedreira, Gordon Mella, Earlene Jordan, Ursula Wollschlaeger, Smita Mengers
MED. DEGREE: Univ. of Maryland '80
TRAINING: Sinai Hosp. of Baltimore '80-'83
BOARD CERT.: Pediatrics '83
HOSPITALS: Shady Grove Adventist, Holy Cross

NORTH POTOMAC

Avneet K. Bawa, MD
12116 Darnestown Rd #L-3, N. Potomac Md 20878
(301)990-6333
MED. DEGREE: Indiana Univ. '86
TRAINING: Univ. of Louisville '86-'89, Kosair Children's & affil. hosps.; Neonatal, pediatric Advanced Life support '91
BOARD CERT.: Pediatrics '89
HOSPITALS: Shady Grove
LANGUAGES: Punjabi
COMMENTS: Being a pediatrician, I feel strongly about giving anticipatory guidance and educating my patients and their families.

GAITHERSBURG

Earlene Jordan, MD
19251 Montgomery Village Ave, Gaithersburg, Md 20879
(301)926-3633
ASSOCIATES: Drs. Sandra Takai, Ursula Wollschlaeger, Cheryl Duncan, Edward Feroli, Gordon Mella, Frank Pedreira, Smita Mengers
MED. DEGREE: Univ. of Maryland '85
TRAINING: Baylor Coll. of Med. affil. hospitals '85-'88
BOARD CERT.: Pediatrics '89
HOSPITALS: Shady Grove, Holy Cross
LANGUAGES: some Spanish SEE Germantown office also

Smita Parikh Mengers, MD
19251 Montgomery Village Ave, Gaithersburg Md 20879
(301)926-3633
ASSOCIATES: Drs. Sandra Takai, Earlene Jordan, Ursula Wollschlaeger, Cheryl Duncan, Edward Feroli, Gordon Mella, Frank Pedreira
MED. DEGREE: Wright State Univ. '89; TRAINING: Georgetown U
HOSPITALS: Shady Grove, Holy Cross
LANGUAGES: Spanish, Gujrati
COMMENTS: Open Sat. and Sun. for emergencies

Ursula Wollschlaeger, MD
19251 Montgomery Village Ave, Gaithersburg Md 20879
(301)926-3633
ASSOCIATES: Drs. Edward Feroli, Gordon Mella, Frank Pedreira, Sandra Takai, S. Mengers, Earlene Jordan
MED. DEGREE: Wayne State Univ. '78; TRAINING: Georgetown
BOARD CERT.: Pediatrics '83
HOSPITALS: Shady Grove, Holy Cross; Georgetown : asst. prof. ped. '83-'88, clinical assoc. prof. '89 -
LANGUAGES: German

SILVER SPRING

Marjorie Barnett, MD
11233 Lockwood Dr, Silver Spring Md 20901 (301)681-1515
MED. DEGREE: Michigan State Univ. '79
TRAINING: Georgetown U.; Children's National Medical Center
BOARD CERT.: Pediatrics '84
HOSPITALS: Columbia, Children's, Georgetown Univ., Sibley, Wash. Hosp. Center, Washington Adventist, Holy Cross
COMMENTS: Our pediatric practice provides care for well and sick children. We are very supportive of breast feeding and young families, but see children from infancy through adolescence.

Linda A. Paxton, MD
344 Univ. Blvd. West #112, Silver Spring Md 20901
(301)681-6730
ASSOCIATES: Drs. Daniel G. Shapiro, Jeff P. Bernstein
MED. DEGREE: Univ. of Maryland '87
TRAINING: Children's National Medical Center '87-'90
BOARD CERT.: Pediatrics '91
HOSPITALS: Holy Cross, Children's National Medical Center

Mildred Sanchez, MD
831 University Blvd East, #34, Silver Spring Md 20903
(301)445-4388
SUBSPECIALTY: Adolescent Medicine
MED. DEGREE: Zaragoza, Spain '74
TRAINING: in Puerto Rico
BOARD eligible pediatrics
HOSPITALS: Washington Adventist, Holy Cross, Silver Spring
LANGUAGES: Spanish COMMENTS: Practice is mostly Spanish-speaking patients and families. Other ethnic groups welcome as staff and myself are totally bilingual. We accept Visa and Mastercard.

Valorie L. Anlage, MD
2415 Musgrove Rd #207, Silver Spring Md 20904
(301)989-0085
ASSOCIATES: Drs. Ann Werner, Diane MacDonald, Steve Brown, Jim Kalliongis, Ed Padow, Al Modlin
MED. DEGREE: Univ. of Rochester '85
TRAINING: Univ. of Rochester '85-'88
BOARD CERT.: Pediatrics '89
HOSPITALS: Holy Cross

Diane L. McDonald, MD
2415 Musgrove Rd, Silver Spring Md 20904
(301)989-0085
ASSOCIATES: Drs. Valorie Anlage, Al Modlin, Ed Padow, Steve Brown, Jim Kalliongis, Ann Werner
MED. DEGREE: Wayne State Univ. '84
TRAINING: Children's Hosp. of Michigan; St. Christopher's Hosp. for Children, Philadelphia
BOARD CERT.: Pediatrics '89
HOSPITALS: Holy Cross, Francis Scott Key, Johns Hopkins

Ann Susan Werner, MD
2415 Musgrove Rd, Silver Spring Md 20904
(301)989-0085
ASSOCIATES: Drs. Diane MacDonald, Valorie Anlage, Al Modlin, Ed Padow, Steve Brown, Jim Kalliongis
MED. DEGREE: Albert Einstein Coll. of Med. '67
TRAINING: Bronx Municipal Hosp. Center '67-'70
BOARD CERT.: Pediatrics '74
HOSPITALS: Holy Cross LANGUAGES: Spanish

VIRGINIA

BURKE

Bernadette N. Wells, MD
8988 Fern Park Drive, Burke Va 22015 (703)978-6061
ASSOCIATES: Drs. Pat A. Balsamo, Jorge Arnoldson, William Rees
MED. DEGREE: Indiana Univ. '78
TRAINING: Bowman Gray Sch. of Med./N.C. Baptist Hosp.
BOARD CERT.: Pediatrics '83
HOSPITALS: Fairfax, Fair Oaks
LANGUAGES: Spanish available
COMMENTS: Private practice in NC for 10 years. Set up and trained personnel for Level II nursery. Involved in clinical teaching of physician assistant and nursing students, EMS and hospital nursing personnel.

FAIRFAX

Urmilla Khanna, MD
10515 West Dr. Fairfax Va 22030 (703)273-8987
MED. DEGREE: Nagpur Univ., India '59
TRAINING: Madras Univ., child health '61; Univ. of Mich. (MS Pharm.) '70; Med. College of Ohio '71-'74; Mercy Hosp. of Toledo '70-'71
BOARD CERT.: Pediatrics '76
HOSPITALS: Fairfax ; Fair Oaks-newborn privileges
LANGUAGES:Hindi, Punjabi, Urdu
COMMENTS: Dr. Khanna and her staff pride themselves on establishing one-on-one relationships with the patients and their families.

Paula N. Fergusson, MD
Virginia Pediatric Group
8316 Arlington Blvd #502, Fairfax Va. 22031 (703)573-2432
ASSOCIATES: Drs. Richard Todhunter, Russell Libby, Samuel Weinstein, Michelle Simon, James Baugh, Lewis Puppo
MED. DEGREE: Med. College. of Virginia '85
TRAINING: Children's National Medical Center
BOARD CERT.: Pediatrics '89
HOSPITALS: Fairfax, Reston, Holy Cross

Michelle L. Simon, MD, PhD
Virginia Pediatric Group
8316 Arlington Blvd #502, Fairfax, Va 22031 (703)280-1321
ASSOCIATES: Drs. Richard Todhunter, Russell Libby, Samuel Weinstein, James Baugh, Paula Ferguson, Lewis Puppo
MED. DEGREE: Univ. of Florida '78
TRAINING: Univ. of Florida - path. '79-'80; neuropath. Univ. of Cal.'80-'82; Georgetown ped. '85-'88; PhD neuroscience '76 and MS Developmental and cell biology Univ. of Cal. Irvine '73
BOARD CERT.: Pathology; Anatomic, Neuropath. '83; Pediatrics '88
HOSPITALS: Fairfax, Reston (Newborns seen at Fair Oaks, Arlington by associates.)
LANGUAGES: French, Spanish available

Mei-Ling Wu Chen, MD
8622 D Lee Hiway, Fairfax Va 22031
(703)698-5488
MED. DEGREE: Kaohsiung Med. Coll. Taiwan '72
TRAINING: Veterans Gen. Hosp., Taiwan; Children's Hosp. Center, Newark, NJ; National Inst. Health fellow/ Cornell Univ. NY; Genetic-endocrinology-metabolism fellow Children's National Med. Center (1 year) and Medical College of Virginia (2 years)
BOARD CERT.: Pediatrics '82
HOSPITALS: Fairfax, Arlington LANGUAGES: Mandarin Chinese
COMMENTS: Emphasize preventive care, family as a whole which affects children's growth /development. Educate young parents (especially first time ones). Bedside teaching of parents and patients. Written instruction with discussion always. As a working mother of 3, married, I like to share my personal experiences with parents about child rearing. I strongly encourage parents to call to discuss medical questions rather than receive advice from friends and news media etc.

Debra Anne Zeh, MD
8303 Arlington Blvd, Fairfax Va 22031 (703)573-2018
ASSOCIATES: Manuel Guillen, MD
MED. DEGREE: State Univ. of NY at Downstate '79
TRAINING: Georgetown Univ.
BOARD CERT.: Pediatrics '84
HOSPITALS: Fairfax SEE also Great Falls office

Lilly Zuckerman, MD
8320 Professional Hill Dr., Fairfax, Va 22031 (703)573-1204
MED. DEGREE: National Taiwan Univ. '79
TRAINING: Baltimore City Hosp, St. Agnes Hosp; also MPH, Harvard Sch. of Public Health
BOARD CERT.: Pediatrics '87
HOSPITALS: Arlington, Alexandria, Reston, Fair Oaks
LANGUAGES: Chinese, Japanese

Noemi Dosa, MD
Fairfax Pediatric Associates PC
3650 Joseph Siewick Dr #101, Fairfax Va 22033
(703)391-0900
ASSOCIATES: Drs. Douglas McDowell, Manijeh Sadr, Diane Dubinsky, William Ohriner
MED. DEGREE: Univ. J.E. Purkyne, Czechoslovakia '68
TRAINING: Great Britain; in U.S. at Georgetown Univ.
BOARD CERT.: Pediatrics '92
HOSPITALS: Fairfax, Fair Oaks
LANGUAGES: Czech

Diane E. Dubinsky, MD
Fairfax Pediatric Assoc., P.C.
3650 Joseph Siewick Dr #101, Fairfax Va 22033
(703)391-0900
ASSOCIATES: Drs. Noemi Dosa, Manijeh Sadr, Douglas McDowell, William Ohriner
MED. DEGREE: George Washington Univ. '82
TRAINING: National Naval Medical Center, Bethesda
BOARD CERT.: Pediatrics '87
HOSPITALS: Fairfax, Fair Oaks
COMMENTS: We provide comprehensive pediatric care to children and adolescents through age 18.

FALLS CHURCH

Beverley J. Bayes, MD
107 N Virginia Ave, Falls Church Va 22046
(703)532-4446
ASSOCIATES: Drs. Lynne Myers, James Stallings, Amin Barakat
MED. DEGREE: Univ. of Toronto
TRAINING: Toronto Gen., Hosp. for Sick Children, Toronto '67
BOARD CERT.: Pediatrics '74, recert. '89
HOSPITALS: Fairfax, Arlington
COMMENTS: We see newborns through college students.

Lynne D. Myers, MD
107 N Virginia Ave, Falls Church Va 22046 (703)532-4446
SUBSPECIALTY: Learning disabilities
ASSOCIATES: Drs. Beverley Bayes, James Stallings, Amin Barakat
MED. DEGREE: State Univ. of NY Downstate '71
TRAINING: Georgetown Univ., 3 years pediatrics
HOSPITALS: Fairfax, Arlington
LANGUAGES: Spanish (just passable)
COMMENTS: Special interest in the "special child" learning disabilities, attention deficit hyperactivity disorder.

GREAT FALLS

Debra Zeh, MD
10134D Colvin Run Rd, Great Falls Va 22066
(703)757-7950 SEE Fairfax office for background

RESTON

Constance Lee Goldberg, MD
1830 Town Center Dr. #205, Reston Va 22090 (703)435-3636
SUBSPECIALTY: Adolescent med.
ASSOCIATES: Drs. Anthony DiPaola, Hope Scott, Stephen Harrison
MED. DEGREE: George Washington Univ. '71
TRAINING: Children's National Med. Center; Ped. chief resident in outpatient & emerg. med. '75
BOARD CERT.: Pediatrics '79
HOSPITALS: Reston, Fairfax
LANGUAGES: German
COMMENTS: Special interest in adolescent medicine. Appointed to Governor's Advisory Board of Child Abuse and Neglect, Richmond.

Ruth Avigan Mann, MD
Reston Pediatric Associates, Ltd.
11305 Sunset Hills Rd #B1, Reston Va 22090 (703)742-0777
SUBSPECIALTY: Adolescent med.
ASSOCIATES: Drs. Ruth McDonald, Martin Forman
MED. DEGREE: McGill Univ. '80
TRAINING: McGill Univ./Montreal Children's Hosp. '80-'81; Children's National Medical Center '81-'82
BOARD CERT.: Pediatrics '85
HOSPITALS: Fairfax, Reston, Fair Oaks
LANGUAGES: French, Hebrew
COMMENTS: Parent educated about medical issues, development, nutrition. Do not overtest or overuse medication. All questions answered. We also have development specialist and nutritionist affiliated with practice.

Ruth I. McDonald, MD, PhD
Reston Pediatric Associates, Ltd.
11305 Sunset Hills Rd #B1, Reston Va 22090 (703)742-0777
ASSOCIATES: Drs. Ruth Mann, Martin Forman
MED. DEGREE: McGill Univ., Montreal '78
TRAINING: Johns Hopkins Univ., Baltimore; PhD Developmental biology '70; continuing educ. courses
BOARD CERT.: Pediatrics '84
HOSPITALS: Fairfax, Reston, Fair Oaks
LANGUAGES: some French (partner-Spanish)
COMMENTS: Delivering continuity to care. Availability - telephone hour 8-9a.m. daily for physician to answer patient calls and questions. Listen to what patient has to say. No double booking of appointments

Hope Taylor Scott, MD
1830 Town Center Dr. #205, Reston Va. 22090 (703)435-3636
ASSOCIATES: Drs. Constance Goldberg, Anthony DiPaola, Stephen Harrison
MED. DEGREE: George Washington Univ. '85
TRAINING: Georgetown Univ. '85-'88, chief resident '88-'89
BOARD CERT.: Pediatrics '89
HOSPITALS: Fairfax, Reston
LANGUAGES: Sign language by staff
COMMENTS: We share calls only among ourselves. Patients may choose the same doctor every visit.

MCLEAN

Yasmin K. Anez MD
8365A Greensboro Dr, Mc Lean Va 22102 (703)356-4444
ASSOCIATES: John Bitar, MD
MED. DEGREE: Georgetown Univ. '76
TRAINING: Georgetown Univ. '83
HOSPITALS: Fairfax, Arlington
LANGUAGES: Arabic, Spanish

SPRINGFIELD

Sharon Seiler Jellinek, MD
NOVA Pediatrics Ltd.
6120 Brandon Ave, Springfield Va 22150
(703)451-3333
SUBSPECIALTY: Adolescent med., sexual abuse, microbiology, advanced llife support
ASSOCIATES: Drs. Ira Seiler, Philip Littleton, Lawrence Seidman, Kathleen Hamilton
MED. DEGREE: Georgetown Univ.
TRAINING: Georgetown Univ.; MS Clinical microbiology '84
BOARD CERT.: Pediatrics '92
HOSPITALS: Fairfax, Alexandria, Potomac LANGUAGES: French
COMMENTS: Old fashioned philosophy. The child comes first, not the insurance company. We stress preventive medicine. Night classes for parents each month by MD in group. Free prenatal consultation visit, 24-hour availability, adolescent med. with gynecologic exams, hypnosis and allergy testing available. Each member in our group has a special area of interest, such as Dr. Hamilton, a board certified pediatric cardiologist. We take time with patients; emphasis towards nutrition, development. SEE office in Woodbridge also

Elaine L. Cockerham MD
Virginia pediatrics and adolescent center
8316 Traford Lane, Springfield Va 22152
(703)569-8400; Adol. med. 644-9444 at 8314 Traford
ASSOCIATES: Drs. H. Donald Knox, Bruce Pfeffer, Martha Hogan, Tania Heller, Lisa Crim
MED. DEGREE: George Washington Univ. 72
TRAINING: Children's National Medical Center; attended regular Ped. update conferences
BOARD CERT.: Pediatrics '77 HOSPITALS: Fairfax
LANGUAGES: German COMMENTS: Separate adolescent office
for patients 12-20. Teenagers can be seen without a parent though we strongly recommend parent involvement. We have nurses trained for lactation advice. prenatal visits, parenting classes and hospital visits after birth. Education programs for parents include home management of asthma and a class for parents of two-year-olds.

Lisa M. Crim, MD
Virginia pediatrics and adolescent center
8316 Traford Ln, Springfield Va 22152
(703)569-8400; 644-9444, Adol. med.
SUBSPECIALTY: Adolescent med.
ASSOCIATES: Drs. Martha Hogan, Tania Heller, Elaine Cockerham, H. Donald Knox, Bruce Pfeffer
MED. DEGREE: Univ. of Cincinnati '87
TRAINING: Georgetown Univ. ; MS physiology Georgetown Univ.
BOARD CERT.: Pediatrics '90
HOSPITALS: Fairfax

Tania Heller, MD
Virginia pediatrics and adolescent center
8316 Traford Ln, Springfield Va 22152
(703)569-8400; 644-9444, adol. med.
SUBSPECIALTY: Adolescent med.
ASSOCIATES: Drs. H. Donald Knox, Bruce Pfeffer, Martha Hogan, Elaine Cockerham, Lisa Crim
MED. DEGREE: Univ. of Capetown, S. Africa, '82
TRAINING: Georgetown Univ.
BOARD CERT.: Pediatrics '87
HOSPITALS: Fairfax, Georgetown Univ., asst. clin. prof.
LANGUAGES: Hebrew, Afrikaans

Martha Hogan, MD
Virginia pediatrics and adolescent center
8316 Traford Lane, Springfield Va 22152
(703)569-8400; 644-9444, adol. med.
ASSOCIATES: Drs. Donald Knox, Bruce Pfeffer, Elaine Cockerham, Tania Heller, Lisa Crim
MED. DEGREE: Georgetown Univ. '68
TRAINING: Georgetown Univ. '68-'71, chief resident '71
BOARD CERT.: Pediatrics '72
HOSPITALS: Fairfax; Georgetown Univ, clin. asst. prof.
COMMENTS: 30-year-old practice with separate facilities for newborns to age 12, and adolescents 12-20. Associated with an onstaff psychiatrist, social worker, allergist, nutritionist and early child developmentalist; evening classes for parents of toddlers, asthmatics and asthmatic patients. Our philosophy is to look at the whole child and ask, "If this were my child, what would I want?" We welcome open communication, feeling it is the key to a good doctor-patient relationship. Two members of the group have been chosen Georgetown Dept. of Ped. "Pediatrician of the Year" - Drs. Don Knox, early 1980s, and Martha Hogan, 1988.

Marsha Shernock, MD
8314 Traford Ln, Springfield Va 22152
(703)451-5200
ASSOCIATES: Deborah Mayergoyz, MD
MED. DEGREE: Georgetown Univ. '76
TRAINING: Long Island Jewish Hosp. '77; Georgetown Univ. '78-'79; MS Roswell Pk., Buffalo NY
BOARD CERT.: Pediatrics '82
HOSPITALS: Fairfax; Georgetown Univ., asst. clin. inst.
LANGUAGES: Nurse:Spanish, French, German

VIENNA

Elizabeth Watts, MD
410 Maple Ave W., Vienna Va 22180
(703)938-2244
ASSOCIATES: Drs. Paul Schweisthal, Richard Schwartz, Robert Knerr, Michael Cassidy
MED. DEGREE: Medical College of Ohio '85
TRAINING: Columbus Children's Hosp./Ohio State Univ.; required continuing educ. credits
BOARD CERT.: Pediatrics '89
HOSPITALS: Fairfax

WOODBRIDGE

Sharon Seiler Jellinek MD
1930 Opitz Blvd, Woodbridge Va 22191
(703)690-3226 SEE Springfield office for background

Kathleen Parente, MD
14904 Jeff. Davis H'way #405, Woodbridge Va 22191
(703)490-1600 SEE Alexandria office for background

Teresa Kosciuk
12616 Lake Ridge Dr., Woodbridge Va 22192
(703)491-4131 SEE Alexandria office for background

Jean M. Massie, MD
12616 Lakeridge Drive, Woodbridge Va 22192
(703)491-4131 SEE Alexandria office for background

ARLINGTON

Isabel J. Ramaswamy, MD
3801 N Fairfax Dr #44, Arlington Va 22203 (703)522-4780
MED. DEGREE: Univ. Sto. Tomas, Philippines '63
TRAINING: DePaul Hosp, Norfolk; Medical College of Virginia
BOARD CERT.: Pediatrics '70
HOSPITALS: Arlington, Fairfax
LANGUAGES: Filipino, Tagalog, some Spanish

Catherine S. Casey, MD
1715 N George Mason Dr #205, Arlington Va 22205
(703)522-7300
ASSOCIATES: Drs. Timothy Daley, William Goldman, Catherine Lischwe, Mary Garrett
MED. DEGREE: Medical College of Virginia '74
TRAINING: Children's Hosp. of Philadelphia '74-'77
BOARD CERT.: Pediatrics '79 HOSPITALS: Arlington, Fairfax
LANGUAGES: American sign language

Catherine A. Lischwe, MD
1715 N. Geo. Mason Dr. #205, Arlington Va 22205
(703)522-7300
ASSOCIATES: Drs. Catherine Casey, William Goldman, Timothy Daley, Mary Garrett
MED. DEGREE: Univ. of Illinois '74
TRAINING: Children's Mem. Hosp./Northwestern Univ., Chicago; also one year child psychiatry
BOARD CERT.: Pediatrics '80
HOSPITALS: Arlington, Fairfax

ALEXANDRIA

Kathleen Parente, MD
4601B Pine Crest Office Park Dr, Alexandria Va 22301
(703)642-1100
ASSOCIATES: Drs. Robert Bregman, Erwin Bondareff, Peter Nachajski, William Fried, Nicholas Kyriazi
MED. DEGREE: Georgetown Univ. '85
TRAINING: Children's National Medical Center '85-'89
BOARD CERT.: Pediatrics '89
HOSPITALS: Alexandria, Fairfax, Potomac
COMMENTS: Friendly practice with 24-hour coverage, daily phone hour, weekend hours, competent nursing staff-all RNs. Sick and well care as a partnership with parents. SEE office in Woodbridge also

Rosario Dancel, MD
6000 Stevensons Ave. #104, Alexandria Va 22304
(703)823-2400
SUBSPECIALTY: Adolescent Med.
MED. DEGREE: Univ. of the East, Philippines '66
TRAINING: Providence Hosp., Georgetown Univ.
HOSPITALS: So. Maryland Hosp.
LANGUAGES: Filipino, Spanish
SEE office in Ft. Washington Md. also

Shahin Parvin, MD
4660 Kenmore Ave #408, Alexandria Va 22304
(703)751-1415
MED. DEGREE: Esfahan Univ., Iran '66
TRAINING: Providence Hosp, Georgetown Univ. Hosp., Baltimore City Hosp.
HOSPITALS: Alexandria, Mount Vernon
LANGUAGES: Farsi

Jacqueline Arnold, MD
1451 Belle Haven Rd, Alexandria Va 22307
(703)765-6093
ASSOCIATES: Drs. Robert Wineland, Ben Wilmot, Dean May, Vito Giannuzzi, William Russell, Sylvia Larkin
MED. DEGREE: George Washington Univ. '87
TRAINING: Georgetown Univ.
BOARD CERT.: Pediatrics '91
HOSPITALS: Fairfax, Mt. Vernon, Alexandria, Potomac

Sylvia A. Larkin, MD
1451 Belle Haven Rd, Alexandria Va 22307
(703)765-6093
ASSOCIATES: Drs. Robert Wineland, Ben Wilmot, Dean May, Vito Giannuzzi, William Russell, Jacqueline Arnold
MED. DEGREE: George Washington Univ. '81
TRAINING: Georgetown Univ. Hospital
BOARD CERT.: Pediatrics '89
HOSPITALS: Mt. Vernon, chair, Dept. of Pediatrics; Alexandria, Potomac, Fairfax
COMMENTS: Homemaker for 11 years before returning to school for MD

Theresa Kosciuk, MD
Alexandria Lake Ridge Pediatric Centers
85 S. Bragg St., Alexandria Va 22312
(703)642-0604
ASSOCIATES: Drs. Jean Massie, Thomas Sullivan, Richard Ryan, Jon Farber
MED. DEGREE: Southwestern Medical School, Dallas '87
TRAINING: Children's Medical Center, Dallas '87-'90
BOARD CERT.: Pediatrics '91
HOSPITALS: Alexandria, Fairfax, Potomac
SEE office in Woodbridge also

Jean M. Massie, MD
Alexandria Lake Ridge Pediatric Centers
85 S. Bragg St. #100, Alexandria Va 22312 (703)642-0604
ASSOCIATES: Drs. Richard Ryan, Thomas Sullivan, Jon Farber, Theresa Kosciuk
MED. DEGREE: Eastern VA Medical Sch. '82
TRAINING: Children's Medical Center, Parkland Mem. Hosp. (Univ. of Texas at Dallas) '85
BOARD CERT.: Pediatrics '87
HOSPITALS: Alexandria, Fairfax, Potomac
SEE office in Woodbridge also

Promise Ahlstrom, MD
Children's National Medical Center
111 Michigan Ave. NW, Washington DC 20010
(202)745-5464
ASSOCIATES: Drs. Lawrence D'Angelo, Tomas Silber, Elda Arce, Kathy Woodward
MED. DEGREE: Univ. of Minnesota '83
TRAINING: Albert Einstein Coll. of Med., Montefiore Med. Ctr., NY; fellow. adolescent medicine
BOARD CERT.: Pediatrics '87
HOSPITALS: George Washington Univ., asst. prof.; Children's National Medical Center
COMMENTS: Geared to medical and psychosocial concerns of adolescents and young adults, including gynecologic care, nutrition and weight issues, routine health care. Satellite office in Shady Grove, Md. (301)424-1755

Karen S. Kuehl, MD
Georgetown Univ. Hosp., 2PHC
3800 Reservoir Rd NW, Washington DC 20007 (202)687-6871
SPECIALTY: Pediatric cardiology
ASSOCIATES: Drs. Lowell Perry, Stephen Shapiro, Frank Galioto, Stanley Beder, John Cockerham, Gillian Carpenter
MED. DEGREE: Harvard Univ. '65
TRAINING: Cleveland Metropolitan Gen. Hosp.; fellow Children's National Medical Center
BOARD CERT.: Ped. '71; Ped. Cardiology '83
HOSPITALS: Georgetown

Kathleen M. Hamilton MD
NOVA Pediatrics Ltd.
6120 Brandon Ave #203, Springfield Va 22150 (703)451-3333
SUBSPECIALTY: Cardiology
ASSOCIATES: Drs. Ira Seiler, Phillip Littleton, Sharon Jellinek, Lawrence Seidman
MED. DEGREE: George Washington Univ. '76
TRAINING: Children's National Medical Center '76-'79; fellow Ped. cardiology '79-'81
BOARD CERT.: Ped. '81; Ped. cardiology '81
HOSPITALS: Fairfax, Alexandria, Potomac
Office also at 1930 Opitz Blvd., Woodbridge, Va 22191
(703)491-2141

Anne S. Frankel, MD
845B Quince Orchard Blvd, Gaithersburg Md 20878
(301)977-2440
SUBSPECIALTY: Child abuse/Sexual abuse/AIDS
MED. DEGREE: Albert Einstein Coll. of Med., NY '68
TRAINING: New England Med. Center, Boston; Fellow Ped. hematology/oncology, Children's Nat'l. Med. Ctr.
BOARD CERT.: Ped. '73, board eligible Pediatric Hematology/Oncology
LANGUAGES: French, Spanish, Italian, Portuguese

Beverly A. Powell, MD
7389 Hidden Knolls Ct., Springfield Va 22153 (703)866-0662
MED. DEGREE: Georgetown Univ. '75
TRAINING: Children's National Med. Center '75-'77; Univ. of Virginia Fellow Mental Hlth; Georgetown U. Fellow child development '78-'79
BOARD CERT.: Pediatrics '79; assoc. member American Academy of Child and Adolescent Psychiatry '89
HOSPITALS: Hosp. for Sick Children, Georgetown, Children's, Fairfax
LANGUAGES: limited sign language
COMMENTS: Practice involves a broad spectrum of specialty services to families of high-risk and handicapped children. The model of service delivery I offer is innovative, flexible and designed to meet the needs of children and parents. Services provided: evaluation of infants and pre-school children with suspected functioning delays; medical care management for youngsters with physical and mental disabilities, including cerebral palsy, mental retardation and neuromuscular disorders.

Patricia O. Quinn, MD
3268 Arcadia Pl NW, Washington DC 20015 (202)966-1561
SPECIALTY: Developmental Pediatrics
MED. DEGREE: Georgetown Univ. '71
TRAINING: Georgetown Univ. '71-'75, including Fellow child development
BOARD CERT.: Pediatrics '77 HOSPITALS: Georgetown
COMMENTS: Practice is limited to evaluating children with developmental disabilities. Dr. Quinn specializes in learning disabilities and hyperactivity in children.

Karen J. Miller, MD
2270 Crows Nest Ln, Reston Va 22091 (703)620-9424
MED. DEGREE: Tulane Univ., New Orleans '77
TRAINING: Georgetown Univ. '77-'80; Post-grad. training in child development, learning disorders
BOARD CERT.: Pediatrics '82; affil. member American Academy of Child & Adolescent Psychiatry
HOSPITALS: Fairfax
COMMENTS: Practice limited to developmental pediatrics, primarily evaluation and management of children with learning disorders.

Louisa Laue, MD
Georgetown Univ. Hosp.
3800 Reservoir Rd, Washington DC 20007
(202)687-8881
SUBSPECIALTY: Endocrinology
ASSOCIATES: Drs. Val Abbassi, Wellington Hung, Douglas Sobel
MED. DEGREE: New York Univ. '83
TRAINING: New York Univ., Georgetown Univ.; also MS
BOARD CERT.: Ped. '90; Pediatric Endocrinology '91
HOSPITALS: Georgetown; National Inst. of Health, adjunct scientist

Naomi L. C. Luban, MD
Children's National Medical Center
111 Michigan Ave NW, Washington DC 20010 (202)745-5292
SPECIALTY: Hemolytic anemias, anemia of the newborn
MED. DEGREE: Mt. Sinai School of Med. NY '72
TRAINING: Children's National Medical Center
BOARD CERT.: Ped. '77; Ped. Hematology/Oncology '78
HOSPITALS: Children's National Med. Center, prof. pediatrics & pathology

Ann Barnet, MD
Children's National Med. Center
111 Michigan Ave NW, Washington DC 20010
(202)745-5454
SPECIALTY: Pediatric Evoked Responses
ASSOCIATES: Faculty assoc. at Children's National Medical Center
MED. DEGREE: Harvard Univ. '55
TRAINING: Children's National Medical Center '79
HOSPITALS: Children's National Med. Center, director Evoked Response Lab.; prof. of Pediatrics and Neurology, George Washington Univ. COMMENTS: The Evoked Response Laboratory is a diagnostic service performing electrophysiological tests for hearing, vision, neurological and somatosensory problems.

Helga Binder, MD
Children's National Med. Center
111 Michigan Ave. NW, Washington DC 20010 (202)745-3080
ASSOCIATES: Drs. Gloria Eng, Barbara Koch
MED. DEGREE: Humboldt Univ., Berlin '57
TRAINING: Knickerbocker Hosp. NY '61-'62; George Washington Univ. - Rehab. resid. '73-'76; Fellow Ped. Rehabilitation Children's National Med. Center
BOARD CERT.: Physical Med./Rehab. '78
HOSPITALS: George Washington, assoc. prof. ped.; Children's, assoc. physiatrist
LANGUAGES: German
COMMENTS: Our experience is in diagnosis and treatment of chronically disabling conditions in children, such as spina bifida, cerebral palsy, neuromuscular diseases, musculoskeletal disorders.

Gloria D. Eng, MD
Children's National Med. Center
111 Mich. Ave NW, Dept. PM/Rehab., Washington DC 20010
(202)745-3080
ASSOCIATES: Drs. Helga Binder, Barbara Koch
MED. DEGREE: Medical College of Illinois (Marquette) '55
TRAINING: Philadelphia Gen.; Children's National Med. Center - Ped. resid., also Hematology and Physical Med. /Rehab.
BOARD CERT.: Pediatrics '60; Physical Med./Rehab '69; American Board of Electrodiagnostic Med. '89
HOSPITALS: Children's National Med. Center, vice-chair Dept. of Med. and Peds.; Assoc. prof. of pediatrics George Washington.
LANGUAGES: Chinese (Cantonese)
COMMENTS: We see disabled children from mild injuries to cerebral palsy, neuromuscular disorders, spina bifida, spinal cord injury etc. The focus is on rehabilitation leading to maximum function.

DISTRICT OF COLUMBIA

Katharine E. Alter, MD
Washington Hosp. Center
110 Irving St. NW #3B-1B, Washington DC 20010
(202)877-7999
SUBSPECIALTY: Pediatric Physical Med. & Rehabilitation
ASSOCIATES: John Aseff, Pamela Ballard, Anne Gawne
MED. DEGREE: Medical College of Ohio '83
TRAINING: Medical College of Ohio
BOARD CERT.:Pediatrics '89; Physical Med./Rehab. '90
HOSPITALS: Washington Hosp. Center, Hosp. for Sick Children, National Rehabilitation Hosp. COMMENTS: Primary areas of interest/specialty: musculoskeletal medicine, i.e. back/neckpain, sports medicine, electrodiagnosis, individuals with disabilities.

Barbara J. Kolack, MD
National Rehab. Hosp., 102 Irving St NW, Washington DC 20010
(202)877-1627
ASSOCIATES: Attending physician staff at National Rehab. Hosp.
MED. DEGREE: Univ. of Connecticut '84
TRAINING: Univ. of California Davis '88; electrodiagnosis also
BOARD CERT.: Physical Med./Rehab. '89
HOSPITALS: National Rehabilitation Hosp.; Washington Hosp. Center, dir. of residency training
COMMENTS: I see patients with acute and chronic musculoskeletal injuries, sports injuries, strokes, spinal cord injuries. I do not see patients without an appointment. I see only adults.

MARYLAND

Anuradha Kulkarni, MD
6188 Oxon Hill Road, Oxon Hill Md 20745 (301)839-6811
SUBSPECIALTY: Electrodiagnostic studies
MED. DEGREE: Bombay Univ. '69
TRAINING: Medical College of Virginia
BOARD CERT.: Physical Med./Rehab. '80
HOSPITALS: Prince Georges', Hadley
LANGUAGES: Hindi, Marathi
OFFICE also at Prince George's Gen. Hosp., Cheverly Md

Deborah L. Bernal, MD
808 Pershing Dr. #104, Silver Spring Md 20910 (301)495-2896
MED. DEGREE: Howard Univ. '83
TRAINING: Sinai Hosp. of Balitmore; Fellow Johns Hopkins Sch. of Med.; Courses in pain management, performing arts medicine, sports medicine, vocational and geriatric rehabilitation
BOARD CERT.: Physical Med./Rehab '87
HOSPITALS: Howard Univ., Sinai
COMMENTS: Dr. Bernal believes in the comprehensive health care team approach. The patient acts as the team leader setting goals with the counsel of physicians. The goal: to maximize function in all aspects of daily life. Positions held: National Medical Association, chair physical medicine/rehab. and scientific council appointment.; secretary physical med/rehab. of Medical Society of DC

VIRGINIA

Katherine L. Maurath, MD
13350 Franklin Farm Road #220, Herndon Va 22071
(703)471-5300
ASSOCIATES: Drs. William A. Hazel, Jr., Dean R. Bennett, Anthony Gristina
MED. DEGREE: Univ. of Cincinnati '80
TRAINING: Good Samaritan Hosp./ Univ. of Cincinnati Med. Center
BOARD CERT.: Physical Med./Rehab. '85
HOSPITALS: Fair Oaks, med. dir.of PM/Rehab. Dept.; Reston, Potomac
COMMENTS: A physiatrist is a non-surgical doctor who specializes in evaluation of disorders of the musculoskeletal and neurologic systems. Also: evaluation of how occupational, recreational, and social activities contribute to the development or maintenance of a problem. A treatment program is then prescribed. It may include medications, exercise, physical therapy, activity modification or surgical referral.

Marija D. Smokvina, MD
1515 Chain Bridge Road, Mc Lean Va 22101 (703)821-2111
MED. DEGREE: Univ. Ljubljana, Yugoslavia '59
TRAINING: Rijeka Gen. Hosp., Yugoslavia '59-'60; Univ. Ljubljana '63-'67; Physical Med./Rehab. resident and fellow NY Univ. and George Washington Univ. '69-'73
BOARD CERT.: in Yugoslavia '67, board eligible in US '73
HOSPITALS: Fair Oaks, Children's
LANGUAGES: Slovenian, Serbo-Croatian COMMENTS: Practice primarily out-patients, referrals by MDs. I provide physical therapy as needed: Deep tissue trigger point massage, electrodiagnosis. New patients for evaluation and consult = 1 hour.

Kathryn E. Grant, MD
1701 N. George Mason Dr, Arlington Va 22205 (703)558-6507
MED. DEGREE: Medical College of Virginia '76
TRAINING: Pediatrics at Medical College of Virginia and Univ. Hosp. San Diego; Temple Univ., PA. - Phys. Med./Rehab.; Fellow Albert Einstein Hosp. NY '81; MS microbiology, Univ. of Kansas '72
BOARD CERT.: Phys. Med./ Rehab. '84
HOSPITALS: Arlington Hosp., Med. dir. of Physical med./ rehab.
LANGUAGES: Spanish
COMMENTS: Patients are generally referred by a primary physician.

Ana T. Acevedo, MD
Mt. Vernon Hospital, 2501 Parker's Lane, Alexandria Va 22306
(703)664-7285
SUBSPECIALTY: Pediatric and Geriatric rehabilitation
ASSOCIATES: Drs. Stephanie Giorlando, Roger Gisolfi, Ali Ganjei
MED. DEGREE: Univ. Central-Caribe '83'
TRAINING: St. Agnes Hosp. '84-'85; Sinai Hosp./ Johns Hopkins '85-'88, resid. in Physical Med./rehab.; Fellow Pediatric rehab. Children's National Med. Center '88-'89
BOARD CERT.: Physical med./rehab. '89
HOSPITALS: Mount Vernon, staff physiatrist
LANGUAGES: Spanish
COMMENTS: Provide services for evaluations of musculoskeletal, soft tissue injuries, sports injuries, electrodiagnostic studies, rehabilitation of stroke patients, closed head and spinal cord injuries.

Stephanie A. Giorlando, DO
Mt. Vernon Hospital, 2501 Parker's Lane, Alexandria VA 22306
(703)664-7285
ASSOCIATES: Drs. Ali Ganjei, Roger Gisolfi, Ana Acevedo
MED. DEGREE: New York Coll. of Osteopathic Med. '83
TRAINING: Saddle Brook Gen. Hosp., NJ; St. Vincent's Hosp. NY
BOARD CERT.: Physical Med./Rehab. '88
HOSPITALS: Mt. Vernon LANGUAGES: French

DISTRICT OF COLUMBIA

Susan E. Otero, MD

1145 19th St. NW #717, Washington DC 20036 (202)785-4187
MED. DEGREE: George Washington Univ. '80
TRAINING: George Washington Univ. - gen. surg.; Nassau County Med. Center, NY - burn Fellow, plastic surg residency; MS biology
BOARD CERT.: Plastic Surg. '90
HOSPITALS: Washington Hosp. Center, chief of plastic & reconstructive surg.;Washington Adventist, Sibley, Providence, National Rehabilitation, Columbia LANGUAGES: some Spanish COMMENTS: I specialize in reconstructive surgery - breast, burn scars, traumatic injuries.

Mary H. McGrath MD

George Washington Univ. Med Ctr.
2150 Penn. NW, Washington DC 20037 (202)994-8141
SUBSPECIALTY: Hand, cosmetic, maxillofacial surgery
ASSOCIATES: Plastic surg. faculty, George Washington
MED. DEGREE: St. Louis U. '70; TRAINING: U. of Colorado; Yale
BOARD CERT.: Surgery '78, Plastic Surg. '79
HOSPITALS: George Washington, prof. of surgery, chair of plastic surgery; Children's
LANGUAGES: All available at George Washington
COMMENTS: Dr. McGrath encourages patient's questions, wishes to discuss her patient's motivations and expectations fully and makes a practice of describing any risks or variations in outcome fully. She enjoys a partnership with her patients in the practice of medicine. She is the first woman chair of plastic surgery in a US medical school and the first woman member of the American Board of Plastic Surgery.

MARYLAND

Diane L. Colgan, MD
9800 Falls Rd #105, Potomac Md 20854 (301)299-6644
MED. DEGREE: Medical College of Pennsylvania '67
TRAINING: Bethesda Naval Hosp. '67-'74
BOARD CERT.: Surgery '74; Plastic Surg. '76
HOSPITALS: Montgomery Gen., chair Plastic Surg.; Suburban, Shady Grove, Sibley, Washington Hosp. Center, Columbia

Roberta Gartside, MD
1800 Town Ctr. Dr #218, Reston Va 22090 (703)742-8004
MED. DEGREE: Temple Univ. '81
TRAINING: Univ. of Vermont ; the Med. Center of Vermont; George Washington Univ.
BOARD CERT.: Surgery '88; Plastic Surg. '90
HOSPITALS: Reston Hosp., chair Plastic Surg.; Fairfax, Fair Oaks, Children's, Countryside Ambulatory Surgery

Carol S. Shapiro, MD
1940 Opitz Blvd, PO Box 4268, Woodbridge Va 22194
(703)494-1163
MED. DEGREE: Medical College of Pennsylvania '65
TRAINING: Philadelphia Gen. Hosp., Georgetown Univ. Hosp.
BOARD CERT.: Plastic Surg. '86;
HOSPITALS: Potomac, Prince William
COMMENTS: Believe in one-on-one patient care.

Linda H. Mosely, MD
2500 N Van Dorn St #128, Alexandria Va 22302
(703)379-6616
SUBSPECIALTY: Hand surgery
MED. DEGREE: Louisiana State Univ. '67
TRAINING: Charity Hosp., New Orleans, intern, med. and gen. surg. residency; Mt. Sinai Hosp., NY, surg. resid.; Univ. of Louisville, gen. surg. '73; Yale Med. Center, plastic surgery '75-'77; also fellowships in clinical and hand surgery at Yale and Univ. of Louisville
BOARD CERT.: Plastic Surg. '81
HOSPITALS: Alexandria, Fairfax, National Hosp. for Orthopaedics/ Rehab.
LANGUAGES: Spanish

DISTRICT OF COLUMBIA

NORTHWEST

Margaret M. Clancy, MD
1015 33rd Street NW, Washington DC 20007 (202)338-5842
MED. DEGREE: Georgetown Univ. '73; TRAINING: Georgetown
BOARD CERT.: Psychiatry '77
HOSPITALS: Psychiatric Inst.; Georgetown faculty, clin. asst. prof.
COMMENTS: Specialize in psychological complications of medical illness, families of sick patients, also women's issues. Principally a female practice.

Roberta M. Gilbert, MD
4400 MacArthur Blvd NW, Washington DC 20007
(202)965-0730
MED. DEGREE: Univ. of Buffalo, NY '62
TRAINING: State Univ. NY, Buffalo; Post-grad. 2-year family therapy course, Menninger Fnd.; 5 years family therapy , the Georgetown Family Center
BOARD CERT.: Psychiatry '75
COMMENTS: I have found Bowen Family Systems Therapy to be an extremely effective form of psychotherapy and my philosophy is more thoroughly explained in my book, "Extraordinary Relationships."

Elizabeth K. Hersh, MD
2121 Wisconsin Ave NW, Washington DC 20007
(202)333-3835
SUBSPECIALTY: Psychoanalysis
MED. DEGREE: New York Univ. '79
TRAINING: Georgetown Univ. '79-'85; MSW Univ. of California at Berkeley
BOARD CERT.: Psychiatry '89 HOSPITALS: Georgetown

Frances E. Rankin, MD
1015 33Rd St NW, Washington DC 20007
1160 Varnum St. NW #312, Washington DC 20017
(202)337-1155
MED. DEGREE: Howard Univ. '69
TRAINING: Freedman's Hosp. '69-'70; Georgetown Univ. '73-'76
BOARD CERT.: Psychiatry '77
HOSPITALS: Washington Hosp. Center, Howard Univ., Providence

Heloise DeRosis, MD
4501 Connecticut Ave NW #104, Washington DC 20008
(202)363-9457
MED. DEGREE: Albert Einstein Coll. of Med. '78
TRAINING: Georgetown Univ.
BOARD CERT.: Psychiatry '83
HOSPITALS: Don't Hospitalize. Affiliated with Georgetown; chair Comm. on Women - Washington Psychiatric Society. COMMENTS: I'm very interested in women's issues, women and depression, relationships, balance between home, work, etc. Have a fairly holistic view and believe a person's own strength is what helps them. I'm a facilitator. I give medications when appropriate.

Barbara J. Novak, MD
3000 Connecticut Ave. NW, Washington DC 20008
(202)332-5359
SPECIALTY: Adult, adolescent and child psych., also psychoanalysis
MED. DEGREE: Univ. of Virginia '81
TRAINING: Pennsylvania Hosp., Inst. of Pennsylvania Hosp., Philadelphia; training in child, adolescent and adult psychoanalysis
BOARD CERT.: Psychiatry '86

Margot P. Onek, MD
4849 Conn Ave. NW, Washington DC 20008 (202)363-7890
MED. DEGREE: Yale Univ. '68
TRAINING: Washington Veterans Admin. Hosp. (George Wash. Univ. service) '68-'69; Georgetown Univ., Psych. resid. '75-'79
BOARD CERT.: Psychiatry '80
HOSPITALS: Georgetown Univ., asst. clin. prof.
COMMENTS: My practice is a general, outpatient psychiatric practice of consultation and evaluation, individual psychotherapy and couples therapy. I do short term therapy, crisis intervention, supportive therapy and longterm dynamic, insight oriented therapy.

Randi Rubovits-Seitz, MD
2623 Woodley Pl NW, Washington DC 20008
(202)234-1621
SPECIALTY: General adult psychiatry, combined psychotherapy & pharmacotherapy
MED. DEGREE: Univ. of Illinois '72
TRAINING:Univ. of Maryland, National Institute of Mental Health
BOARD CERT.: Psychiatry '77 HOSPITALS: George Washington Univ., clin. prof. of psychiatry

Lise C. Van Susteren, MD
4545 Linnean Ave NW, Washington DC 20008
(202)686-3314
MED. DEGREE: Univ. of Paris '82
TRAINING: American Hosp. of Paris; Tokoin Lome, Togo (W. Africa); St. Elizabeth's Hosp. DC
BOARD CERT.: Psychiatry '89
HOSPITALS: Georgetown Univ. Hosp., assoc. clin. prof.
LANGUAGES: French COMMENTS: I see psychotherapy as a means of achieving freedom, obtaining satisfaction and joy in living. To quote J.J. Rousseau, "Happiness and social harmony through self knowledge and self mastery."

Peggy J. Pazzaglia, MD
1755 S St. NW, Washington DC 20009 (202)363-7792
SPECIALTY: psychopharmacology
ASSOCIATES: Drs. Bernard Vittone, Terrence Ketter, Lauren Marangell
MED. DEGREE: Univ. of Texas, Houston '74
TRAINING: Univ. of Texas, Houston
BOARD CERT.: Psychiatry '90
HOSPITALS: National Inst. of Mental Health
COMMENTS: Cognitive/behavioral therapy usually with therapist as adjunct with pharmacology for depression/anxiety, phobias.

Kelley L. Phillips, MD
1616 18th St. NW #109, Washington DC 20009
(202)337-8051
SUBSPECIALTY: women's issues, depression
ASSOCIATES: Inst. for Research on Women's Health, founding member
MED. DEGREE: Univ. of Ottawa '74
TRAINING: McMaster Univ. , Canada '78; MPH Johns Hopkins - public health; Royal Coll. Phys., Surg., Canada '82
BOARD CERT.: Psychiatry '83 COMMENTS: Health and mental health policy, quality of care, outcome measures.

Colleen A. Conley, MD
Childrens National Med. Center
111 Michigan Ave NW, Psych. Dept., Washington DC 20010
(202)745-5386
SPECIALTY: child, adolescent, general psych., ped. psychopharmacology and eating disorders
ASSOCIATES: Children's Dept. of Psychiatry
MED. DEGREE: Univ. of Colorado '78
TRAINING: George Washington Univ. '78-'81; child psych. fellows Children's National Med. Center, George Washington Univ. '81-'83
BOARD CERT.: Psych '84; Child and Adol. Psych. '84
HOSPITALS: Children's COMMENTS: I try to help patients and families understand and feel as if seeking psychiatric treatment is a strength and a commitment to resolving problems, rather than seeing it as a sign of weakness or failing as often is felt with seeking mental health services being stigmatized negatively.

Judith Fingert Chused, MD
1805 Randolph St NW, Washington DC 20011
(202)726-9273
SUBSPECIALTY: Psychoanalysis
MED. DEGREE: Harvard Univ. '67
TRAINING: Case Western Reserve Univ., Cleveland; Psych resid. - Case Western, George Washington Univ.; child psych., George Washington; Psychoanalysis, Washington Psychoanalytic Inst.
BOARD CERT.: Psych '76; Psychoanal: child, adol, adult '80
HOSPITALS: George Washington Univ., clin. prof. psych. and pediatrics; Children's COMMENTS: I do many psychiatric consultations (1-4 visits) to help adults and children find the appropriate therapy and therapist. My own practice is limited to intensive psychodynamic therapy and psychoanalysis.

Sue Bailey, DO
5301 Wisconsin Ave. #320, Washington DC 20015
(202)966-0050
ASSOCIATES: Drs. Maria Lehnert, Lisa Hochheiser
MED. DEGREE: Philadelphia Coll. Osteopathic Medicine '77
TRAINING: Georgetown Univ., Johns Hopkins Univ. fellow
BOARD CERT.: Psychiatry '83
HOSPITALS: Georgetown, clin. faculty
LANGUAGES: some Spanish COMMENTS: Standard psychotherapy with pragmatic goal directed approach.

Naomi Heller, MD
5225 Conn Ave NW, Washington DC 20015 (202)966-0112
MED. DEGREE: Harvard Univ. '60
TRAINING: Beth Israel Hosp., Boston; St. Elizabeth's Hosp. DC; Washington School of Psychiatry, adv. psychotherapy program
BOARD CERT.: Psychiatry '75
HOSPITALS: George Washington, clin. prof., attending physician
LANGUAGES: minimal Portuguese
COMMENTS: General outpatient psychiatry with adults — eclectic outlook — often combine psychotherapy with medication.

Christine W. Kehne, MD
5225 Conn. Ave, Washington DC 20015 (301)986-0047
SPECIALTY: Adult, child, adolescent, forensic psychiatry
MED. DEGREE: Johns Hopkins Univ. '49
TRAINING: George Washington Univ., St. Elizabeth's Hosp., DC General, US Public Health Serv. fellow in child psych.; Forensic training and other continuing medical educ. course work
BOARD CERT.: Psychiatry '61; Child and adolescent psych. '61
LANGUAGES: German, French COMMENTS: Eclectic, developmental, social-psychological, psychoanalytically oriented psychotherapy; psychopharmacological intervention as indicated.

Ellen Liebenluft, MD
5410 Conn. Ave NW #109, Washington DC 20015 (301)654-6160
SPECIALTY: Mood disorders, depression in women particularly, psychotherapy and psychopharmacology
MED. DEGREE: Stanford Univ. '78
TRAINING: Herrick Mem. Hosp, Berkeley; Georgetown Univ.
BOARD CERT.: Psychiatry '84
HOSPITALS: National Inst. of Mental Health, researcher

Catherine S. May, MD
1301 20th St. NW #913, Washington DC 20036 (202)466-3455
SPECIALTY: Psychotherapy, psychopharmacology, adult psychiatry
MED. DEGREE: Indiana Univ. '80
TRAINING: Univ. of Maryland, St. Elizabeth's Hosp. DC
BOARD CERT.: Emerg. Medicine; psychiatry board eligible
HOSPITALS: George Washington Univ., clin. asst. prof. of psych.

Geraldine Schaeffer, MD
2201 L St NW #109, Washington DC 20037 (202)785-0077
MED. DEGREE: Medical College of Pennsylvania '58
TRAINING: Albert Einstein Med. Center, Phil.; Georgetown Univ.
BOARD eligible Psychiatry
HOSPITALS: George Washington Univ., asst. clin. prof.
COMMENTS: Individual psychotherapy - psychodynamic and psychopharmacologic. Enhance self-knowledge and self-understanding to resolve conflicts and widen potential for realizing opportunities and expanding positive experiences for improving relationships and the quality and enjoyment of life.
See Arlington office also

Cynthia B. Stevens, MD
3 Washington Circle NW #405, Washington DC 20037
(202)775-9091
SUBSPECIALTY: Psychoanalysis
MED. DEGREE: Georgetown Univ. '85
TRAINING: Georgetown Univ.; George Washington Univ.; '91 grad. Washington Psychoanalytic Inst.
BOARD CERT.: Psychiatry '90
HOSPITALS: George Washington Univ., asst. clin. prof.; Washington Psychoanalytic Inst. faculty LANGUAGES: some German
COMMENTS: I am a psychiatrist and psychoanalyst with a particular interest in self-esteem issues in young professionals and insight-oriented psychotherapy. I also do short-term psychotherapy and psychopharmacology.

Abby Wellman, MD
George Washington Univ. Med. Center
2150 Penn. Ave NW, Washington DC 20037 (202)994-5476
ASSOCIATES: Medical faculty associates of George Washington
MED. DEGREE: Univ. of Maryland '85
TRAINING: George Washington Univ. '85-'89
BOARD eligible Psychiatry
HOSPITALS: George Washington COMMENTS: I am primarily a therapist with medication used only if needed.

Inez Jones White, MD
2141 K St NW #605, Washington DC 20037 (202)659-9716
MED. DEGREE: Medical College of Pennsylvania '67
TRAINING: Mt. Carmel Mercy Hosp., Detroit; St. Elizabeth's Hosp.; George Washington Univ.; continuing education certification
BOARD CERT.: Psychiatry '77
HOSPITALS: Washington Hosp. Center, George Washington
COMMENTS: Eclectic with analytic training during residency

MARYLAND

BETHESDA

Constance Anton, MD
5415 W. Cedar Lane #208-B, Bethesda Md 20814
(301)530-7738
SUBSPECIALTY: Psychoanalysis
MED. DEGREE: Boston Univ. '69
TRAINING: Santa Barbara Gen. & Cottage Hosp. '69-'70; George Washington Univ.; Grad. Washington Psychoanalytic Inst. '87
BOARD CERT.: Psychiatry '86
HOSPITALS: George Washington Univ., volunteer, Dept of Psych.

Lindsay L. Clarkson, MD
4400 East West Hwy #1104, Bethesda Md 20814 (301)654-5072
SUBSPECIALTY: Psychoanalysis
MED. DEGREE: Duke Univ. '79
TRAINING: Duke Univ.; Washington Psychoanalytic Inst.
BOARD CERT.: Psychiatry '89
HOSPITALS: Georgetown, adjunct faculty, counseling and psychological services

Ellen E. Cronin, MD
4401 East West Highway #202, Bethesda 20814 (301)907-3353
MED. DEGREE: Yale Univ. '68
TRAINING: Johns Hopkins Univ.; Fellow short-term psychotherapy
BOARD eligible Psychiatry HOSPITALS: Holy Cross

Maria M. Lehnert, MD
3 Bethesda Metro Ctr., Bethesda Md 20814 (301)961-1949
SUBSPECIALTY: Eating disorders, survivors of sexual abuse
ASSOCIATES: Dr. Sue Bailey
MED. DEGREE: New York Medical Coll. '84
TRAINING: Univ. of Connecticut Health Center
BOARD eligible Psychiatry
HOSPITALS: Suburban; Georgetown, asst. dir. eating disorders
LANGUAGES: Portuguese, Spanish

Anne C. Mazonson, MD
Old Georgetown Mental Health Assoc.
10401 Old Georgetown Rd, #309, Bethesda, Md 20814
(301)897-0099
SPECIALTY: Adult psychiatry, eating disorders
ASSOCIATES: Drs. Deborah Pollack, Daniel Levine, Douglas Kay
MED. DEGREE: Univ. of Maryland '87
TRAINING: George Washington Univ., chief resid. in Psych.; MA Wesleyan Univ. BOARD eligible Psychiatry HOSPITALS: Suburban, George Washington, asst. clin. prof, attending staff

Frances K. Millican, MD
5100 Acacia Ave, Bethesda Md 20814 (301)530-2870
SUBSPECIALTY: Psychoanalysis, adult & child
MED. DEGREE: Univ. of Tennessee '48
TRAINING: St. Elizabeth's Hosp. DC; Veterans Admin. DC; Children's National Med. Ctr.; MS biochemistry; cert. by American Psychoanalytic Assoc. in adult, child and adol. psychoanalysis
BOARD eligible adult and child Psychiatry
HOSPITALS: Georgetown, assoc. clin. prof. COMMENTS: Do family and child evaluations, brief and long-term psychotherapy

Deborah R. Pollack, MD
Old Georgetown Mental Health Assoc.
10401 Old Georgetown Rd #309, Bethesda Md 20814
(301)897-0099
ASSOCIATES: Drs. Daniel Levine, Douglass Kay, Anne Mazonson
MED. DEGREE: Univ. of Maryland '81
TRAINING: Georgetown Univ. Hosp. '81-'86; continuing educ. credits - American Psychiatric Assoc.
BOARD CERT.: Psychiatry '87
HOSPITALS: Suburban; Georgetown, asst. clin. instr.
COMMENTS: I'm interested in anxiety disorders, women's issues and Type A behavior traits in particular. I use various modalities of treatment, including cognitive, insight-oriented and behavioral techniques alone, or with medication if indicated.

CHEVY CHASE

Cecile R. Bassen, MD
4701 Willard Ave #210, Chevy Chase Md 20815
(301)656-7558
SUBSPECIALTY: Psychoanalysis
MED. DEGREE: Duke Univ. '76
TRAINING: New England Med. Center, Boston '77-'78; McLean Hosp., MA. '78-'80; Georgetown Univ. '80-'81; Washington Psychoanalytic Inst. '82-'89
BOARD CERT.: Psychiatry '83 HOSPITALS: Faculty: Washington Psychoanalytic Inst., the Washington Psychoanalytic Fnd., the Washington School of Psychiatry, U.S. Univ. of Health Sciences. COMMENTS: Psychotherapy and psychoanalysis. I also do consultations aimed at helping each individual decide whether he or she wishes to pursue psychotherapy, and which type of therapy would be most helpful.

Susan J. Blumenthal, MD, MPA
4701 Willard Ave #212, Chevy Chase, Md 20815 (301)718-7774
SUBSPECIALTY: depression, anxiety disorders, women's issues
ASSOCIATES: Drs. Molly Strauss, Beth Morrison
MED. DEGREE: Univ. of Tennessee '76
TRAINING: Stanford Univ. '76-'80; MPA (Public Administration) Harvard Univ. '82; Fellow, National Inst. of Mental Health '80-'81
BOARD CERT.: Psychiatry '82
HOSPITALS: National Inst. of Mental Health, chief, Behavioral Medicine Research branch; Georgetown Univ., clin. prof.
COMMENTS: Dr. Blumenthal is an expert in suicide, depression and women's health issues and a leader in behavioral medicine and women's health research. Committees include the National Commission on Sleep Disorders Research and the Group for the Advancement of Psychiatry. She serves on the board of directors of the National Women's Health Resource Center and chairs the Scientific Advisory Board of the Starbright Foundation, dedicated to improving the quality of life of seriously ill children.

Suzanne Griffin, MD
35 Wisconsin Circle #345, Chevy Chase Md 20815
(301)986-1481
SUBSPECIALTY: Psychopharmacology, PMS, post-partum disorders, chronobiology, light treatment
ASSOCIATES: Richard Greenburg, MD
MED. DEGREE: Medical Univ. of S. Carolina '77
TRAINING: Dartmouth Medical School, chief resident Psychiatry '80
BOARD CERT.: Psychiatry '82 HOSPITALS: Georgetown, clin. asst. prof.; Psychiatric Inst. of Washington

Carol Cole Kleinman, MD
5480 Wisconsin Ave #1006, Chevy Chase Md 20815
(301)654-1810
SUBSPECIALTY: Forensic psychology, Psychoanalysis
MED. DEGREE: George Washington Univ. '80
TRAINING: Univ. of Maryland Hosp., Baltimore; also JD George Washington National Law Center '69
BOARD CERT.: Psychiatry LANGUAGES: Spanish

Martha Brown Martin, MD
4701 Willard Ave #204, Chevy Chase, Md 20815
(301)951-0969
SUBSPECIALTY: Psychoanalysis
MED. DEGREE: Georgetown Univ. '79
TRAINING: Greenwich Hosp., (Yale affil. internship); Georgetown Univ.; Washington Psychoanalytic Inst. grad. '92
BOARD CERT.: Psychiatry '83
HOSPITALS: Georgetown, clin. asst. prof.

Elizabeth Morrison, MD
4701 Willard Ave #212, Chevy Chase Md 20815
(301)652-2100
MED. DEGREE: Univ. of Cincinnati '78
TRAINING: Univ. of Colorado
BOARD CERT.: Psychiatry '84
HOSPITALS: Sibley, sec.-treas., Dept. Psych.; Suburban
COMMENTS: Outpatient evaluation, diagnosis and treatment of adults and late adolescents, including but not limited to affective disorders (depression, anxiety, etc.), personality disorders, life crisis issues, psychoses. Special interest in post-partum depressions and couples therapy. Treatment philosophy is psychodynamic, insight oriented and psychopharmacology where indicated.

Jill Savege Scharff, MD
6612 Kennedy Dr, Chevy Chase Md 20815 (301)951-3630
SPECIALTY: Psychoanalysis, child & adult; Couple, family therapy
MED. DEGREE: Aberdeen Univ., Scotland '67 ; MD exam in DC '76
TRAINING: Woodend Gen. Hosp., Aberdeen; Royal Edinburgh Hospitals; Tavistock Clinic, London; Fellow Child and adol. psych., George Washington Univ. and Children's National Med. Center; child and adult psychoanalysis certif., American Psychoanalytic Assoc. '90
BOARD CERT.: Psych. '76; Child psych. '77
HOSPITALS: Washington School of Psych., chair-elect object relations program; Georgetown U., assoc. clin. prof.
COMMENTS: Intensive, long-term, in-depth therapy for character change, difficulties with intimate relationships, work inhibition, and blocks against development through the life cycle.

Molly M. Strauss, MD
4701 Willard #212, Chevy Chase Md 20815 (301)652-2664
MED. DEGREE: Duke Univ. '78
TRAINING: Univ. of Washington, Seattle
BOARD CERT.: Psychiatry '84 HOSPITALS: Suburban
COMMENTS: General psychiatry practice. I see adults and adolescents for psychotherapy and/or medication and do consultations for non-psychiatrist therapists.

Lucy R. Waletzky, MD
2 Wisconsin Circle #530, Chevy Chase Md 20815 (301)654-3638
SPECIALTY: Psychotherapy and sex therapy for those with medical illnesses and physical disabilities only
ASSOCIATES: Stephen Hersh, MD
MED. DEGREE: Columbia Univ. NY '68
TRAINING: Harlem Hosp. '69; Mount Sinai Hosp., NY '69-'73
BOARD CERT.: Psychiatry '77
HOSPITALS: Medical Illness Counseling Center, co-dir.

BETHESDA

Lucie Greenblum, MD
5415 Kirkwood Dr, Bethesda Md 20816
(301)320-6885
SEE Arlington office for background

Bonnie R. Anthony, MD
6901 Whittier Blvd, Bethesda Md 20817 (301)229-7028
SPECIALTY: Psychiatry and Psychoanalysis, adult and adolescent
MED. DEGREE: Georgetown Univ. '75
TRAINING: Georgetown Univ. '75-'78; Veterans Admin. Hosp, chief resident '77-'78; PhD Physiology, Columbia Univ. '69; Grad. Baltimore-DC Inst. of Psychoanalysis
HOSPITALS: Montgomery Gen.
COMMENTS: Eclectic practice, willing to take reduced fee patients.

Ann C. Birk, MD
8600 Split Oak Cir, Bethesda Md 20817 (301)365-4447
MED. DEGREE: Albany Medical College '70
TRAINING: Albany Medical Center, Sheppard & Enoch Pratt Hosp.; Grad. Baltimore-Washington Inst. for Psychoanalysis
BOARD CERT.: Psychiatry '78
HOSPITALS: Suburban; Georgetown, asst. clinical prof.
COMMENTS: Individual and couples psychotherapy, short term and long term goals set. Seek to understand underlying conflicts and factors which are responsible for symptoms. Adolescents and adults.

Liliana L. Borensztein, MD
6306 Marywood Rd, Bethesda Md 20817 (301)493-0262
MED. DEGREE: Univ. de Buenos Aires, Argentina '80
TRAINING: Providence Hosp., St. Elizabeth's Hosp., DC
BOARD CERT.: Psychiatry '90
HOSPITALS: St. Elizabeth's Hosp.
LANGUAGES: Spanish
COMMENTS: Medication and psychotherapy. Practice limited to adults.

Sandra Cohen, MD
Metropolitan Psychiatric Group
4520 East West Highway, Bethesda Md 20817 (301)656-9520
SPECIALTY: Adult, child and adolescent psychiatry
ASSOCIATES: Metropolitan Psychiatric Group includes psychiatrists, psychologists, social workers
MED. DEGREE: New York Medical College '79
TRAINING: Duke Univ. Med. Center; Fellow, child psych.
BOARD CERT.: Psychiatry '85

Sandra G. Hershberg, MD
Asked that street address not be published, Bethesda Md 20817
(301)229-6570
SUBSPECIALTY: Psychoanalysis
MED. DEGREE: Yale Univ. '75
TRAINING: Case Western Reserve Univ., Cleveland; Mt. Sinai NY; Fellow Child Psych. Univ. of California, LA; psychoanalysis training
BOARD CERT.: Psych. '80; Child Psych. '83
HOSPITALS: George Washington; Children's National Med. Ctr.
COMMENTS: Particular areas of interest, expertise - female development, sexual abuse, eating disorders, child/adol. psychiatry, children of parents with handicaps, psychological aspects of medical illness issues related to pregnancy and post-partum difficulties.

Linda R. Kessler, MD
Home office, asked that address not be published
Bethesda Md 20817
(301)229-3629
SUBSPECIALTY: Psychoanalysis, women's issues
MED. DEGREE: Tulane Univ. '74
TRAINING: Tulane Univ. '74-'76; National Inst. of Mental Health, clin. assoc., '76-'77; Grad. Washington Psychoanalytic Inst.
BOARD CERT.: Psychiatry '78
COMMENTS: I am especially interested in a variety of issues that are important to women, such as self-esteem, interpersonal relationships, women as mothers and post-partum depression and the effects of previous abuse. I am experienced in using anti-depressant and antianxiety medication when indicated.

Susan G. Lazar, MD
Asked that address not be published
Bethesda Md 20817 (301)365-0373
SUBSPECIALTY: Psychoanalysis
MED. DEGREE: Albert Einstein Coll. of Med. NY '70
TRAINING: Univ. of Virginia; Tufts New England Med. Center; Certif. in Psychoanalysis by American Psychoanalytic Assoc. '88
BOARD CERT.: Psychiatry '76
HOSPITALS: George Washington, clin. prof. of psychiatry; teaching analyst Wash. Psychoanalytic Inst.
COMMENTS: Evaluations and long-term psychodynamic, psychotherapy and psychoanalysis.

Louise Y. Postman, MD
6807 Hillmead Rd, Bethesda Md 20817
(301)469-9089 SEE Rockville office for background

ROCKVILLE

Louise Y. Postman
Psychiatric and Psychotherapy Services
15225 Shady Grove Rd #301, Rockville Md 20850
(301)990-9400
SUBSPECIALTY: women's issues, sexual abuse
ASSOCIATES: Partner, Ann L. Rogers, LCSW
MED. DEGREE: Boston Univ. '65
TRAINING: Boston Floating Hosp. '65-'66; Mass. Mental Health Center '66-'67; Georgetown Univ. '67-'69
BOARD CERT.: Psychiatry '76; administrative psychiatry certificate
HOSPITALS: Psychiatric Inst. of Montgomery County; Shady Grove, Suburban, Psych-Systems of Bethesda
LANGUAGES: Spanish COMMENTS: Services pointed particularly towards women, women's issues, sexual abuse, psychopharmacology, multiple personality disorder, dissociative disorders, acute psychiatric emergencies and hospitalizations, group therapy, family and individual therapy, chronically mentally ill adults and adolescents. SEE Bethesda office also

Ann-Louise S. Silver, MD
500 W. Montgomery Ave, Rockville Md 20850
(301)424-8300
SUBSPECIALTY: Psychoanalysis
ASSOCIATES: Chestnut Lodge Hosp. medical staff
MED. DEGREE: Johns Hopkins Univ. '66
TRAINING: Baltimore City Hospitals, Ped. and Internal med.; Johns Hopkins Univ., psych.; Grad., Washington Psychoanalytic Inst., Washington School of Psychiatry family therapy program
BOARD CERT.: Psychiatry '76
HOSPITALS: Chestnut Lodge Hosp.
COMMENTS: Psychoanalytic and intensive insight-oriented therapy, full range of mental, emotional illnesses.

Deborah L. Feldheim, MD
11513 West Hill Dr, Rockville Md 20852
(301)816-9278
SUBSPECIALTY: Psychoanalysis
MED. DEGREE: State Univ. of NY at Buffalo '84
TRAINING: George Washington Univ.; Chestnut Lodge Hosp.; Washington Psychoanalytic Inst.
BOARD CERT.: Psychiatry '89
HOSPITALS: Chestnut Lodge Hosp.

Sherry D. Goldman, MD
11404 Old Georgetown Rd #105, Rockville Md 20852
(301)881-0855
SPECIALTY: Child, Adolescent, Adult Psychiatry
MED. DEGREE: George Washington Univ. '79
TRAINING: Children's National Med. Center, ped. and primary care, '79-'82; Sinai Hosp. of Baltimore, chief resident ped. '82-'83; George Washington Univ. , psych. '83-'86
BOARD eligible psychiatry
HOSPITALS: Children's National Med. Ctr., volunteer clin. staff
COMMENTS: I have a special interest in children with Attention Deficit Hyperactivity Disorder, learning disabilities and their families, as well as school consultation, parenting skill and social skills development. When indicated, pharmacotherapy.

Shirley Barrie Papilsky, MD
6110 Executive Blvd. #910, Rockville, Md 20852
(301)468-7321
SPECIALTY: Adult, adolescent, child psychiatry
ASSOCIATES: Rachel Ritvo, MD
MED. DEGREE: Univ. of Cape Town, S. Africa '72
TRAINING: Groote Schuur Hosp. S. Africa; National Inst. of Mental Health; St. Elizabeth's Hosp. DC; Fellow Children's National Med. Center and George Washington Univ.
BOARD CERT.: Psych '89; Child Psych '90

Rachel Z. Ritvo, MD
6110 Executive Blvd. #910, Rockville Md 20852
(301)468-0117
SPECIALTY: Child psychotherapy, adult psychoanalysis
ASSOCIATES: Shirley Papilsky, MD
MED. DEGREE: Yale Univ. '77
TRAINING: Fairfax Hosp. '77-'81; Children's National Med. Center, child psych.'81-'84; St. Elizabeth's Hosp. DC '84-'87; candidate Baltimore-Washington Inst. of Psychoanalysis
BOARD CERT.: Psych. '88; Child psych. '90
COMMENTS: Emphasis is on individual insight-oriented psychotherapy for children and a few adults, psychoanalysis with adults, psychopharmacology of children, parent counseling.

Norma N. El. Shammaa, MD
4708 Powder House Dr., Rockville, Md 20853 (301)774-4220
MED. DEGREE: Cairo Univ. '66
TRAINING: Episcopal Hosp., Philadelphia '70-'73; Albert Einstein Med. Center, Philadelphia '73-'76
BOARD CERT.: Psychiatry '79 HOSPITALS: Montgomery Gen.
LANGUAGES: Arabic, some French

POTOMAC

Nancy C. Clark, MD
10125 Darmuid Green Drive, Potomac Md 20854
(301)983-3173
MED. DEGREE: Georgetown Univ. '80
TRAINING: George Washington Univ. '80-'84
BOARD CERT.: Psychiatry '88

DARNESTOWN

Theresa A. Kurtz, MD
13012 Chestnut Oak Drive, Darnestown Md 20878
(301)921-1012
SPECIALTY: Child, adolescent, adult psychiatry
MED. DEGREE: Univ. of Rochester '80
TRAINING: Georgetown Univ. '80-'83; Fellow Georgetown Univ., child, adolescent psych. '83-'85
BOARD CERT.: Psych '85; Child psych '87

SILVER SPRING

Linda Frey, MD
11141 Georgia Ave #402, Silver Spring Md 20902
(301)949-8822
MED. DEGREE: George Washington Univ. '78
TRAINING: Vanderbilt Univ.,Nashville; Univ. of Maryland; MA Univ. of Wisconsin, Hispanic-Amer. studies
BOARD CERT.: Psychiatry '83
HOSPITALS: George Washington, Holy Cross, Washington Adventist (Chair Psychiatric review comm.)
LANGUAGES: Spanish, some French, Portuguese
COMMENTS: I have a particular interest and experience in cross cultural issues, depression, panic disorders. My approach is eclectic, with emphasis on psychodynamics. I am skilled in psycho-pharmacology and prescribe psychotropic medication judiciously.

Catherine E. Ostell, MD
8818 Georgia Ave, Silver Spring Md 20910 (301)340-7150
SUBSPECIALTY: Women's issues
MED. DEGREE: Univ. of Massachusetts '85
TRAINING: Univ. of Vermont, Med. Center Hosp. of Vermont
BOARD CERT.: Psychiatry '91
HOSPITALS: Chestnut Lodge Hosp.; Montgomery County Mental Health Clinic
COMMENTS: General adult psychiatry, including psychotherapy (insight-oriented and supportive) and medications. Especially interested in women's issues, including psychiatric problems in pregnancy and PMS.

Margaret Altemus, Md
7722 Carroll Ave, Takoma Park Md 20912 (301)853-2071
MED. DEGREE: Georgetown Univ. '83; TRAINING: Yale Univ. '87
BOARD CERT.: Psych '88
HOSPITALS: National Inst. of Mental Health, sr. staff fellow, clin. research in obsessive compulsive and eating disorders

VIRGINIA

BURKE

Ruth E. Imershein, MD
Burke Family Counseling & Consultation Center
5206 B Rolling Rd, Burke Va 22015 (703)356-5802
MED. DEGREE: George Washington Univ. '77
TRAINING: Medical College of Wisconsin; Fellow child psych. at Children's National Med. Ctr.
BOARD CERT.: Psychiatry
COMMENTS: I do psychiatric consultations for non-MD mental health professionals SEE Fairfax office also

FAIRFAX

Katherine A. Ferguson, MD
3921 Old Lee Highway #73A, Fairfax Va 22030
(703)273-0218
SPECIALTY: Adults and older adolescents
MED. DEGREE: George Washington Univ. '79
TRAINING: George Washington Univ. '83
BOARD CERT.: Psychiatry '85
HOSPITALS: Outpatient mostly; Dominion, Fairfax
COMMENTS: Practice individual psychotherapy, psychiatric and psychopharmacologic evaluations and medication monitoring. Range of problems treated include: depression (including post-partum)and mania, anxiety and obsessive-compulsive disorders, post-traumatic stress disorders (including survivors of incest), some psychotic and eating disorders, dual diagnosis patients (substance abuse).

Stephanie Heidelberg, MD
11330 Lafferty Lane, Fairfax Va 22030 (703)385-5772
SPECIALTY: Adults only, couples, mediation
MED. DEGREE: Louisiana State '69
TRAINING: Tulane Univ. Med. Center '74; Continuing educ. certificate
BOARD CERT.: Psychiatry '78
COMMENTS: Practice out of home office.

Patricia A. Majewski, MD
Commonwealth Psychotherapy Associates
3921 Old Lee Hwy #73-A, Fairfax Va 22030 (703)691-8513
ASSOCIATES: Katherine A. Ferguson, MD; several psychotherapists (social workers, PhDs)
MED. DEGREE: Univ. of Florida '81
TRAINING: Medical Univ. of S. Carolina '82-'85
BOARD CERT.: Psychiatry '88
HOSPITALS: Dominion, Fairfax COMMENTS: Adult and adol. psychiatry with special interests in eating disorders, adult survivors of sexual/physical abuse, cult-ritual abuse, schizophrenia and personality disorders. Individual psychotherapy and psycho-pharmacology. Also available through associates: Couples/family therapy, eating disorders, support group and nutritional counseling.

Ruth E. Imershein, MD
3650 Joseph Siewick Dr. #408, Fairfax Va 22033
(703)620-0901 (handicap accessible)
SEE Burke office for background

FALLS CHURCH

Adrian Brown, MD
6408-P Seven Corners Place, Falls church Va 22044
(703)237-6783
SUBSPECIALTY: Eating disorders, psychopharmacology
ASSOCIATES: Drs. David Daniel, Susan Trachman, Cynthia Cohen
MED. DEGREE: Univ. of Florida '86
TRAINING: George Washington Univ. '86-'90
BOARD CERT.: Psychiatry '91 HOSPITALS: Dominion
LANGUAGES: Portuguese, Spanish, French

Marilyn Lewis Renfield, MD
200 Little Falls St #205, Falls Church Va 22046 (703)241-8833
SPECIALTY: Child, adolescent, adult
MED. DEGREE: George Washington Univ. '65
TRAINING: George Washington -Internal Med. child & adult psych; Children's National Med. Center - Ped., Neonatology Fellow; Georgetown Univ., behavioral and developmental pediatrics; Holistic med., Berkeley, CA
BOARD CERT.: Ped. '71, Neonatal-perinatal med. '75
HOSPITALS: Refer to associates at Springwood, Fairfax and Dominion Hospitals when necessary
COMMENTS: I practice primarily psycho-dynamic psychotherapy for children,

adol. and adults. I use all therapy modalities — individual, couples, behavioral, cognitive, interactive, existential, logotherapy, humanistic and medication. I see an entire range of issues, e.g., depression, life transition, post-partum, maternal/ paternal bonding, school failure, job-related issues, stress and eating disorders, attention deficit hyperactivity disorder. I treat the whole person in the context of their social, emotional and spiritual world.

Miriam Woodall Roland, MD
200 Little Falls St. #205, Falls Church Va 22046 (703)241-1275
SPECIALTY: Adults, couples, older teens
MED. DEGREE: Univ. of Texas, Galveston '76
TRAINING: Hershey Med. Center/Penn State Univ. '76-'79; MA English Louisiana State Univ. '67; Ongoing continuing educ. courses
BOARD CERT.: Psychiatry '82
COMMENTS: Outpatients only. Psychodynamically oriented and do primarily insight-oriented psychotherapy. I use a full range of psycho-pharmacology but do not see patients for medication only. I see adults, couples and high school teens in a broad, general practice.

MCLEAN

Elizabeth L. Finch MD
Family Counseling Center, coord. of child and adolescent services
1495 Chain Bridge Rd #201, McLean Va 22101
(703)821-3404
ASSOCIATES: Family Counseling Center - broad range of mental health services by MDs, PhDs, and social workers. Multiple offices in three states.
MED. DEGREE: Univ. of Cincinnati '78
TRAINING: Univ. of California LA - psych resid., child psych. fellow; Children's Hosp., LA - pediatrics.
BOARD CERT.: Psychiatry '74; member, Amer. Academy of Psychiatry and Law, Amer. Professional Society on the Abuse of Children
HOSPITALS: Dominion; Arlington for referrals; also asst. clin. prof. psychiatry, George Washington Univ.; assoc. physician, Metropolitan Psychiatric Group; attending psychiatrist, Psychiatric Inst. of Washington
LANGUAGES: some French
COMMENTS: I do what works without strict adherence to one philosophy, expecially with children. Sexual abuse evaluations, medication, long and short-term play and adult therapy, custody evaluation, infertility.

Pamela M. McCurdy, MD
1307 Dolley Madison Blvd 3C, McLean Va 22101
(703)893-2962
SPECIALTY: adult and child
MED. DEGREE: Univ. of Oklahoma '75
TRAINING: Childrens National Medical Center- child psych.; Georgetown Univ. Hosp.- adult psych.
BOARD CERT.: Psych. '88; Child psych '90

Lillian Marlene Payne, MD
6458 Madison Ct., McLean Va 22101 (703)821-1018
SPECIALTY: Child, adult
MED. DEGREE: Northwestern Univ. '72
TRAINING: Northwestern Mem. Hosp. '72-'73; Georgetown Univ. Adult psych '73-'75, Fellow Child psych '75-'77
BOARD CERT.: Psych '78; Child Psych '80
HOSPITALS: No inpatient. Georgetown Univ., asst. clin. prof.

Kathy J. Smith, MD
6760 Old McLean Village Drive, McLean, Va 22101
(703)356-5423
SPECIALTY: Adult, adolescent, child
MED. DEGREE: Michigan State Univ. '83
TRAINING: Univ. of Michigan; Yale Univ.
BOARD CERT.: Psych. '89: Child psych. '91
HOSPITALS: Georgetown, clinical asst. prof.; Dominion Hosp., medical exec. comm. COMMENTS: Psychotherapy and medication management. Mood disorders, anxiety and eating disorders. Outpatient and inpatient psychiatry.

Elizabeth W. Johnston, MD
1010 Spencer Rd, McLean Va 22102 (703)356-8325
SUBSPECIALTY: Psychoanalysis
MED. DEGREE: Univ. of Michigan '49
TRAINING: St. Joseph's Mercy Hosp., MI. '49 '50; St. Elizabeth's Hosp. DC '54-'57; American Psychoanalytic Assn. '68
COMMENTS: With no hospital afiliation, I do not prescribe medications, but am willing to work with medicated patients provided the patient keeps me informed as to the situation.

SPRINGFIELD

Harriet Soheil, MD
8507 Grigsby Dr, Springfield Va 22152 (703)866-3043
MED. DEGREE: Tabriz Univ. Iran '61
TRAINING: Howard Univ., five years
BOARD eligible psychiatry LANGUAGES: Farsi

VIENNA

Valerie J. Buyse, Md
2110-D Gallows Rd, Vienna Va 22182 (703)893-2429
MED. DEGREE: Boston Univ. '79
TRAINING: Univ. S. California, LA; Tufts New England Med. Center, Psych, Fellow in adv. psychotherapy
BOARD CERT.: Psych '77; certified clinical hypnotist
HOSPITALS: Fairfax; Georgetown, asst. clin. prof.

ARLINGTON

Geraldine Schaeffer, MD
1101 S. Ridge Rd #115, Arlington Va 22202 (202)785-0077
SEE L St. NW DC for background

Melissa Chaffee, MD
3803 N. Fairfax Dr, Arlington Va 22203 (703)525-1754
ASSOCIATES: Joseph Sebastian, MD
MED. DEGREE: State Univ. of NY at Buffalo '87
TRAINING: George Washington Univ.
BOARD CERT.: Psychiatry '92
HOSPITALS: Arlington, George Washington, assoc. clin. prof.

Lucie Greenblum, MD
3900 Fairfax Dr, Arlington Va 22203 (703)527-0160
SUBSPECIALTY: Psychoanalysis
MED. DEGREE: Univ. of Paris '73
TRAINING: Doctor's Hosp. DC, St. Elizabeth's Hosp. DC; also grad. of Baltimore-Washington Inst. for Psychoanalysis
BOARD CERT.: Psychiatry '80
LANGUAGES: French SEE office in Bethesda also

Marjorie A. Harelick, MD
6427 N Washington Blvd, Arlington Va 22205 (703)532-9174
SPECIALTY: Children, adult individual psychotherapy and psychopharmacology
MED. DEGREE: Ohio State Univ. '69
TRAINING: Highland Hosp., Oakland, '69-'70; St. Elizabeth's Hosp. DC, Psych resid. '70-'72; Child psych fellow, Woodburn Center, Annandale '72-'74
BOARD CERT.: Psychiatry '76

Janieth K. Wise, MD
1701 N. George Mason Dr, Arlington Va 22205 (703)558-6579
SUBSPECIALTY: Addiction, hypnosis
MED. DEGREE: Medical Univ. of S. Carolina '74
TRAINING: W.S. Hall Psychiatric Inst., Columbia SC; Practical hypnosis '78
BOARD CERT.: Psych. '81; Certified addictionologist '88
HOSPITALS: Arlington, director medical addiction treatment
COMMENTS: American Psychiatric Assn. certificate of achievement '80, '83,'86. Behavioral cognitive approach with a systems model; the patient is ultimately responsible for his/her recovery.

Lillibeth Boruchow, MD
3557 N. 36th St, Arlington Va 22207 (703)243-6377
MED. DEGREE: Ohio St. Univ. '63
TRAINING: Georgetown/DC Gen.; Georgetown, med. & psych resident
BOARD eligible psychiatry
HOSPITALS: Arlington Hosp., chr. Quality assurance; Georgetown, asst. clin. prof.

ALEXANDRIA

Pamela A. Quarles, MD
5249 Duke Street #200, Alexandria Va 22304 (703)751-3300
SPECIALTY: General adult practice
MED. DEGREE: Univ. of Pennsylvania '79
TRAINING: Univ. of California Davis '79-'82; George Washington Univ. '82-'83
BOARD CERT.: Psychiatry '84

Elaine R. Green, MD
303 Kentucky Ave, Alexandria Va 22305 (703)836-3438
SPECIALTY: Adult
MED. DEGREE: Univ. of Kansas '74
TRAINING: Univ. of Kansas '74-'76; National Inst. of Mental Health '76-'78; Washington School of Psychiatry - advanced Psychotherapy
BOARD CERT.: Psychiatry '86
HOSPITALS: Alexandria, Mt. Vernon
COMMENTS: Adult practice consists of 50% individual psychotherapy and 50% psychiatric consultations to other clinicians and medication management.

Betsy Jane Cooper, MD
1800 Diagonal Rd #600, Alexandria Va 22314 (703)684-4456
SUBSPECIALTY: Geriatric Psychiatry
MED. DEGREE: Meharry Medical Coll. '74
TRAINING: Grady Mem. Hosp. '74-'76; Hahnemann Hosp., Philadelphia '78-'82
BOARD CERT.: Psychiatry '84
HOSPITALS: Arlington
COMMENTS: Adult psychiatry, with emphasis on geriatric psychiatry, medication consultation and monitoring. Nursing home or in-home consultation available.

Barbara R. Hoar, MD
1446 Duke St., Alexandria Va 22314 (703)548-4333
SPECIALTY: Adult, child, family therapy
MED. DEGREE: George Washington Univ. '70
TRAINING: Children's National Med. Center - child psych. '70-'73; St. Elizabeth's, DC - adult psych '73-'76
HOSPITALS: St. Elizabeth's Hosp. - half-time position in crisis unit for children - outpatient
COMMENTS: Very helpful in career planning and support as well as combining needs of career and family.

Alberta M. Vallis, MD
1846 Park Rd NW, Washington DC 20010 (202)234-5713
SPECIALTY: Child Psychiatry - 2 1/2 to 12 years old
MED. DEGREE: Howard Univ. '62
TRAINING: Cook County, Chicago '63; St. Elizabeth's Hosp. DC - Gen. psych. '63-'66; Children's National Med. Center, child psych. '66-'68; substance abuse training
BOARD eligible psychiatry
HOSPITALS: Children's
COMMENTS: Children need structure and parents need professional guidelines to avoid serious emotional problems later in life. The right school and beginning will make a difference.

Clara Aisenstein, MD
5035 Rockwood Pkwy NW, Washington DC 20016
(202)966-2467
SPECIALTY: Psychiatry, Child Psychiatry, infant
ASSOCIATES: Besides practice, acting director, Youth-Parent Infant Development program at DC Comm. in Mental Health Service
MED. DEGREE: Univ. of Buenos Aires '64
TRAINING: Hospitals in Buenos Aires '64-'66; Univ. of California, Berkeley '67-'69; Fellow child psych. James. J. Putnam Children's Center, Boston '70-'72; resident and fellow, National Inst. of Mental Health, St. Elizabeth's Hosp. '72-'74
BOARD CERT.: Psych. '75; Child psych. '78
HOSPITALS: Sibley , assoc. med. staff; Georgetown, assoc. clin. prof. of psych. / child psych; Providence (consultant in neonatology); Psychiatric Inst. of Washington
LANGUAGES: Spanish, Portuguese, Yiddish
COMMENTS: Psychodynamic, family-oriented, mother/infant relationships, education evaluations, multi-family member, court evaluations, special problems of women, especially psychological effects of relationships.

Lynn Staton Dworsky, MD
7307 MacArthur Blvd #201, Bethesda Md 20816 (301)229-1004
SUBSPECIATLY: Child psychiatry
MED. DEGREE: Univ. of Texas '74
TRAINING: Univ. of Wisconsin Hospitals, Madison; George Washington Univ. '75-'77; Fellow child psych. Children's National Med. Center '77-'79; training in family violence, child sexual abuse, adult survivors of childhood sexual abuse, multiple personality disorder and hypnotherapy.
BOARD CERT.: Psych. '80; Child psych. '82
HOSPITALS: Psychiatric Inst. of Washington, Suburban
COMMENTS: Eclectic approach with psychoanalytic orientation; hypnotherapy used to help with recovery of traumatic memories with sexual abuse survivors. Adult women's incest survivors group therapy with female co-therapist. Available for medical evaluations as well as psychotherapy. See children in play therapy. Family therapy.

Polly Harding Craft, MD
Reginald S. Lourie Center for Infants and Young Children
11710 Hunter's Lane, Rockville Md 20852 (301)984-4444
SPECIALTY: Child Psychiatry/infant/early childhood
ASSOCIATES: Medical dir. of The Lourie Center, which has 40 staff members, specializing in child pyschiatry, psychology, speech and language
MED. DEGREE: Medical College of Wisconsin '76
TRAINING: Medical College of Wisconsin - Int., resid. and child psych fellow. through '81
BOARD CERT.: Psychiatry '86
HOSPITALS: Washington School of Psychiatry faculty; previously asst. prof. Medical Coll. of Wisconsin COMMENTS: I see children and families of kids 6 and under through the Lourie Center. I see a few private patients, latency-age children or adults, at the center. Preferred focus: early intervention, enhancing parent-child relationships, short or long-term dynamic Rx as indicated.

Maya C. Bhatia, MD
101 S. Whiting St. #212, Alexandria Va 22304 (703)660-6674
SPECIALTY: Psychiatry, child psychiatry, pediatrics
MED. DEGREE: Bombay Univ., India '66
TRAINING: Children's National Med. Center, Georgetown Univ. Hosp, Michigan State Univ.
BOARD CERT.: Psych '78; Ped. '73; Child psych '81
HOSPITALS: Children's National Med. Center
LANGUAGES: Hindi

Susan Hasselquist, MD
George Washington Univ. Med. Center
2150 Penn. Ave NW, Washington DC 20037 (202)994-4108
ASSOCIATES: Morgan Delaney, MD
MED. DEGREE: Univ. of Wisconsin '78
TRAINING: George Washington Univ.
BOARD CERT.: Pulmonary '90
HOSPITALS: George Washington, asst. prof.

Revathy Murthy, MD
6130 Landover Road, Landover Md 20785 (301)322-7737
MED. DEGREE: Lady Harding Med. College, India '68
TRAINING: Riverside Methodist, Prince George's Gen. Hosp./DC General - Georgetown medicine
BOARD CERT.: Int. med. '78; Pulm. '90; board eligible critical care
HOSPITALS: Washington Adventist, Holy Cross, Doctors of Lanham, Prince George's, Leland
LANGUAGES: Hindi, Malayal, Tamil COMMENTS: 90% consultation in pulmonary. I spend time with patients, explain their disease, procedures planned. Always return phone calls.

Gita C. Bakshi, MD
9406 Old Georgetown Rd, Bethesda Md 20814 (301)530-0331
MED. DEGREE: Delhi Univ., India '76
TRAINING: State Univ. of NY; Univ. of California, San Francisco, pulm. fellow; also National Inst. of Health
BOARD CERT.: Int. Med. '80; Pulm. '84; Crit. Care '89
HOSPITALS: Suburban, Holy Cross, Shady Grove, Washington Adventist

Ylene Ann Larsen, MD
5454 Wisconsin Ave, Chevy Chase Md 20815 (301)656-7374
ASSOCIATES: Drs. Robert W. Langevin, Peter G. Hamm, D. Scott Cohen
MED. DEGREE: Georgetown Univ. '78
TRAINING: Georgetown Univ. '78-'81, Pulmonary '81-'83
BOARD CERT.: Int. med. '84; Pulmonary, Crit. care
HOSPITALS: Georgetown Univ., asst. clin. instr.; Sibley, director of Medical Intensive Care LANGUAGES: Spanish
COMMENTS: I primarily take care of adults with lung problems. Many are seriously ill. People will be disappointed if they need a doctor who is never late and answers their calls promptly. My patient's needs are triaged because of the nature of caring for critically ill patients and I am not by nature a time-oriented person.

Ann Medinger, MD
2440 M St NW #606, Washington DC 20037 (202)775-0860
SUBSPECIALTY: Crit. care/Internal Med.
ASSOCIATES: Drs. Gary Miller, Byron Cooper (cross coverage)
MED. DEGREE: Univ. of Pennsylvania '71
TRAINING: Univ. of Wisconsin, Madison
BOARD CERT.: Int. Med.'74,'81 ; Pulm.'78, critical care'87
HOSPITALS: Sibley, Wash. Hosp. Center, George Washington, Veterans Admin. Med. Center, dir. pulmonary function lab; Columbia

Juliana Simmons, MD
Washington Hosp. Center Cancer Institute
110 Irving St. NW, Washington DC 20010 (202)877-3925
ASSOCIATES: Drs. R. L. White, Michael Porrazzo
MED. DEGREE: Indiana Univ. '65
TRAINING: St. Vincent Hosp. Indianapolis '65-'66, Diagnostic Rad. '66-'67, Therapeutic Rad. '68-'70
BOARD CERT.: Radiology '70
HOSPITALS: Washington Hosp. Center Cancer Inst., chair, Dept. Radiation Oncology
COMMENTS: The hospital's cancer center is new. Patient care is the priority. We look at the whole patient with financial, nutritional, psycho-social support as well as diagnosis, radiation therapy. There is a warm family feeling in our department.

Allison Brown LaVigne
Greater SE Comm. Hospital, Rad. Oncology Dept.
1310 Southern Ave SE, Washington DC 20032 (202)373-5940
ASSOCIATES: Drs. Alfred Goldson, Ebrahim Ashayeri, Olubunmi Abayomi
MED. DEGREE: Univ. of California, Irvine '87
TRAINING: Kaiser Permanente, Los Angeles; Rad. Onc. Howard U.
BOARD eligible Radiology (therapeutic), written exam '91; oral board pending
HOSPITALS: Greater SE, Howard Univ.

Kaethe Wechsler-Jentsch, MD
George Washington Univ. Med. Center
901 23rd St. NW, Washington DC 20037 (202)994-4680
SUBSPECIALTY: Gynecologic, pediatric oncology
ASSOCIATES: Drs. Charles Rogers, Leonidas Harisiadis, Alan Ney
MED. DEGREE: Freie Univ., Berlin '64
TRAINING: Auguste Viktoria Kik. U., Berlin; Univ. of Vienna; George Washington Univ. '79-'81
BOARD CERT.: Radiology '81 (therapeutic)
HOSPITALS: George Washington, assoc. prof.
LANGUAGES: German

Judith L. Bader, MD
Suburban Hospital
8600 Old Georgetown Rd, Bethesda Md 20814 (301)530-3100
SUBSPECIALTY: Pediatric Hem./Oncology
MED. DEGREE: Yale Univ. '71
TRAINING: Univ. of California, San Francisco '71-'74; National Cancer Inst., Rad. Onc. '81-'84; Stanford Univ. fellow Pediatric Hematology/Oncology '74-'76
BOARD CERT.: Radiology '84; Ped. '74; Ped. Hema./Onc.
HOSPITALS: Holy Cross, Suburban pending
LANGUAGES: French

Christine D. Berg, MD
Georgetown Univ. Vincent T. Lombardi Cancer Research Center
9711 Medical Center Dr. #111, Rockville Md 20850
(301)762-5595
SUBSPECIALTY: Breast cancer
ASSOCIATES: Drs. Anatoly Dritschilo, K. William Harter, K.C. Lee, Michael Kuettel, Neelofur Shah, David Thomas, Gregory Gagnon, John Torrisi
MED. DEGREE: Northwestern Univ. '77
TRAINING: Northwestern Mem. Hosp., Chicago '77-'81; Georgetown Univ. Rad/Onc.'84-86; Fellow Med. Oncology, National Cancer Inst., '81-'84
BOARD CERT.: Radiology '86; Med. Oncology '83; Internal Med.'80;
HOSPITALS: Georgetown, asst. prof.; Shady Grove Adventist
COMMENTS: also Georgetown Univ. office (202)784-3320. Full-time faculty of Georgetown Med. School. Also clinical director of our radiation therapy facility adjacent to Shade Grove Adventist Hosp. We treat up to 50 patients a day for a variety of malignancies.

Susan F. Stinson, MD
2121 Medical Park Dr. #4, Silver Spring Md 20902
(301)681-4422
MED. DEGREE: Tufts Univ. Sch. of Med. '84
TRAINING: Faulkner Hosp., Boston; National Cancer Inst. - Rad. Onc. resid.
BOARD CERT: Radiology '91
HOSPITALS: Holy Cross COMMENTS: Medical director, Clinical Radiologists. Comprehensive radiation oncologic treatment given in our out-patient facility.

Lynn Merrill Ludmer
Washington Hosp. Center, rheumatology sect.
110 Irving St. NW, Washington DC 20010 (202)877-6374
ASSOCIATES: Drs. Marcia Coe, Werner Barth
MED. DEGREE: Univ. of Maryland '84
TRAINING: Univ. of Maryland; Washington Hosp. Center
BOARD CERT.: Int. Med. '87; BOARD eligible rheumatology
HOSPITALS: Washington Hosp. Center

Caroline Samuels, MD
DC General Hosp. (Georgetown Dept of Medicine)
19th & Mass Ave., Washington DC 20003 (202)675-7970
ASSOCIATES: Kenneth Grant, MD
MED. DEGREE: Univ. of Connecticut '75
TRAINING: Georgetown Dept. of Med./DC Gen. Hosp.; fellow Rheum. George Washington Univ. Med. Center
BOARD CERT.: Int. med. '78; Rheum. '86
HOSPITALS: DC General;Georgetown , asst. clin. prof.

Marcia D. Coe, MD
Washington Hospital Center
110 Irving St. NW #2A-38B, Washington DC 20010
(202)877-6374
ASSOCIATES: Drs. Werner F. Barth, chairman; Lynn Ludmer (Drs. Ludmer and Coe work half-time, sharing a position.)
MED. DEGREE: Temple Univ. '84
TRAINING: Washington Hosp. Ctr., int., resid. and fellowship
BOARD CERT.: Int. med. '87; Rheum. '90
HOSPITALS: Washington Hospital Center
COMMENTS: Many of my patients are women due to the predominance of females in most rheumatic diseases.

Patience H. White MD
Children's National Med. Center
111 Mich. Ave NW, Washington DC 20010 (202)745-5483
SEE Penn. Ave. office for background on adult rheumatology practice

Susan Lacks, MD, MPH
2141 K St. NW #407, Washington DC 20037 (202)223-4141
SUBSPECIALTY: Arthritis, connective tissue disease
ASSOCIATES: Drs. Joel Guiterman, Joseph Laukains, Jack Summer
MED. DEGREE: Duke Univ. '80
TRAINING: George Washington Univ. - Int. Med. '80-'83, Rheum. '84-'86; MPH Johns Hopkins '87
BOARD CERT.: Int. Med. '83; Rheum. '86
HOSPITALS: George Washington, asst. prof.

Patience H. White, MD
George Washington Univ.
2150 Pennsylvania Ave NW, Washington DC 20037
(202)994-4416
SPECIALTY: Adult rheumatology (George Washington)
Pediatric rheum. (Children's National Med. Center) (202)745-5483
ASSOCIATES: Drs. David Borenstein, William Feltz, Karyl S. Barron
MED. DEGREE: Harvard Med. School '74
TRAINING: Harvard teaching hospitals for int., resid.; Brigham & Women's Hosp. - adult rheum.; ped. rheum. and pediatrics, London
BOARD CERT.: Int. med. '78; Rheum. '82
HOSPITALS: Dir. Dept. of Adult and Ped. Rheumatology at George Washington Univ. and CNMC; also assoc. prof. George Washington
COMMENTS: I enjoy working with families and patients over many years to help them feel as best they can with a chronic condition, such as arthritis. Because I am a full-time academic physician, I am involved in teaching and research, thus all my patients have the opportunity to meet the many doctors working with me and participate in clinical research studies.

Dorothy Nicholson-Elbaor MD
101 S.Whiting St., Alexandria Va 22304 (703)751-8804
ASSOCIATES: Harvey Schwartz, MD
MED. DEGREE: Boston Univ. '81
TRAINING: George Washington Univ.
BOARD CERT.: Int. Med. '84; Rheum. '90
HOSPITALS: Alexandria, Mount Vernon
Office also at 2616 Sherwood Hall Lane, #205, Alexandria 22306.

Grace S. Rozycki, MD
Washington Hosp. Center
110 Irving St. NW 4B-46, Washington DC 20010 (202)877-5190
SUBSPECIALTY: Surgical critical care
ASSOCIATES: Drs. Howard R. Champion, Mario Golocovsky, Mark Buchly, Bikram Paul, Duncan Harviel
MED. DEGREE: Medical College of Virginia '80
TRAINING: Medical College of Va.; Univ. of Tennessee Med. Center '81-'86; trauma and surgical critical care fellow '86-'88
BOARD CERT.: Surgery '89, Surgical critical care '89
HOSPITALS: Dep. dir. of Trauma and Surg. crit. care, sec., Dept of Gen. Surgery, Washington Hosp. Center

Elizabeth G. Adams, MD
1140 Varnum St NE #202, Washington DC 20017 (202)526-7555
MED. DEGREE: George Washington Univ. '73
TRAINING: Children's Hosp.; Wash. Hosp. Center, 2nd intern., gen. surg. resid. Chief resident final year
BOARD CERT.: Gen. Surgery recertfication '91
HOSPITALS: Providence, Washington Hosp. Center
LANGUAGES: French, Filipino

Denise J. Hunt, MD
1160 Varnum St NE #214, Washington DC 20017
(202)529-0527
ASSOCIATES: David R. Hunt, MD
MED. DEGREE: Howard Univ. '84
TRAINING: Surgery - Howard Univ. Hosp. '84-89; also laparoscopic cholecystectomy
BOARD CERT.: Surgery '91
HOSPITALS: Clin. instr. Providence, Howard Univ.; Montgomery Gen., Howard County Gen., Leland, Doctors
COMMENTS: We believe in combining traditional values and ideals of medicine with the latest technological advances to assure quality care for our patients.
SEE office also in Olney Md

Gail D. Pearson, MD
1140 Varnum St. NE #103, Washington DC 20017
(202)529-4903
MED. DEGREE: Tufts Univ. School of Med. '79
TRAINING: Rhode Island Hosp., Buffalo Gen. Hosp.
BOARD eligible general surgery
HOSPITALS: Providence, Columbia
LANGUAGES: French (some) COMMENTS: I try to be very sensitive to the patient's needs. I try my best to see them on time and expect them to be on time for their appointments.

Katherine Alley, MD
2440 M St. NW #326, Washington DC 20037 (202)457-0606
SUBSPECIALTY: breast disease
ASSOCIATES: Richard Flax, MD
MED. DEGREE: George Washington Univ. '74
TRAINING: George Washington Univ. '74-'79, general surgery
BOARD CERT.: Surgery '82
HOSPITALS: Columbia Hosp. for Women, Sibley, George Washington, asst. clin. professor of surgery
LANGUAGES: minimal Spanish

Shawna C. Willey, MD
2440 M St NW #706, Washington DC 20037 (202)331-1234
ASSOCIATES: Drs. Norman H. Isaacson, Stanley M. Knoll
MED. DEGREE: Univ. of Iowa '82
TRAINING: George Washington Univ.; laparoscopic cholecystectomy
BOARD CERT.: Surgery '89
HOSPITALS: Asst. clin. prof, George Washington; Columbia Hosp. for Women; Reston COMENTS: Interest in breast disease, laparoscopic surgery, anorectal disease. I do fine needle aspiration.
SEE office in Reston also

Denise J. Hunt, MD
18111 Prince Philip Dr. #327, Olney, Md 20832
(301)559-9048 SEE office on Varnum St. NE also for background

Denise Mack Fraser, MD
3299 Woodburn Rd, Annandale Va 22003
(703)698-8030
ASSOCIATES: Drs. Robert L. Pinnar, Daniel G. Turgeon
MED. DEGREE: Univ. of Rochester '85
TRAINING: Pennsylvania Hosp., Philadelphia; Fairfax Hosp. trauma surgeon
BOARD eligible surgery
HOSPITALS: Fairfax, Fair Oaks, Reston ; Patient care and surgical case review committees at Fairfax; Infectious disease comm., Fair Oaks; Operating room comm., Reston.
COMMENTS: I would like to provide the best quality medical care in a strongly male dominated field. SEE also Reston office

Denise Mack Fraser
1830 Town Center Pkwy, Reston Va 22090
(703)709-9701 SEE Annandale office for background

Shawna C. Willey, MD
1800 Town Center Pkwy, Reston Va 22090
(703)435-8700 SEE NW DC office for background

Susan D. Stein, MD
2440 M Street NW, Washington DC 20037 (202)463-8548
ASSOCIATES: Bradley H. Bennett, MD
MED. DEGREE: Medical College of Pennsylvania '77
TRAINING: George Washington Univ.; Fellow Carle Clinic - colon rectal surgery; also laparoscopy, laparascopic cholecystectomy
BOARD CERT.: Gen. Surgery '83; Colon/rectal Surg. '83
HOSPITALS: Holy Cross, Suburban, Sibley, George Washington, Columbia
SEE also Silver Spring office

Susan D. Stein, MD
2101 Medical Park Dr., Silver Spring Md 20902
(301)681-6437 SEE M St. NW for background

Allyson A. Askew, MD
3301 Woodburn Rd #205, Annandale Va 22003
(703)560-2236
ASSOCIATES: Earl Hodin, MD
MED. DEGREE: Tulane Univ. '82
TRAINING: New York Hosp./Cornell Med. Center '82-87; Children's Hosp. of Oklahoma '87-89
BOARD CERT.: Surgery '88, Pediatric surgery '90
HOSPITALS: Fairfax, Arlington
COMMENTS: I treat all general surgery problems in infants and children ages newborn to 18 years.

Pamela W. Coleman, MD
3619-14th St. NW, Washington DC 20010
(202)291-0007
MED. DEGREE: Howard Univ. '81
TRAINING: Albert Einstein NY/Montefiore Hosp '81-'86; training in laser and lithotripsy surgery
BOARD CERT.: Urology '88
HOSPITALS: Providence, Howard, Sibley, Columbia and Washington Hosp. Center

Jean L. Fourcroy, MD, PhD
6310 Swords Way, Bethesda Md 20817
(301)897-5563
SPECIALTY: consultant only
MED. DEGREE: Medical College of Pennsylvania '74;
TRAINING: George Washington Univ. '79; Univ. of California, San Francisco PhD; MA San Jose State Univ.
BOARD CERT.: Urology '81
HOSPITALS: Walter Reed Army med.
COMMENTS: Patient is a partner in her care, and with appropriate guidance can help control her care.

Janice L. Arnold, MD
1830 Town Center Dr. #301, Reston Va 22090
(703)742-7757
MED. DEGREE: Univ. of Chicago '86
TRAINING: State Univ. of NY at Buffalo; Univ. of Chicago - Resid., Urology Dept. of Surg.; laser and shockwave therapy of kidney stones
BOARD CERT.: Internal Med. '82; Urology '91
HOSPITALS: Reston , Columbia Hosp. for Women, Washington Hosp. Center
COMMENTS: Thorough evaluation and understanding of the disease entity begins with careful, thorough questioning and examination of the patient. We make every effort to allow each individual to ask all questions necessary to obtain a workable understanding of their illness.

GLOSSARY

ADHD: Attention deficit/hyperactivity disorder, a syndrome affecting primarily children and adolsecents. It is marked by learning and behavior disabilities.

ALLERGY/IMMUNOLOGY: disorders affecting the immune system, such as asthma, eczema and reactions to foods, drugs or insect bites.

ANESTHESIOLOGY: relief and maintenance of a stable condition during and following a surgical or diagnostic procedure.

AYUR VEDIC MEDICINE: a nonpharmacologic, natural approach to treatment of chronic illness, disease prevention and health promotion.

CARDIOVASCULAR MEDICINE: Also called cardiology, a subspecialty of internal medicine involving diseases of the heart, lungs and blood vessels.

CHOLECYSTECTOMY: The removal of the gall bladder by surgery.

CHOLECYSTECTOMY, LAPAROSCOPIC: The removal of the gall bladder through a tube inserted through a small incision in the abdominal wall.

CHRONOBIOLOGY: The study of biological rhythms and how they affect health, including mental health.

CLINICAL CARDIAC ELECTROPHYSIOLOGY: A field of expertise within the internal medicine subspecialty of cardiology, involving technical procedures to evaluate heart rhythms and determine treatment for them.

COLON AND RECTAL SURGERY: After four years of general surgery, a surgeon may complete an additional year of training in the colon/rectal areas to be board certified in this specialty.

COLPOSCOPY: An examination of the vagina and cervix using a lighted instrument called a colposcope.

COMEDONE EXTRACTION: Removal of comedones, or blackheads, caused by a buildup of oil in the skin.

CRITICAL CARE MEDICINE: A subspecialty of internal medicine for the management of life-threatening disorders in intensive care units and other hospital units.

CRYOSURGERY: The use of subfreezing temperature to destroy tissues.

DERMATOLOGY: Treatment of disorders of the mouth, skin, hair, nails, scalp external genitalia, with extensive training in skin cancers and other tumors.

DERMATOPATHOLOGY: A subspecialty of pathology, which entails the monitoring of skin diseases by examination of tissue and skin scrapings.

ECHOCARDIOGRAPHY: The use of sonograms to view the heart.

EMERGENCY MEDICINE: Decision-making to prevent death or disability in emergency situations. These specialists are usually hospital-based.

ENDOCRINOLOGY: A subspecialty of internal medicine that treats the internal endocrine glands, such as thryoid and adrenal. Common disorders include diabetes, metabolic, menstrual and sexual problems.

FAMILY PRACTICE: Treatment of a wide variety of ailments in patients of all ages.

GASTROENTEROLOGY: A subspecialty of internal medicine which treats digestive organs of the stomach, liver, bowels and gallbladder.

GERIATRICS: A subspecialty of family practice or internal medicine for treatment of disorders common to the elderly.

HEMATOLOGY: A subspecialty of internal medicine dealing with diseases of the blood, spleen, and lymph glands.

HOLISTIC MEDICINE: Medical care that considers the physical, social, emotional and spiritual needs of the patient.

HOMEOPATHY: A branch of medicine, made popular early in the century, that uses the smallest dose of a drug to make a person well.

HYSTEROSCOPY: Visual inspection of the cervical and uterine area through a hysteroscope, an instrument through which polyps or specimens can be removed for biopsy.

IMMUNODERMATOLOGY: A subspecialty of dermatology involved in the cause, diagnoses and treatment of skin diseases affecting the immune system.

INFECTIOUS DISEASES: A subspecialty of internal medicine involving the treatment of infectious diseases in all body organs.

INTERNAL MEDICINE: Treatment of all types of illnesses in adolescents and adults, with special training in the internal orgrans of the body.

LAPAROSCOPY: The examination of the abdominal cavity with an instrument consisting of a lighted tube with a magnifying lens. The tube is inserted through a small incision in the abdominal wall.

LITHOTRIPSY: Use of shockwave therapy in the treatment of kidney stones.

MATERNAL-FETAL MEDICINE: A subspecialty of obstetrics/gynecology, involving complications of pregnancy.

NEONATAL-PERINATAL MEDICINE: A subspecialty of pediatrics involving the care of sick newborns.

NEPHROLOGY: A subspecialty of internal medicine that treats disorders of kidneys, high blood pressure and fluid/mineral imbalances.

NEUROLOGICAL SURGERY: Surgical treatment of disorders of the nervous system.

NEUROLOGY: Treatment of disorders of the brain, spinal cord, nervous systems and related structures.

OBSTETRICS/GYNECOLOGY: Treatment of disorders of the female reproductive system.

ONCOLOGY, MEDICAL: A subspecialty of internal medicine involving the diagnosis and treatment of all types of cancer and other tumors.

OPHTHALMOLOGY: Treatment of all aspects of eye and vision care.

ORTHOPAEDIC SURGERY: Medical and surgical treatment of disorders of the extremities, spine and related structures.

OTOLARYNGOLOGY: Head and neck surgery, and treatment of disorders of the ears and respiratory systems.

PATHOLOGY: Examines the causes and nature of diseases, using laboratory methods to diagnose and recommend treatment.

PEDIATRICS: Treatment of the ailments of children, from birth through adolescence.

PELVISCOPY: Advanced laparoscopic procedure in which a lighted instrument is inserted through the abdominal wall. But instead of just a diagnostic tool, with pelviscopy, cysts and other abnormalities in the pelvic area can be surgically removed through the scope.

PHARMACOTHERAPY: The treatment of mental disturbances through the use of drugs and medicines.

PHYSIATRIST: A specialist in physical medicine and rehabilitation, who treats disabilities involving the musculoskeletal, neurologic, and other body systems.

PHYSICAL MEDICINE AND REHABILITATION: Treatment of patients with disabilities involving the musculoskeletal, neurologic, cardiovascular and other body systems. This specialist is known as a physiatrist.

PLASTIC SURGERY: Repair and reconstruction of body defects, including limbs, breast, face and external genitalia.

PREVENTIVE MEDICINE: Promotion and maintenance of good health and well-being.

PSYCHIATRY: Treatment of mental, addictive and emotional disorders, including depression, anxiety, sexual dysfunction and substance abuse.

PSYCHOANALYSIS: A method of treating some mental disorders through analysis of character, personality and mind.

PSYCHOLOGY: The study of the mind and its functions.

PSYCHOLOGY, FORENSIC: The psychological state of a person's mind appplied in a legal setting, such as testifying as an expert witness in court.

PSYCHOPHARMACOLOGY: The study of the making, ingredients, uses and actions of drugs used in the treatment of psychiatric disorders.

PSYCHOTHERAPY: The treatment of mental disturbances.

PULMONARY DISEASES: A subspecialty of internal medicine involved with treatment of diseases of the lungs, including pleurisy, bronchitis and asthma.

REPRODUCTIVE ENDOCRINOLOGY: A subspecialty of obstetrics/gynecology, involving problems of the endocrine system and infertility.

RHEUMATOLOGY: A subspecialty of internal medicine that treats diseases of joints, bones and related structures.

RADIATION ONCOLOGY: Treatment using radiant energy to treat diseases, particularly malignant tumors.

SCLEROTHERAPY: The injection of a medication into a vein to allow fibrous tissue to form within it. It is commonly used to treat varicose veins.

SIGMOIDOSCOPY: Examination of the rectum and sigmoid colon (part of the left large bowel) through a long, lighted tube.

SONOGRAPHY: A diagnostic method that uses ultrasonic sound waves to reflect and photographically record clear outlines of organs and tissues.

SURGERY: Treatment of a broad variety of conditions affecting all bodily parts through surgical means.

SURGERY OF THE HAND: A subspecialty of plastic surgery and general surgery, involving the repair and reconstruction of defects of the hand.

TERATOLOGY: The study of substances that interfere with the normal development of the fetus.

UROGYNECOLOGY: The study of female bladder abnormalities.

UROLOGY: Treatment of disorders of the adrenal gland and reproductive and urinary systems.

UVEITIS: Eye inflammation or swelling of the uveal tract of the eye. It may cause an irregularly shaped pupil or opaque deposits on the cornea.

INDEX

ORDER FORM

Please send ________ copy (copies) of the Guide to Women Physicians in the Washington D.C. area at $12.95 per copy, plus $1.75 for shipping and handling for the first book and $0.75 for each additional book.

Virginia residents please add an additional 4.5% (58 cents for one book) for state sales tax. If you have any questions, call Rocky Run Publishing, Inc. at 703-759-0244.

NAME____

ADDRESS____

CITY______________________________STATE______ZIP___________

PHONE____

Mail order form with check or money order to:

Rocky Run Publishing, Inc.
P.O. Box 456
McLean, VA 22101